TEACHING READING

SOLVING PROBLEMS IN THE TEACHING OF LITERACY
Cathy Collins Block, *Series Editor*

RECENT VOLUMES

Teaching Reading

Strategies and Resources for Grades K–6

Rachel L. McCormack
Susan Lee Pasquarelli

THE GUILFORD PRESS
New York   London

©2010 The Guilford Press
A Division of Guilford Publications, Inc.
72 Spring Street, New York, NY 10012
www.guilford.com

Printed in the United States of America

This book is printed on acid-free paper.

Last digit is print number: 9   8   7   6   5   4   3   2   1

Library of Congress Cataloging-in-Publication Data

McCormack, Rachel L.
   Teaching reading: strategies and resources for grades K–6 / Rachel L. McCormack, Susan
Lee Pasquarelli.
      p. cm. — (Solving problems in the teaching of literacy)
   Includes bibliographical references and index.
   ISBN 978-1-60623-483-9 (hardcover: alk. paper) — ISBN 978-1-60623-482-2 (pbk.: alk. paper)
   1. Reading teachers—Training of.   2. English language—Composition and exercises—
Study and teaching (Elementary)   3. Reading (Elementary)   I. Pasquarelli, Susan
Lee.   II. Title.
   LB2844.1.R4M35 2010
   372.41—dc22
                                                                          2009037260

About the Authors

Rachel L. McCormack, EdD, is Associate Professor of Literacy Education at Roger Williams University in Bristol, Rhode Island, where she teaches undergraduate and graduate courses in reading and writing methods and children's literature. She is a frequent presenter at national conferences; her research interests include strategies for improving comprehension, literature discussions, and teaching reading to children with hearing disabilities.

Susan Lee Pasquarelli, EdD, is Professor of Literacy Education at Roger Williams University in Bristol, Rhode Island. For the past 3 years, she has been conducting research in urban classrooms on using multicultural literature to teach children in grades 1–6 about tolerance and diversity. Dr. Pasquarelli teaches undergraduate and graduate courses in reading and writing methods and adolescent literature.

Preface

Teachers of reading have one important goal: to prepare children to be independent, strategic readers in real life. This text is intended to help teachers and reading specialists achieve this goal by providing research-based instructional strategies for teaching phonological/phonemic awareness, phonics, fluency, vocabulary, all aspects of comprehension, and writing in response to literature. The strategies are geared toward teaching diverse learners in grades K–6.

This book includes many special features: sample scripted lessons; classroom-ready instructional materials; and photographs of classroom-literate environments with bulletin boards and other elements that support effective reading instruction.

HOW TO READ THIS TEXT

Interacting with the Text

This book is meant to be interactive. We hope you will read it with some type of writing implement in your hand. We know that good teaching requires practice, reflection, and more practice, so we provide many opportunities for you to do these things. We ask you questions periodically, and provide space for you to jot down your responses or additional questions you may have. Sometimes we ask you to engage in a theoretical exercise; many of these exercises are applications of what we have described in the chapters' sections on pedagogy. At other times, we make suggestions for implementing ideas in the future. We urge you to fill in the charts and figures as you read, and to use the white spaces in the text to record additional notes and reflections. As a result, the text can become a *record of your growth* as a teacher of reading, in addition to being a good reference for teaching reading.

How the Book Is Organized

After Chapter 1, which encourages you to think about what makes a good teacher of reading, we have organized this text according to the key literacy categories: contexts for literacy learning (Chapter 2); phonological/phonemic awareness, phonics, and fluency (Chapter 3); vocabulary (Chapter 4); comprehension (Chapters 5–8); writing in response to literature (Chapter 9); culturally responsive classrooms (Chapter 10); and reading assessment (Chapters 11–12). We conclude with a discussion (Chapter 13) of your continued professional development. Much of this volume is devoted to comprehension instruction, and this emphasis is deliberate. When we work with teachers on their reading programs, most of their questions are about comprehension; we have tried to answer them.

In each chapter, we remind you of the good work of experts who have preceded us. Their work has been the basis for our own practice, and we often begin a chapter by discussing the guiding principles derived from their work. Also included in this section are our own current investigations.

Most of each chapter, however, is devoted to bringing best practices to life with many illustrations from our own classroom experiences and those of teachers with whom we have worked. Photographs of classrooms, student work, and other artifacts accompany our descriptions.

Near the end of each chapter (except Chapter 13), we provide a Key Terms Chart for that chapter. We encourage you to pause and reflect on the vocabulary and concepts, and to jot down your understanding of the terms. We have selected the words and concepts that are critical to your background knowledge as teachers of reading. Knowing how to define and apply the key terms is essential for an excellent teacher of reading. We urge you to use them when thinking and talking about teaching reading.

In the final section of each chapter from 2 through 12, we guide you through a self-study review process, which is described step by step below. You may find this process particularly useful if you systematically need to collect, analyze, and submit evidence of your knowledge and performance as a teacher for a teacher education program or for state certification. However, we would argue that the process of self-study is critical to good teaching and that all teachers should engage in it, regardless of their requirements.

THE SELF-STUDY REVIEW PROCESS

If you interact in writing with each chapter, you will have a record of your thoughts, ideas, and implementation of the topics presented. At the ends of Chapters 2–12, we ask you to reflect on these interactions by engaging in a self-study review. To help you, we have placed a Self-Study Review Chart (as shown here in Figure P.1) at the end of each of these chapters.

The chart's first column asks you to name an *artifact*. An artifact is any lesson or learning event you create as a result of trying out the ideas in this book. Your artifacts may include a drawing of a literate classroom, a plan for a reading lesson, or any other learning event you design as a result of interacting with this book. The chart then asks you to consider each artifact in terms of five categories of good pedagogy: (1) teacher instructional actions and language; (2) provisions for individual differences; (3) variety of modes of communication; (4) critical thinking and active engagement; and (5) opportunities for assessment. We selected these categories after researching professional teaching standards from state to state and identifying those that were consistent across the states. We then restructured them into broad categories that represent good pedagogy and an understanding of how students learn. We now outline the self-study review process.

SELF-STUDY REVIEW CHART

Name of Artifact	Teacher Instructional Actions and Language	Provisions for Individual Differences	Variety of Modes of Communication	Critical Thinking and Active Engagement	Opportunities for Assessment

FIGURE P.1. Self-Study Review Chart.

From *Teaching Reading: Strategies and Resources for Grades K–6* by Rachel L. McCormack and Susan Lee Pasquarelli. Copyright 2010 by The Guilford Press. Permission to photocopy this figure is granted to purchasers of this book for personal use only (see copyright page for details).

Step 1: Try the Best-Practice Suggestions in Each Chapter

Each chapter has model learning events for best-practice teaching of reading. If you are reading this book on your own, we hope you will design lessons and other learning events that you might like to try out in your own classroom. If you are using this book as a course text, you may be assigned to create lessons or other best-practice tasks as course assignments. Whenever you are able, we encourage you to try them out in real classrooms.

Step 2: Gather Your Artifacts for Self-Study Review

If you design a lesson plan, you will probably have a written plan, instructional materials you have designed for the children, and a companion assessment. All of these materials can be considered artifacts for self-study. These artifacts will allow you and others to evaluate your performance in a given area of reading instruction, such as fluency, vocabulary, or comprehension.

Step 3: Reflect on the Artifacts You Have Collected

Reflect on the artifacts you have collected that show evidence of using the five standards-derived categories discussed above. That is, look at them for evidence of (1) teacher instructional actions and language; (2) provisions for individual differences; (3) variety of modes of communication; (4) critical thinking and active engagement; and (5) opportunities for assessment. The following questions are intended to help you understand each category and to guide your reflection.

Teacher Instructional Actions and Language

- Does the artifact contain components of direct instruction providing clear explanations, scaffolds, guided practice, and independent practice?
- Does the artifact reflect a variety of explanations, analogies, and demonstrations tailored to help meet the needs of all students?

Provisions for Individual Differences

- Does the artifact reveal accommodations of individual differences, including prior knowledge, cultural background, native language, specific challenges, and learning differences?

Variety of Modes of Communication

- Does the artifact support a variety of ways students and teachers can communicate to promote student learning?
- Does the artifact reflect opportunities for growth in written communication by all students?

- Does the artifact illustrate the use of technological advances in communication to enrich the discourse during the lesson?
- Does the artifact demonstrate the use of discussion—listening and responding to the ideas of others?

Critical Thinking and Active Engagement

- Does the artifact suggest opportunities for students to solve problems?
- Does the artifact reflect opportunities for students to develop higher-level cognitive skills?
- Does the artifact reflect opportunities for students to engage in intellectual risk taking?
- Does the artifact include opportunities for students to discuss and understand multiple perspectives?
- Does the artifact reveal opportunities for students to work collaboratively and independently?

Opportunities for Assessment

- Does the artifact support appropriate formal or informal assessment strategies with individuals and groups of students?
- Does the artifact reflect provisions for sufficient feedback to plan for future instruction and professional development?
- Does the artifact demonstrate provisions for the students to evaluate their own work?

Step 4: Take Time to Evaluate the Strength of Each Artifact

What did you learn about yourself as a teacher of reading from each of your artifacts? How does each artifact reflect the professional standards of good pedagogy? We suggest using the Self-Study Review Chart at the end of each chapter from 2 to 12 (again, see Figure P.1 for an example) to note your answers. Also, record at the bottom what went well, so that when you teach this lesson to another class, you will be sure to retain the best parts.

Step 5: Make the Necessary Changes to the Lesson, and Attach These to the Original Artifact

Chances are great that the process of self-evaluation will generate new ideas. If so, be sure to include these new ideas in the chart. Make the revisions to an artifact as soon as you think of them; this way, there is less chance of forgetting your ideas. This process will show your growth as you reflect on your work. Ask yourself, "How can I improve the lesson next time I try this?" or "How can I make this plan better?"

Step 6: Organize and Store Your Artifacts in a Hard-Copy or Electronic Portfolio

As the final step of your self-study, gather the chapter Self-Study Review Chart and the artifacts for each chapter, including your revisions. Then devise a way to organize and store them. For example, you may want to organize them according to the chapter topics, as they represent a wide range of topics in teaching reading. You may elect to store everything in a binder or portfolio, or you may decide to transfer everything to an electronic portfolio program. Whatever you decide, set it up so that storing your artifacts becomes an ongoing process. We are sure that as you progress through the text and participate in chapter-by-chapter self-study reviews, your teaching of reading will improve.

RACHEL L. MCCORMACK
SUSAN LEE PASQUARELLI

Acknowledgments

We, the authors of this book, are literacy colleagues at Roger Williams University, friends, and partners in many projects. While writing this book, we also took courses in the Italian language. As second-language learners, we found ourselves taking a fresh perspective on literacy learning that has found its way into this book. We think it was our success in learning the language that drove us to balance the demands of writing a book, fulfilling our beloved teaching duties at the university, and practicing Italian verb tenses. Whenever we had an experience of "getting it right," we found ourselves motivated to learn more. Our success led to more success. We hope this book inspires you to help young children "get it right."

In Chapter 1 of this book, we quote two Boston University professors who have had an important impact on our own teaching: Dr. Roselmina Indrisano and Dr. Jeanne Paratore. You will recognize them when we refer to "our revered professors." Our debt of gratitude to them both is very great.

We would also like to acknowledge our students in the Roger Williams University MA in Literacy program, who have generously offered their thoughts, comments, and revisions as they tried out our instructional materials in their own classrooms. They will recognize their influence in our writing.

This book would not have been as colorful without lesson ideas and photographs of bulletin boards, classrooms, and children's work. For these materials, we would like to thank and acknowledge the following teachers and reading specialists who have generously allowed us into their classrooms:

Dale Blaess, Carey School, Newport, Rhode Island
Christina Camardo, Underwood School, Newport, Rhode Island
Michelle Carney, The Atlantis Charter School, Fall River, Massachusetts
Rachael Ficke, The Atlantis Charter School, Fall River, Massachusetts
Sybil Grayko, Carey School, Newport, Rhode Island
Sue Moore, Carey School, Newport, Rhode Island
Liz Rosenthal, Carey School, Newport, Rhode Island
Aaron Sherman, Carey School, Newport, Rhode Island
Meghan Snee, Dighton–Rehoboth Schools, Dighton, Massachusetts

For some of the beautiful charts and other figures, especially those that defied our computer drawing ability, we thank our faculty secretary, Mary Gillette.

Rachel L. McCormack is grateful to her husband, Bill, who took over 100% of the cooking and cleaning during the last revisions; and her children, Patrick and Ian, who patiently waited for everything until "after the book is done." She also thanks her niece and nephew, Polly and Christian, for sharing their work and their love for reading.

Susan Lee Pasquarelli thanks her children, Rachael and Erik, for their words of encouragement: "You go, Mom!" She also thanks them and her whole extended family for the multitude of text and picture messages she received during the busiest part of this writing, so she would not miss out on any of the family news.

Finally, we thank Chris Jennison of The Guilford Press, who believed in our project and gave us sterling advice about writing a volume that our students might actually read and enjoy.

In Chapter 9, you will read a short vignette that we wrote in Italy this past winter. To practice our new language skills and to have time to work on this book together, we packed up our computers and books and headed to Siracusa, Sicily, to finish writing this volume. We would be remiss if we did not acknowledge our Sicilian friends, Salvo and Giordana Baio, and Irene Randazzo Rizza, who encouraged us to put away our writing night after night to eat sumptuous Sicilian food and practice the Italian language with the locals. To them we say, "Grazie mille!"

This is the first book that we have written together, and we dedicate it to our students, who will be our first critics.

Contents

TEACHING READING

CHAPTER 1

Investigating Our Own Literacy

What Makes a Good Teacher of Reading?

If you are reading this book, you are—or will become—a teacher of reading. Anyone who uses any text to teach children any subject teaches reading. Our primary goal in writing this book is to *show* you, as best we can, what good reading instruction looks like and sounds like. Throughout this text, you will find many lessons, activities, and suggestions. We have used all of these with children in public school classrooms, so we have had the benefit of modeling everything we present to you. Through your interaction with this text, we hope to give you a clear picture of effective reading instruction.

Good instruction is ultimately defined by its goal. Our goal as teachers of reading is to prepare students to be independent, strategic readers in real life. Let us begin this book by looking at what this goal means.

PREPARING STUDENTS TO BE INDEPENDENT, STRATEGIC READERS IN REAL LIFE

It is not enough that our students do well in our classrooms; the true measure of good teaching is our students' reading performance when they are on their own. Johnston (2002) gives this sage advice: "Set your gaze on the endpoint." Our endpoint consists of students who can independently read and understand any text.

Readers become independent when they can read *strategically*—that is, when they learn strategies for decoding and deciphering unknown words and can monitor their comprehension in a variety of texts and situations. In other words, we are preparing students for reading in real life outside the classroom. This goal has implications for the way we teach.

In Real Life, We Do Not Read Something Aloud Unless We Have Read It Silently First

In many classrooms, children are expected to read aloud a great deal of the time, and too often they must do so without having had the chance to read the text silently first. We know many people, including ourselves, who have been asked to do readings at weddings or other public occasions. After the initial panic, we agree to do it, but we request a copy of the text before the event. We want to practice reading it before we must read it aloud under "high-stakes" circumstances. We do not want to make mistakes because we would be embarrassed. It is not fun to make a mistake in public.

Children who are good readers (and some who are developing readers) love to read aloud. There are many ways to foster this love for reading. Chapter 3 gives several examples of fluency-building oral reading activities that are fun and motivating, but they provide for silent practice first. In the real world, most of the reading our students will do will be silent reading. So, if we are preparing our children to be readers in the real world, we should trust them to read silently, give them substantial practice in being fluent, and check in as often as we need to with one-on-one assessment of their oral reading.

In Real Life, Texts Are Not Read to Us First

It would be ideal if we woke up every morning and had someone read the newspaper to us while we went about our morning routine. But, of course, that's not *reading*. That's *listening*. In order to read the newspaper, we have to contend with the text on our own, reading it silently. Teachers who read everything to their students are doing them a great disservice. We think it is better to ask ourselves these questions: What texts can our students read on their own? (Let them.) What texts do they need help with? (Help them.)

Every Content-Area Text Is Different

Students encounter a wide range of texts during the school day. Reading a fictional story (narrative text) is different from reading a text about rocks and minerals (expository text). The two types of texts are set up differently. Their text structures and text features vary. So it makes sense that each teacher has a responsibility to teach his or her students how to read the text they will be using. In most elementary classrooms, one teacher teaches all the content areas. In some of the upper elementary grades, teachers may departmentalize their instruction so that one teacher teaches language arts and social studies, for example, and another teaches math and science. Nevertheless, the premise is the same: Each must teach the students to negotiate the text. Dispensing with a text in a content area is not a good practice; it does not help students who will have to read and understand text in every content area in real life.

Reading a Lot Really Matters

Reading has many benefits, and these benefits increase as we increase the amount of reading our students do in a variety of texts and contexts. Their background knowledge increases, and their knowledge of text structures and complex syntactic structures improves.

Good readers often choose to read; conversely, struggling readers often avoid it. So good readers get lots of practice getting better, and struggling readers often do not. Stanovich (1986) refers to these outcomes as the *Matthew effects in reading*. The term *Mat-*

thew effects is a reference to a verse in the Biblical gospel of Matthew (Matthew 25:29), the gist of which is that "the rich get richer and the poor get poorer." Using this analogy, let us imagine two cycles in reading. As illustrated in Figure 1.1, good readers are likely to be ones who have had the benefit of rigorous instruction in decoding and comprehension. They are given opportunities for sustained practice; they get better at reading; they choose to read more; "the rich get richer," and the cycle continues. On the other hand, struggling readers may have received less-than-optimal instruction when they started to learn to read; they have limited skills in reading; they do not choose to read on their own; their reading does not improve; "the poor get poorer," and the cycle continues.

Allington and Cunningham (2007) also remind us that reading a lot really matters. They advocate *wide reading*—an abundance of reading in a great variety of texts and contexts—and describe the many benefits students obtain from this practice, ranging from increased vocabulary knowledge to achievement in high-stakes circumstances.

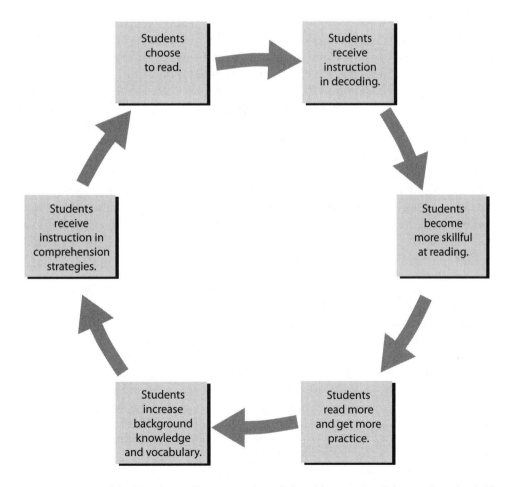

FIGURE 1.1. One of the Matthew effects in reading ("the rich get richer," for good readers). The converse of this effect ("the poor get poorer") occurs for struggling readers. Based on Stanovich (1986).

Work done by Anderson, Wilson, and Fielding (1988) provides further evidence of the effects of wide reading on achievement in reading. In their study, they investigated the independent reading habits of fifth graders in and out of school. What did they find? The students who typically scored at the 98th percentile on state tests read approximately 65 minutes independently per day (both in and out of school), which translated to about 4½ million words a year. These were the "rich" students, in Stanovich's analogy. However, the students who typically scored at the 50th percentile read about 4½ minutes independently per day, which translated into approximately 200,000 words a year. These were students who might hardly, if ever, get a chance to read silently. These were students who went home and did *not* choose to read. These were the "poor" students, in Stanovich's analogy. The more able students—the ones who probably didn't need it as much—were reading 20 times more words than their less able peers. These two groups of students had unequal access to learning simply because of the amount of text they read on a day-to-day basis.

Not All Reading Situations Are the Same

As adults in the real world, we read for many different reasons. The way we read is determined by the type of text and our purpose (or the purposes others set for us). So it is reasonable to say that each and every act of reading we do is different.

Look at the chart in Figure 1.2. In the first column, we list several different types of texts. The second column is for noting the purposes for reading the texts. In the first row is a real-life reading situation: reading an entertainment magazine while waiting for an appointment with the dentist. We often read this kind of text while waiting for the dentist to call us into the office. It helps pass the time. If we are anxious about the appointment, it helps get our mind off the procedure. If we happen to have many choices for reading material, we choose to read something that is easy, informative, and of interest to us. We do not choose to learn something difficult or to read something lengthy. We also know that the dentist is not going to ask us questions about the magazine to assess our comprehension. So the text (entertainment magazine) and the purpose we set (passing time while we wait to be called) determine our reading behavior (skimming the text and choosing things to read that are of interest).

The second row of the chart offers a very different situation: reading directions for a task. The stakes are very different now; carefully reading and thoroughly understanding the text are necessary to get things done. The text (directions to assemble a bookcase) and the purpose (successfully assembling the bookcase) have a direct effect on the way in which we read. We will have to reread sections many times as we do the assembling, particularly if this is the first bookcase we have assembled. We may employ other strategies, such as reading aloud to purposefully slow down our reading. We may have to ask someone questions about a term or tool or technique. The reading may be interactive and collaborative. We keep the directions close at hand. Reading directions to assemble a bookcase differs greatly from reading while waiting for an appointment, but they are both examples of ways we read in the real world.

On the chart, we have suggested other situations in which adult readers use text to get things done or for pleasure. Take a few minutes to jot down what you, as a reader, experience in each of these situations. You will see that every reading situation is different and puts different demands on you.

TEXT +	PURPOSE =	BEHAVIOR
Entertainment magazine	To pass time while waiting to go into the dentist's office.	I skim the magazine and find articles of interest. I know I'm not accountable for remembering the information. I am merely reading for pleasure.
Directions for assembling a bookcase	To guide me through the task of assembling.	I read the text over once and see which parts of the task I can do without help. I get started and reread the directions that need careful attention. I may have to read the directions several times. I keep the directions close to me.
Course text		
Novel (for a book group)		
Novel (for pleasure)		
Recipe		

FIGURE 1.2. Text + purpose = behavior.

The concept of *text + purpose = behavior* is a crucial one to teach, especially to our developing and reluctant readers. Those students are the ones who often think that they have to remember everything they read after reading aloud once, because that is the way they do most of their reading. Consequently, they often dislike reading, and their dislike escalates as they get older. These students, in particular, need to know that there are low stakes as well as high stakes in reading. They need to get experience and practice in all kinds of reading, so that they will choose to read more outside of school and when they are adults. However, they will not choose to read if the stakes are always high. When students' reading is oral, their mistakes are always public. They may rarely, if ever, get to choose their own purposes and texts. They may rarely, if ever, get a chance to solve problems privately. It is no wonder to us that there are large numbers of adolescents and adults who never read.

Learning to Read Well Is Really Hard, So We Need as Much Help as We Can Get

One of our revered professors began her classes on teaching reading with this saying: "Let them in on the secret: Learning to read is hard work." We always remember this advice, and we pass it on to our own students. Our more able readers make reading look easy. Our developing readers think there is something wrong with them if they have to read something more than once, or if they have to decipher an unknown word they encounter in the text, or if they have to stop for a while and think about what they read. What they don't know (and we don't always tell them) is that *good* readers do those things—that good readers encounter problems while reading, and good readers fix them up. Learning to read well in a variety of situations is hard, and we are always developing more skills as adult readers.

We Cannot Improve as Readers Unless We Are Willing to Step Outside Our Comfort Zone

Learning something new involves taking a bit of risk and stepping out of our initial comfort zone. We learn this from Vygotsky (1978), a Russian psychologist who first described a concept known as the *zone of proximal development*. Vygotsky asserted that a task a child does in collaboration with a "more knowledgeable other" *today* will be accomplished independently *tomorrow*. In order for this to happen, learners have to take the chance of trying something difficult, but know that there is someone available to help them achieve success. The zone of proximal development is wide; in fact, it is probably wider than their initial comfort zone. By presenting students with an appropriate level of challenge within their zone of proximal development, and giving them the appropriate amount of support, we can guide all students in their attempts at learning to be excellent readers.

We worry about our most fragile students a great deal. We worry about the effects that challenges might have on their self-esteem. And so we feel that we should not encourage them to step outside of their comfort zone; this zone is very narrow. This is the reason why we may read everything to them and explain everything in detail. Ironically, attempting to make them feel good about themselves may take away their opportunities to think, take chances, set goals, stumble, and get themselves back up again. Another revered professor used to chastise us when we argued in support of this practice: "You want to build their self-esteem? Teach them to read!"

Every Child Has the Rights to Excellent Instruction by Qualified Teachers of Reading

The International Reading Association (2000) has published a position statement that includes a set of reading rights to be honored for all children. See *www.reading.org* for a list of these rights. As teachers, we have a responsibility to prepare our students for the reading demands they will encounter as adults. The demands on today's readers are far greater and the stakes are higher than in the past. This is why we need to prepare students for the real-life demands they will encounter in reading. That is what this text is about: preparing teachers to prepare students for these demands. If you are still reading, we have accomplished what we set out to do. We are confident, if you have come this far, that you will find this text useful and informative.

From what you have read so far, and from your own experience, what do you think makes a good teacher of reading? Record your ideas in the space below. We have started it for you.

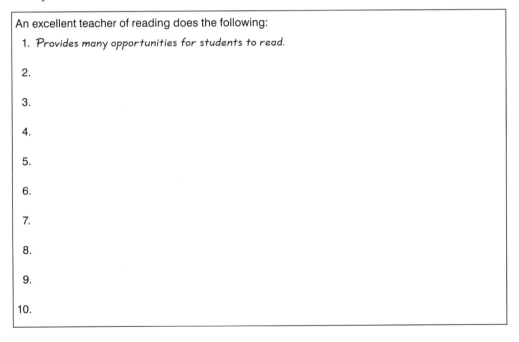

An excellent teacher of reading does the following:

1. *Provides many opportunities for students to read.*

2.

3.

4.

5.

6.

7.

8.

9.

10.

In Chapter 2, we begin the process of guiding you through an interactive investigation of research-based reading instruction. We describe the physical environment for delivering reading instruction and supporting literacy learning, as well as the routines that should be part of the everyday instruction in teaching reading to children in grades K–6.

Before you read the next chapter, take a few moments to assess your comprehension of this chapter by referring to the Key Terms Chart in Figure 1.3 (page 8). Try to write definitions for the terms in your own words.

KEY TERMS FOR CHAPTER 1

In this chapter, the following key terms are essential to your understanding of reading instruction. Think about what they mean, and try to define them in your own words.

Matthew effects in reading

wide reading

text + purpose = behavior

zone of proximal development

FIGURE 1.3. Key Terms Chart for Chapter 1.

CHAPTER 2

Creating a Literacy-Rich Classroom Environment

PAM'S CLASSROOM

Pam, a third-grade teacher, is sitting at a table with five students. She is leading this group of developing readers in reading "A List," a chapter in *Frog and Toad Together* (Lobel, 1972). The students are highly engaged and animated while reading with Pam. "Toad is so silly," cries Marco. "Doesn't he know you don't need a list to tell him to get up?" Pam enjoys these small groups of learners, as she is able to give them individual attention, and the students know that they are encouraged to speak freely and engage in conversations without raising their hands.

Occasionally Pam sweeps her eyes around the classroom, to keep up with what is going on in other areas. She sees a group of students in a center called "Word Sorts." They are taking turns leading the group as they participate in sorting the words they learned during a lesson the day before.

In the classroom library, Pam observes two pairs of students who are reading books on predators and prey—two concepts they are learning in science. They are reading to each other, occasionally stopping to talk about the information they are obtaining. Another group of students are at the computers, researching information about adopting wolves. Pam has set the computers on the website the students need, and given explicit directions about how to navigate the website and record the information. Once again, the students are talking softly to each other, pointing and helping each other.

After approximately 20 minutes, a chime goes off. The students stop what they are doing and pay attention to Pam as she gives directions. The students who are in the classroom library move to the word study center. The students who have been reading with her go to the classroom library to choose books to read on their own. The students in the computer center stay there and are given the extra time they need to work on their research. The students rotate one more time in the hour dedicated to centers.

Establishing an efficiently-run classroom is hard work. Although it took Pam a great deal of time and effort at the beginning of the year to build the structure and provide the practice, it has paid off for the students in her productive classroom.

CLASSROOM CONTEXTS THAT FOSTER MOTIVATION TO READ

Researchers have learned a great deal about the effects of motivation on students' attitudes about reading and performance while learning to read. They agree strongly that motivation improves performance (Gambrell, 1996, 2004; Guthrie & Wigfield, 2000). We have drawn upon Gambrell's (1996, pp. 194–197) guidelines for creating classrooms that foster motivation to read:

- Students are motivated to read when the environment is literacy-rich.
- Students are motivated to read when they are involved in choosing texts and materials they want to read.
- Students are motivated to read when they have opportunities to engage in sustained, independent reading.
- Students are more motivated to read when they have opportunities to discuss with others what they have read.
- Students are more motivated to read when literacy activities recognize and value their cultural identities.

HIGHLY EFFECTIVE CLASSROOMS

In Cunningham and Allington's (2007) review of the studies of highly effective classrooms, they have drawn the following conclusions (pp. 7–9) about what it takes to provide an environment in which all students can learn to read and write well:

- The most effective classrooms provide balanced instruction.
- Children in the most effective classrooms do a lot of reading and writing.
- Science and social studies are taught and integrated with reading and writing.
- Meaning is central, and teachers emphasize higher-level thinking skills.
- Skills are explicitly taught, and children are coached to use them while reading and writing.
- Teachers use a variety of formats to provide instruction, as well as a wide variety of materials.
- Classrooms are well managed, with high levels of engagement.

At the beginning of this chapter, you have read about Pam's classroom, a well-designed learning space that invites, encourages, and inspires her students to read and write. Although an attractive physical environment is not a guarantee or a substitute for effective reading instruction, it can clearly contribute to the overall comfort and motivation of the learners within its walls. It is clear that Pam has put a great deal of thought into the physical space in her classroom, and she uses the space effectively to support the literacy routines that she has put in place. In the rest of this chapter, we discuss ways you can establish a positive learning environment, with well-designed, literacy-rich physical spaces, and consistent daily routines that support the development of excellent readers.

BEST PRACTICES YOU WILL SEE IN THIS CHAPTER

✓ Setting up a literacy-rich classroom.

✓ Using a word wall.

✓ Using flexible grouping.

✓ Teaching reading in a variety of contexts and using a variety of materials.

THE PHYSICAL SPACE

We have little, if any, control over the size of the spaces given to us to deliver reading instruction. The spaces may range from cramped closets (where reading specialists are often delegated to work with students one on one or in small groups) to large, airy classrooms with high ceilings and windows that open to let in fresh air. Most classroom spaces fall somewhere in between. The good news, however, is that once we are given the space, much of what is inside *is* within our control, and we have the freedom to create an inviting and motivating environment in which our students can thrive. Assuming that this is, or will be, the case for you, we offer you suggestions for designing a space that sustains and supports excellent reading instruction.

Seating

An efficiently running classroom has a variety of seating for the students: desks and chairs, benches, rocking chairs, and beanbag chairs. We like to think of students' desks as their home bases, not the places where they spend the entire day learning. Students' desks can provide the space to store some personal materials, such as writing instruments and notebooks, and can serve as personal space in which to write or read. Moveable desks are also ideal for group work or projects, as the desks can be moved close together. The dynamic nature of the seating has many possibilities for supporting literacy learning.

In younger grades, trapezoid, rectangular, and round tables make it easy for students to work together; in the upper elementary grades, larger bodies require more substantial personal spaces, so desks work well. We have seen classrooms in which desks are grouped so that one empty desk serves as a place to store supplies (extra pencils, erasers, markers, etc.). Or the empty desk can hold baskets of books that students can read during transition periods, center time, or independent reading.

Wall Space

The classroom walls offer optimum opportunities to support literacy learning. We encourage you to be thoughtful about the kinds of print you display on the walls. Too much print is overwhelming. We advise against purchasing ready-made posters and wall displays that simply decorate the room and fill up space. These are often distracting, and the students stop noticing them after they have been up for a while. We encourage you to display purposeful print that the students can interact with and refer to throughout the day. Figure 2.1 depicts an example of an interactive wall display. The

FIGURE 2.1. Exemplary interactive classroom wall display.

photo shows a part of the classroom where students gather with the teacher each day to discuss the days of the weeks, months of the year, and daily weather, among other topics. The number chart and tally pockets help the students calculate how many days they have been in school that year. Students also log the weather and use graphs to aggregate the data they collect.

Another example of an interactive wall space is a *word wall* (Cunningham, 2005; Wagstaff, 2001). At first glance, a word wall may simply resemble an organized display of words. However, as Figure 2.2 explains, word walls are anything but simple. Word walls frequently display words in alphabetical order that students use frequently in their writing, including their own names, the teacher's name, and the name of the school. High-frequency words are added gradually as the students begin encountering them. A first-grade word wall featuring high-frequency words is illustrated in Figure 2.3.

Words on a word wall can also be displayed according to spelling patterns or content-area themes. The spelling patterns might coincide with your word study, and

---

- A developmentally appropriate collection of words for students to study in the classroom.
- A cumulative collection to which new words are added as they are introduced and needed.
- A visual scaffold that temporarily assists students in reading and writing.
- A conversational scaffold that structures the ways students study, think about, and use words.

FIGURE 2.2. What is a word wall? Based on Brabham and Villaume (2001).

FIGURE 2.3. First-grade word wall.

the words on the word wall reinforce the patterns learned. Or during a theme or unit of study in one of the content areas (such as math, social studies, or science), word walls can contain the words the students will see and write often during that unit as a means of reference, and then the words are removed at the end of the unit. No matter how the words are arranged, the words should be clearly written and accessible to all students from wherever they sit. In Figure 2.4, we summarize Cunningham's (2005) guidelines for using word walls.

The classroom walls can also display print that reinforces the classroom routines, rules for procedures, responsibilities, and other important information that may stay the same throughout the year. These can be written by you and your students together. When students assist in devising rules and procedures, their voices are heard and their ideas are honored; they take ownership of an efficient classroom. Most of the print, however, should be dynamic, and it should be revised or changed periodically. For example, strategies for reading and writing become part of the wall display, and the contents change as the strategies are added to the students' repertoire.

- Be selective.
- Limit words to common words students need frequently in writing.
- Add words gradually—five a week.
- Make words accessible and easily read by all children.
- Practice words by chanting and writing them.
- Use a variety of activities to provide sufficient practice in using the words.
- Make students accountable for spelling word wall words in all writing they do.

FIGURE 2.4. Guidelines for using word walls. Based on Cunningham (2005).

Student work on display is an example of meaningful and purposeful print on the walls. In addition to completed work, work in progress should be displayed, to showcase the development of a piece of writing. Classroom walls can exhibit anything that showcases the students' strengths. Other ideas for student work are listed below:

- Written responses to literature
- Book reviews
- Graphic organizers and other strategies for organizing text designed by individual or groups of students
- Word problems or word stories in mathematics
- Science journal entries
- Research reports
- Art
- Computer-generated materials
- Published books

Dedicated Spaces

Dedicated spaces are areas set aside for a specific purpose. They contribute to an organized literacy classroom. Such spaces provide a sense of security and ownership for your students, especially if they are involved in the designing and maintenance of the spaces. The dedicated spaces that we recommend include a common meeting area, classroom library, quiet reading space, computer center, writing center, and resource center. We elaborate on each type of area below.

Common Meeting Area

The common meeting area is a place in a busy classroom where everyone meets to serve a common purpose. It is the place where students gather for morning meeting or participate in calendar activities. Students can also meet in the common meeting area during reading instruction to learn or debrief a strategy, engage in whole-class instruction, or watch a demonstration of answering an open-response question.

In many classrooms, the common meeting area is designated by a carpet and contains something to write on (a whiteboard or easel). The area should be large enough for all the students to sit comfortably. The students should know that whenever they meet in the common meeting area, there is a common goal or purpose.

Classroom Library

We can immediately recognize a well-designed classroom, because the classroom library is the focal point. Its prominent position in the classroom space gives the strong message that reading is vital to learning in the classroom.

Effective teachers know that the classroom library is more than a set of shelves for storing books. These teachers also know that the library is a dynamic place. They continually scrutinize the space: They give a great deal of thought to the way the books are organized, the materials and texts that are included in the space, and the procedures surrounding the selection of books. We know that the materials in classroom libraries, as in other types of libraries, should be well organized, accessible, and multidimensional.

The classroom library should include a wide variety of texts and genres, and should be highly accessible. Worthy and Roser (2004) humorously refer to this as "flood ensurance," since it will enable you to accommodate a "flood" of eager readers! They define *access* as appropriateness, appeal, and sufficiency. They remind us that "students who have ready access to a wide range of reading materials are more likely to read, and to make more progress, than those who do not" (p. 184). The International Reading Association (2000) makes recommendations about specific numbers of books that students should have access to: seven per child in each classroom library, plus two more per child each year for books that are no longer timely or that have been damaged.

Like public libraries, classroom libraries should contain a balance of expository and narrative texts, and should also include other kinds of print materials (such as magazines, newspapers, and reference texts). Narrative and expository materials should be shelved separately, as they represent very different kinds of reading, and they may be chosen for very different purposes. Duke's (2000) investigations remind us of the importance of including expository texts both in elementary classroom libraries and in our instruction.

Books can be labeled by categories and stored in a variety of colorful bins and shelves. In Figure 2.5, you can see books stored in this way; they are arranged in categories and well labeled. Books can be also showcased in a separate display to complement a science unit, a social studies unit, or a genre or author study. Showcasing books is another way to make them highly accessible for the students.

To help your students discover what is in the classroom library, you can choose a few books each week to preview and endorse. In addition, any new acquisitions to the classroom library should be introduced. These books will often be chosen by the students during self-selected reading, as they have received the stamp of approval by the teacher.

FIGURE 2.5. Books in storage bins.

To maintain the efficacy of your classroom library, we suggest the following:

- Ensure that there are books representing the cultures of all readers in the classroom.
- Ensure that there are books that all readers can read independently.
- Review the books on the shelves for condition, appropriateness, and accuracy.
- Rotate the books on the shelves periodically.
- Showcase certain books that complement a unit in the content areas.
- Use a variety of shelves, bins, and containers to display the books in creative ways.
- Involve the students in organizing the classroom library by sorting and labeling the texts and devising guidelines for using the library space.

As with any literacy space or center, certain procedures and routines need to accompany the use of the space. In many classrooms, we see rules and procedures written by children for using the classroom library. We think this is a great idea. In this way, students and teachers work together to create an optimum library space.

Figure 2.6 is a chart for rating your classroom library. If you are a practicing teacher, take the time to evaluate your own classroom library—your most important literacy space. Then, using what you have recorded, make a plan for improving this space. If you do not have your own classroom, visit the classroom of a peer, and use the chart as a way to inventory your peer's classroom library.

Quiet Reading Space

Aside from the classroom library, there should be a space designated as the quiet reading area. We understand that a highly productive classroom will not always be quiet, but it should include at least one quiet space. At least some students in a busy classroom may need and seek a quiet space. The space need not be large; in fact, a small space is better. A comfy armchair or beanbag chair, a small rug, and more shelves with limited books can serve effectively for this space. Figure 2.7 (page 18) depicts an example of a quiet space for reading and writing.

Computer Center

The computer center is a fundamental learning space in the 21st century. It is no longer an option; it is a necessity. Kuhn and Morrow (2005) explain that despite initial difficulties with using technology in classrooms (not enough computers, non-user-friendly computers), the implementation of computers in classrooms is increasing in the United States. Kuhn and Morrow go on to explain that there is a cause-and-effect action in play: As computers and other technology become increasingly sophisticated, they also become more user-friendly; as they become more user-friendly, they become more prolific; as they become more prolific, teachers and students are more at ease using them.

If students have computers at home, school use of computers reinforces the home–school connection; if students do not have computers at home, the classroom is an indispensable place for them to learn and practice the technology they will be expected to know and use with relative ease. Because students in grades K–6 spend the majority of

HOW DOES YOUR CLASSROOM LIBRARY RATE?

0: Not yet

1: Need more

2: Growing

3: Excellent

Does your classroom library have . . .	0	1	2	3
Current and appropriate reference materials?				
Expository texts containing accurate information?				
Narrative texts representing all levels of reading ability in the classroom?				
Narrative texts representing all children in the classroom?				
Narrative texts representing our multicultural world?				

Texts representing a variety of genres children love?
    Realistic fiction
    Fantasy
    Traditional tales
    Historical fiction
    Biographies
    Poetry
    Informational text				

Picture books?				
Wordless picture books?				
Current children's magazines in good condition?				
Current newspapers?				
Well-organized shelves and bins?				
Displays that showcase authors, themes, topics, or genres?				

FIGURE 2.6. Rate your classroom library.

FIGURE 2.7. A quiet reading space.

their school day within the classroom setting, it makes sense for them to have access to technology within the classroom walls, rather than going to a computer lab once or twice a week.

The directions for using computers and other technology should be clearly demonstrated by the teacher, and then written out and strategically placed in the computer center for reference. There are many high-quality educational websites for students to use during their computer time; these sites continue to change and improve. As you have read at the start of this chapter, Pam integrates the computers into her center time, while she works with small reading groups. If students use headphones, computers can be part of a quiet area also devoted to reading.

Writing Center

The writing center stores writing materials and provides a space where students can work on writing projects independently or in small groups. The writing materials should be accessible, and the writing center should be stocked with the kinds of things students will need and can get themselves. Morrow (2005), Bromley (2007), and Diller (2003) provide suggestions for the types of materials writing centers should have. Suggestions are also given in Figure 2.8.

Diller (2003) has suggested positioning a writing center (she calls it a "work station") near a word wall, for easy accessibility when students are working independently or in small groups in the center. A small table and chairs allows students a comfortable and temporary place to work. Several types of paper, including blank books, should be

---

- Assorted paper
- Pens, pencils, markers
- Table and chairs
- Reference materials
- Books, photographs, and pictures for models and ideas
- Strategies for revising/editing
- Ideas for writing topics
- Student writing in various stages
- Author's chair

FIGURE 2.8. Materials for the writing center.

a staple of the center materials; pens, pencils, and markers should also be available in abundance.

Students of all ages need books, magazines, photographs, and other visual aids to give them ideas for topics and to provide models of good writing. Reference materials such as dictionaries and thesauruses should be accessible as well. The walls of the writing center can contain specific suggestions for writing topics and can clearly post the strategies the students have already learned for revising and editing their work. It is also a good idea to display student writing in various stages, so they have models of writing in progress.

A chair specifically designated for sharing work, the *author's chair* (Calkins, 1994), can be stored in the writing center and used when students are sharing their work in small groups or with the whole class. We discuss the author's chair further in connection with the writing workshop, later in this chapter.

Resource Center

A resource center has shelves for various types of materials. These include core content-area texts for science, social studies, and math; manipulatives for math; science supplies for hands-on learning events; atlases and maps for social studies; and dictionaries for all subjects. They should be well labeled and organized, and students should be able to find them easily. You can also store published anthologies of literature used for your reading program and leveled texts used for small-group reading instruction in the resource center, as these would not normally be part of your classroom library.

TRY THIS

Visit a classroom of a teacher you consider to be a highly effective literacy instructor, who has an appealing and well-organized classroom. Look at the space carefully and ask yourself these questions:

- How are the students' desks arranged?
- Is there a common meeting area?
- Where is the classroom library?
- Is it organized according to the guidelines in this chapter?
- Is the information on the walls dynamic and interactive?
- Are there dedicated spaces for students to work independently?
- Are there sufficient materials?
- Are centers well labeled with clear directions?

Now, using the good ideas you have gathered from observing one or more effective classrooms and the information in this chapter, design a classroom in the space provided on the following page.

- First, choose a grade level for your classroom.
- Next, decide on the types of centers and dedicated areas you want to include.
- Then consider the kinds of grouping you will want to use.
- Finally, make a sketch of your ideal space. Share your sketch with your peers.

Sketch it here.

Now record the materials you need to include in each of the spaces designated below. Use observations you have made of a literacy-rich classroom and the ideas you have read in this text. What would you choose for each area? What specific materials are necessary for each area to be effective? Make a list in each column, and share your ideas and questions with your peers.

Walls	Classroom Library	Writing Center	Resource Center	Computer Center

MANAGING LITERACY SPACES, EVENTS, AND MATERIALS

The well-designed literacy spaces we have described provide excellent opportunities for the students to get sustained practice in a skill or strategy recently taught, to work independently, and to extend their knowledge beyond what has already been taught. They also provide opportunities for the students to work collaboratively in a more informal setting. Diller (2003) reminds us that the literacy spaces should not replace good instruction or be places where students merely keep themselves busy.

In most cases, the students will move to these spaces on their own, either individually and/or in small groups. Many inquisitive bodies moving in and around a classroom space can be chaotic if specific procedures are not in place. At the very least, there should be (1) clear directions for each space; (2) sufficient materials and resources to work independently; (3) bins, folders, and other types of containers for storing and organizing completed work and works in progress; and (4) reference materials and books to assist the students.

Students need to be taught how to navigate through literacy spaces, and this can be done the same way you would teach any new skill: through demonstration and guided practice. Reutzel and Morrow (2007) suggest a procedure for introducing each center one at a time, over a period of weeks. They begin by explicitly modeling the use of each space (and the materials contained in the space), followed by guided practice. Then the children can begin to use the space independently. Eventually the students will understand the procedures for each center and the routines for moving among several centers in the same classroom.

Grouping

Deciding how to group students effectively is a common concern of teachers in a literacy learning classroom. Types of grouping include whole-class instruction, teacher-led homogeneous groups, teacher-led heterogeneous groups, student-led heterogeneous groups, peer dyads, and individual learning. The ways in which we group students are dependent on a few factors: (1) the particular literacy event, (2) the type of text used, and (3) the makeup of the class. The way you arrange your classroom is related to the kinds of grouping you plan.

Paratore (2000) suggests using many grouping options to allow all children equal access to learning. See Figure 2.9 (page 22) for an explanation of the grouping practices.

Daily Routines That Support Literacy Learning

Throughout this text, you will learn about specific ways to teach reading, from word study to strategy instruction to fostering engagement in literature. In this section, we present a broad model that defines the *kinds of reading* our students need to do, the *kinds of support* we must provide, and the *kinds of texts* our students require in order to be accomplished readers. Paratore (2000) refers to this model of reading instruction as *multiple grouping*, and it includes three daily literacy events: *community reading, just-right reading,* and *on-your-own reading* (see Figure 2.10 on page 23). Below, we describe Paratore's framework for excellent reading instruction; this passage is adapted from

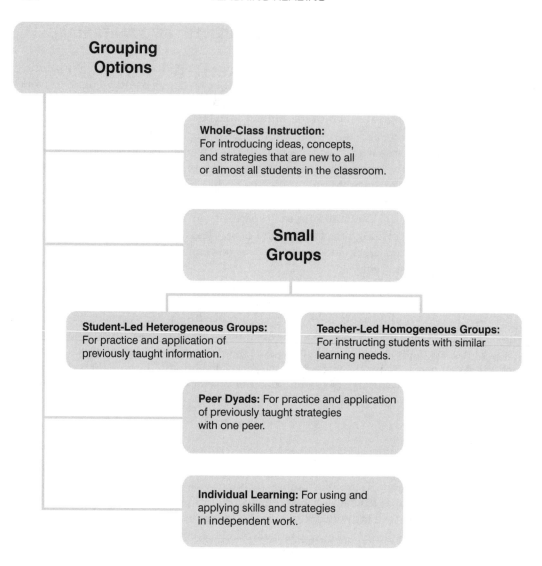

FIGURE 2.9. Grouping options. Based on Paratore (2000; see also Paratore & McCormack, 2005).

Paratore and McCormack (2005, pp. 101–105).* Some of the practices described are more fully explained in Chapter 3 of the present book.

Community Reading

In community reading, children read or listen and respond to text that will support the development of language and concepts appropriate at their grade level. Community reading is intended to achieve two major purposes. The first is to provide every child with access to grade-appropriate curriculum, and by so doing, to provide opportuni-

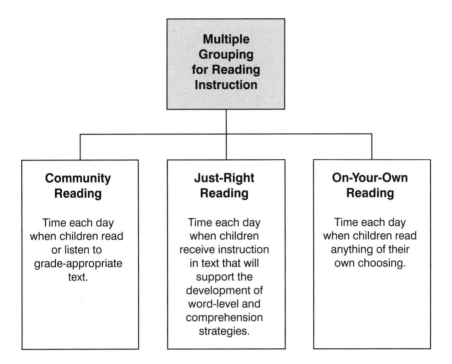

FIGURE 2.10. Multiple grouping for reading instruction. Based on Paratore and McCormack (2005).

ties for every child to acquire grade-appropriate vocabulary, concepts, and language structures. The second purpose is to create contexts that support the development of the classroom as a learning community, where a focus on the same text or topic by children of differing ability levels enables all children to interact and provides an opportunity for them to learn from one another.

In classrooms where teachers use a basal reading program, children may read a selection from the anthology during the community reading period. In classrooms where trade books frame the reading program, children generally read a teacher-selected trade book or choose from a selection of thematically related trade books during the time period.

Because all children read the same text, or a collection of texts, about the same topic or theme during this particular time period, these lessons typically begin with whole-class instruction, during which children prepare for reading by making predictions, reviewing key vocabulary and concepts, and posing questions. Although time allocations differ in every classroom, on average, teachers allocate about 45–60 minutes to the community reading component of the literacy program.

During the period when children read text, small groups are usually formed on the basis of children's reading needs. In one group, children who are capable readers are directed to read the text on their own and to complete a teacher-assigned cooperative learning activity. The assigned task is selected precisely to motivate students to reflect on, and respond to, the texts in ways that will clarify meaning or challenge their thinking.

In choosing the comprehension tasks, we are guided, in particular, by three criteria. First, the tasks we assign must be consistent with strategies previously taught. For example, after we have provided explicit instruction in story mapping to the whole class, we might ask children to work with partners to construct a story map of the next story. Second, the tasks we assign must also engage students in higher-level thinking. So, for example, after constructing a story map, we might ask students to consider the connections between a character's actions and story outcomes. What if the character had acted differently? How would that different behavior have changed the outcome? Third, we plan comprehension activities that we expect could be useful to students during subsequent lessons. For example, students might save story maps in a journal or notebook and, after a few weeks, review their collection of maps and compare or contrast events or characters.

In another group the teacher may assist struggling readers. For some children, grade-level text represents "frustration-level" material, and without teacher guidance and support, some students are likely to fail. In these cases, the teacher's responsibility is to mediate text difficulties in ways that prevent frustration. That is, the teacher must intervene with strategies and practices that make the text readable. Such intervention strategies include (1) reading all or part of the text aloud before children are expected to read it on their own; (2) providing instruction in vocabulary that is essential to comprehending the selection; (3) engaging children in choral or echo readings; or (4) assigning buddy reading. Students who need to develop word-reading accuracy and fluency may be given additional opportunities to reread parts or all of the text individually, with a partner, or with the teacher. After children have finished reading the text, they work with the teacher to complete the same comprehension task their higher-performing peers completed on their own or in small groups. In the teacher-led lesson, struggling readers are given more explicit instruction when required by the text. That is, they may be reminded of text structure and guided to use the structures when recalling or retelling important ideas. Or the teacher may focus on specific vocabulary, concepts, or language structures and discuss how the writing style influences their understanding of the text.

After all children have read and responded to the text, the groups reconvene as a whole class or as small heterogeneous groups to share what they have read and learned that day. See below for a graphic representation of the community reading segment of daily literacy instruction.

Story Introduction (Whole Class)
- Preview text, develop background knowledge, make predictions.

Reading the Selection (Needs-Based Groups)

No Help	With Help (Teacher-Led Group)
• Silent reading	• Read-aloud by teacher
• Partner reading	• Rereading with teacher or partner
• Partner response (oral)	• Group response (oral)
• Individual response (written)	• Individual response (written)

Responding to the Selection (Heterogeneous Groups or Whole Class)
- Small-group or whole-class discussion or strategy lesson

Just-Right Reading

In the just-right reading period, small groups are formed to provide children with instruction with text that is "just right" for them—that is, text they can read with 90–95% accuracy, a level that is widely believed to be optimal for acquiring word knowledge, fluency, and accuracy. Just-right reading groups are usually small (four to eight children) and typically last for 20 minutes or so. This group-based model allows the teacher to work with more than one child at a time. In addition, it includes three important tasks in each lesson: reading a focal book, engaging in systematic and explicit word study, and rereading familiar books.

For able and advanced readers, the just-right reading period offers opportunities to return to the text during community reading for explicit instruction in word-level or comprehension strategies, or, when appropriate, to read beyond the grade-level text and receive instruction that will challenge them cognitively, linguistically, and motivationally.

On-Your-Own Reading

On-your-own reading encompasses activities more widely known as *sustained silent reading* or "drop everything and read." It is the time of day when children choose to read any book or text of interest to them, and, if they wish, to share their responses with teachers and peers.

Designing a Literacy Plan

A well-designed literacy plan or schedule can include and integrate all kinds of text reading described above. You can see an example of how they can be coordinated in Figure 2.11 (page 26). We suggest that you devise a consistent schedule. If you schedule a separate block of time for on-your-own reading, we suggest using the guidelines in Figure 2.12 (page 26) for creating an independent reading program, which were inspired by the work of Cunningham and Allington (2007).

PROMOTING PEER TALK

We know that in order for children to become competent language users, they need frequent experiences of *talking* to each other in the classroom (Cazden, 2001). To our dismay, we also know that this practice is often highly discouraged. In many classrooms we observe, students are given little time to socially construct meaning. Most lessons are offered as recitations, with the predominant *participation structure* being one in which the teacher initiates (I), a student responds (R), and the teacher evaluates the response (E). This structure is referred to as the *I-R-E structure* and offers little time for open student talk (Mehan, 1979). A classroom transcript of a discussion with an I-R-E structure is below. Each is marked with an (I) for *initiation*, an (R) for *response*, and/or an (E) for *evaluation*.

> (I) TEACHER: We are studying mammals. What makes a mammal different from other animals?
>
> (R) STUDENT 1: It is warm-blooded.

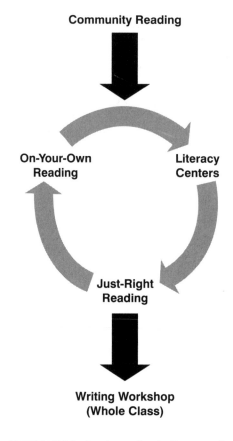

FIGURE 2.11. An example of a literacy plan.

- Create a program that will promote independent reading both in and out of school.
- Begin the program in kindergarten.
- Allow 10–15 minutes a day for independent, in-school reading in grades K–2.
- In grades 3–5, increase the amount to 15–20 minutes per day.
- Above grade 5, continue to increase the amount of time for independent reading.
- Have designated periods of time devoted to independent reading.
- Establish a no-wandering rule.
- Encourage students to talk about what they've read.
- During independent reading, the teacher should also read. During sharing time, the teacher should share what he or she has read.

FIGURE 2.12. Guidelines for creating an independent reading program. Based on Cunningham and Allington (2007).

(E) (I) TEACHER: Yes, you are right. What else?

(R) STUDENT 2: It carries its baby inside? I mean, mammals don't lay eggs like birds.

(E) (I) TEACHER: Yes! Very good! Mammals do carry their babies inside and give birth to live young. Are we mammals?

(R) STUDENT 3: Yes, we are mammals.

(E) (I) TEACHER: Very good. We are all mammals. We are warm-blooded, and our mothers gave birth to us alive. Mammals also have some sort of fur or hair that sets us apart from egg-laying animals. So can anyone think of another characteristic of a mammal?

Do you notice in the transcript that the teacher is doing most of the talking? Figure 2.13 shows graphically how the I-R-E structure gives much more opportunity for teacher talk than student talk. Encouraging student talk helps children clarify their thoughts, assists them in understanding what they have read, and helps them develop confidence as language users (Paratore & McCormack, 1997). With opportunities to practice, students are able to use both the language of the curriculum (school talk) and the language of personal identity (home talk) (Cazden, 2001).

By building specific experiences for your students to talk together, you can create authentic ways for your students to practice becoming more competent language users. By *listening* to them talk, you have a unique opportunity to discover the ways in which they negotiate meaning. You will often find your own pedagogical language replicated in their voices. What better way to assess their knowledge and the efficacy of your teaching? Promoting peer talk provides your students with rich opportunities for personal interactions, and it gives sanction for them to discuss their observations about their world and themselves in an authentic way.

Discussions of the books students read with others and on their own provide one context for helping students construct meaning about the world around them. These discussions are not limited to talking about narrative text; rather, the discussions should

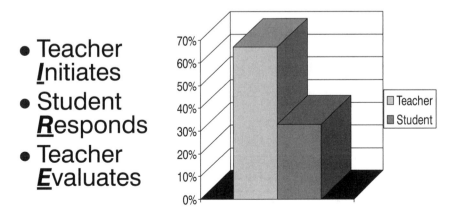

FIGURE 2.13. Proportion of teacher talk to student talk in I-R-E participation structure.

include talking about the many expository books they read to gain information about the world around them.

Supporting Good Book Discussions

Fostering good discussions takes time and patience. We have used practical suggestions from the work of Lapp, Flood, Ranck-Buhr, Van Dyke, and Spacek (1997) and Roser, Strecker, and Martinez (2000) to devise the following guidelines for nurturing critical thought and insightful talk in the classroom. The guidelines are also summarized in Figure 2.14.

Choose Good Books

The books you choose will affect the quality of the discussions. Select books that have strong plots, good characterization, and worthwhile themes. Expository texts should be engaging, accurate, and well presented.

Model Good Discussion Behaviors

APPROPRIATE TURN TAKING

Taking turns is not instinctive; it has to be taught. Modeling turn-taking behavior in front of the class with parent volunteers, teacher aides, and other support staff in your classroom is one way to show your students how to "get the floor." It is important to establish a list of rules to govern the active participation of *all* students.

LISTENING

Teaching active listening skills is important before young children can participate in a group discussion. Children are likely to think about and dwell on what they want to say *next*, instead of listening to what another student is saying *now*. You can teach your students these aspects of active listening: (1) making eye contact with the speaker; (2) showing they are listening by responding with nonverbal language, such as nodding their heads when they are in agreement; and (3) appreciating the speaker's message.

- Choose good books.
- Model good discussion behaviors:
  Appropriate turn taking
  Listening
  Speaking
- Arrange seating strategically.
- Encourage students to think on their feet.
- Gradually relinquish control of the discussions.

FIGURE 2.14. Guidelines for promoting good discussions.

SPEAKING

It is very important to model appropriate speaking behaviors before your students participate in discussion groups. Rules and routines must be clearly established. For example, students need to see modeled: (1) constructive, positive talk; (2) talk that keeps the conversation flowing from point to point; and (3) talk that clarifies, initiates, and/or questions.

Arrange Seating Strategically

Whether the whole class or part of the class is participating in the discussion, the students should be seated so that they can have face-to-face interactions. This can be done by arranging the students in a circle on the floor or at their desks. You should situate yourself within the group without being in a position to be the "leader" of the discussion, but rather just one participant. If students think you are leading, they will defer to you as the voice of authority.

Encourage Students to Think on Their Feet

Many students think they are only allowed to speak in a discussion if they know "the right answer." You can encourage them to use talk to clarify their thinking.

Gradually Relinquish Control of the Discussions

As students begin to show competence in the give and take of discussions, your role should change from discussion leader to discussion facilitator. At some point, your presence will not be essential to the discussions, and the students can engage in their own constructive discussions of the books they read.

Using Small-Group Formats

Book circles, literature circles, or book clubs (Kong & Fitch, 2002–2003; Raphael & McMahon, 1997; Raphael, Florio-Ruane, & George, 2001) can be highly structured, small-group contexts for teaching reading and talking about books; they can also be more informal contexts for students to talk about the books they have self-selected and are reading on their own (McCormack & Carney, 2005). In the formal contexts, teachers can begin with the whole class to teach a strategy or introduce a genre. Students can then meet in groups to read and discuss a common book. They may follow their discussion with a written assignment or journal entry. Following the written assignment, the whole class can reconvene to debrief the strategy the students have learned and to discuss their books.

In the informal contexts, the students can meet periodically in small groups to share their self-selected books. This practice can take place at any grade level, and the groups can be led by the students themselves. It is ideal to let the students establish their own guidelines for talking about books and for participating in the discussions, as illustrated in Figure 2.15.

1. Come to the group prepared.
2. Listen to the leader's directions.
3. Be respectful and helpful to each other.
4. Have lots of conversations about the books.
5. Have fun!

FIGURE 2.15. Student-devised rules for literature circles.

We provide more elaboration of the value of peer talk in Chapter 12, when we discuss assessing vocabulary, comprehension, and response.

TRY THIS

In order to understand what book discussions look and sound like in real classrooms, schedule a time to observe and listen to a teacher-led discussion. If possible, try to observe a peer-led discussion as well. Use the questions in Figure 2.16 to guide your observation. What have you learned about the discussion between teacher and students or among students? How would you facilitate the discussion to make it different? How would you change the participation structure?

WRITING WORKSHOP

Writing workshop is the ultimate format for teaching process writing (Calkins, 1994; Graves, 1994), and it perfectly illustrates what we mean by a teaching and learning

Observe the members of a discussion group. Use these questions to guide your observations.

- How can you describe the participation structure?
- Did any student emerge as the leader? How did you know?
- How did the participants get the floor? Maintain the floor?
- What were the purposes of the talk?
  Initiating
  Questioning
  Agreeing
  Seeking clarification
  Challenging
  "Upping the ante"
  Elaborating/explaining
  Other
- To what extent did everyone participate?
- Was there overlapping talk? If so, was it appropriate?
- Was any of the discourse off topic? If so, was it redirected? If so, how?

FIGURE 2.16. Participation structure exercise.

event that encompasses all the guidelines of best practice. It provides instruction in a variety of grouping options; allows substantial opportunities for peer interaction; contains authentic and meaningful instruction; and engages all learners in the acts of reading, writing, listening, and speaking. In writing workshop, students are active learners of the process of planning, drafting, revising, editing, and publishing their own writing, the way real writers do.

Although students should be writing all day, in every subject, a writing workshop format provides direct instruction in the writing process, specific genre elements, and grade-appropriate writing conventions (such as grammar, capitalization, and punctuation). A large block of time within the writing workshop structure allows for sufficient practice. We suggest that you set aside up to 1 hour one or two times a week in grades K–2, and 1–2 hours one or more times a week in grades 3–6. We agree with writing experts that writing instruction should be structured around the standards your students need to meet and the genres you need to teach (Pasquarelli, 2006a).

A typical writing workshop has four basic components: reading, mini-lesson, writing/conferring, and sharing (see Figure 2.17). We like to see each writing workshop session begin with immersing the students in the genre you are teaching. This may only take a few minutes each session, as you read to or with your students some excellent examples of the genre you are studying.

The next component of writing workshop is a mini-lesson focusing on a strategy for revising or editing the writing pieces the students are working on. Each mini-lesson should center on a piece of real writing, preferably your own.

After the mini-lesson, the students continue working on their writing pieces, applying the strategy they learned in the mini-lesson to their own pieces of writing. Mini-lessons should not be followed by worksheets; rather, the students' writing pieces become their "personal worksheets" as they apply the strategy you have taught to revise or edit their own writing. During the writing time, students can engage in peer conferences, working collaboratively to improve their pieces. You can also confer with students in small groups or one on one, focusing on process or product.

At the end of writing workshop, you can choose two or three students to share their finished pieces or works in progress by taking the *author's chair* (Calkins, 1994), the chair of honor (see Figures 2.18 and 2.19 on page 32). This is a time for positive feedback. See Figure 2.20 (page 33) for the kinds of comments the students can expect from their peers. Final draft pieces or pieces in varying stages of development can be displayed in the classroom, specifically in the writing center.

- *Reading the genre with, by, and to children:* Immerse the students in the genre by sharing lots of examples of great writing.
- *Mini-lesson:* Teach a strategy to revise or edit their writing by applying the strategy to a piece of your own writing.
- *Writing and conferring:* Guide students to apply the strategy to their writing while they plan, draft, revise, and edit their work. Meet with students one on one or in small groups.
- *Sharing:* Choose two or three students to take the author's chair.

FIGURE 2.17. Components of writing workshop.

> *This is a great opportunity to share your writing with others!*
>
> - Hold your piece so you can see it, but without covering your face. Smile.
> - Read slowly and with expression.
> - Look up from time to time and make eye contact with your audience.
> - Call on a few classmates for their comments.
> - Thank your classmates for their input.

FIGURE 2.18. Directions to students for taking the author's chair.

We have had success using a writing workshop format to teach writing, beginning in kindergarten. There are many good resources for implementing writing workshop in your classroom. We suggest that you consult a writing text for an elaboration on how to carry out an effective workshop. For example, for younger students, the text *Scaffolding Young Writers: A Writer's Workshop Approach* (Dorn & Soffos, 2001) is an explicit text for setting up a workshop model in your classroom. For older elementary students, *Teaching Writing Genres across the Curriculum* (Pasquarelli, 2006b) is an excellent resource for teachers to help students skillfully negotiate the writing tasks they will need as they get older.

FIGURE 2.19. Student taking the author's chair.

FIGURE 2.20. "What can I expect my classmates to say when I take the author's chair?": Examples of positive peer comments.

The chart below lists the kinds of grouping options effective teachers use throughout the literacy curriculum. Reflect on the kinds of literacy events that occur on a typical school day. Then, indicate how they can be carried out through a variety of grouping configurations. A few are already listed as a model.

Literacy Event	Whole Class	Teacher-Led Homogeneous Groups	Student-Led Heterogeneous Groups	Peer Dyads	Individual
Literature circles	×		×	×	
Independent reading				×	×

FOLLOWING GINA: COMMUNITY READING THROUGH THE EYES OF A THIRD GRADER

Let us follow Gina as she navigates a flexibly grouped classroom, and participates in some of the reading routines described in this chapter.

Gina is an energetic and gregarious third grader. She loves to read, but she still struggles a bit with decoding new words. Although she often feels challenged, she is quite cheerful. In the common meeting area, Gina's teacher introduces the whole class to the core reading selection of the day: *A Picture Book of Thomas Alva Edison* (Adler, 1996), which is a selection from the district-adopted reading list. The biography is challenging because of the number of new and difficult words Adler presents to the reader, but Gina's teacher shows how Adler defines each word explicitly in the sentence following the words, and provides a detailed illustration on each page. The whole-class instruction is a great format for introducing the selection and getting the students ready to read on their own.

As this text is too difficult for Gina and several of her classmates to read completely on their own, Gina joins a group of six children at a table with her teacher, while the other students read the selection about Edison on their own. The teacher spends the next 20 minutes guiding the reading of Gina's group along. Sometimes he reads to them, and sometimes he asks them to read parts of it alone. All the while, he is reviewing how Adler structures the vocabulary support. Gina is animated and talkative during this group session, especially when her teacher starts asking questions about Thomas Edison. At the end of the session, the students choose two pages to read together. They practice these a few times.

Gina now joins all her classmates back in the common meeting area. Gina's teacher asks, "So what do you think about Thomas Alva Edison?" The students laugh, and they start talking about Edison's quirkiness, drawing specific examples from the text. Then Gina's teacher says, "Turn to the person next to you and talk about some of Thomas Edison's inventions." Gina turns to a boy who was not in her small group, and they begin to list some of the inventions mentioned in the book. After this peer talk activity, one student says, "He invented the telephone." Gina looks aghast, but politely says, "No, *Alexander Graham Bell* invented the telephone. Thomas Edison *improved* it." She is proud of herself, because that was precisely what they had talked about in her small group. To finish the lesson, Gina's teacher says, "How about if we read a couple of pages together? Let's read the part when Thomas Edison was a boy and worked as a candy butcher. Can you find those pages?" Of course, Gina finds those pages quickly. Those were the *exact* pages her group practiced!

Before you read the next chapter, take a few moments to assess your comprehension of this chapter by referring to the Key Terms Chart in Figure 2.21. Try to write definitions in your own words.

REFLECTION ON ARTIFACTS FOR YOUR SELF-STUDY

For your self-study, record on Figure 2.22 (page 36) the artifacts you created while you read this chapter.

KEY TERMS FOR CHAPTER 2

In this chapter, the following key terms are essential to your understanding of reading instruction. Think about what they mean, and try to define them in your own words.

word wall

dedicated spaces

multiple grouping

community reading

just-right reading

on-my-own reading

participation structures: I-R-E versus peer talk

writing workshop

author's chair

FIGURE 2.21. Key Terms Chart for Chapter 2.

SELF-STUDY REVIEW CHART FOR CHAPTER 2

Name of Artifact	Teacher Instructional Actions and Language	Provisions for Individual Differences	Variety of Modes of Communication	Critical Thinking and Active Engagement	Opportunities for Assessment

FIGURE 2.22. Self-Study Review Chart for Chapter 2.

CHAPTER 3

Developing Foundations for Fluent Readers

Phonological/Phonemic Awareness, Phonics, and Fluency

Learning to read is hard work. Reading is a complex process influenced by an assortment of cognitive, linguistic, and affective factors. As difficult as it is, children usually follow a somewhat standard developmental course in learning to read that begins well before they arrive at school. Clay (1979) has described this early process as *emergent literacy*. Children can learn a great deal about books, print, and writing from many sources before coming to school. They learn the functions (the reasons why we have print) and the forms (all kinds of writing) of written communication through their experiences with environmental print—signs, labels, and billboards. They learn that symbols represent sounds and words. They learn that print conveys meaning. This awareness is supported when home environments nurture literacy through storybook reading, writing experiences, trips to museums, and other outings.

We know of many children who come to school with thousands of hours of literacy instruction derived from those very experiences: from storybook reading to learning about letters and sounds from popular children's television programs. For other children, trips to the grocery store are opportunities for them to observe printed labels and associate them with things they know. For still other children, their classrooms will be the only places where they read and enjoy books, write for a variety of purposes, and "talk the talk" of the classroom.

Our students develop as excellent readers, in great part, because of the time they spend with teachers and other students who make learning to read the top priority in the early grades. We have a responsibility to provide our students with the best experiences we can to prepare them to be independent, strategic readers.

In this chapter, we describe the foundations of strategic reading: phonological and phonemic awareness, knowledge of phonics and high-frequency words, and fluent reading.

BEST PRACTICES YOU WILL SEE IN THIS CHAPTER

✓ Teaching phonological and phonemic awareness.

✓ Choosing approaches and contexts to teach phonics.

✓ Teaching high-frequency words.

✓ Teaching fluency.

✓ Using the fluency development lesson.

✓ Choosing books that help build fluency.

TEACHING PHONOLOGICAL AND PHONEMIC AWARENESS

What Are Phonological and Phonemic Awareness?

Phonological awareness is the consciousness of sounds in words (Adams, 1990; Yopp, 1995). When children have phonological awareness, they can hear and manipulate the sounds and chunks of sounds in spoken language. They enjoy and appreciate words that rhyme, and they delight in hearing, reciting, reading, and rereading poems and rhyming books. They know that our spoken language is divided into separate words, and the evidence of this is seen in their writing, when they can separate the words that they have previously written as connected strings of letters. They understand the concepts of *syllables*, *onsets* (beginnings of letters up to the vowel in a syllable or a one-syllable word), and *rimes* (the vowel and everything after in a syllable or a one-syllable word). *Phonological awareness* is a broad term and includes the concept of *phonemic awareness*.

When children have *phonemic awareness*, they understand and can manipulate the individual *phonemes*—the smallest speech sounds—in words. They can tell you that the word *dog* is like *log* because you can take the *d* sound away and replace it with an *l* sound. They can listen to the sounds made by the letters *c-a-t* and know the word is *cat*. Conversely, they can listen to the word *cat* and tell you the sounds made by the letters *c-a-t*.

The prevalent thinking is that there is a reciprocal relationship between phonemic awareness and reading (Armbruster, Lehr, & Osborn, 2001; Snow, Burns, & Griffin, 1998). Being able to detect and manipulate phonemes in our spoken language helps a child to read, and the act of reading promotes growth in phonemic awareness. Adams (1990) refers to students' phonemic awareness as a major predictor of reading success.

How to Teach Phonological/Phonemic Awareness

Teaching phonological and phonemic awareness takes a bit of planning, but after a short while, many of the focused lessons can become second nature to you and your students. There are few, if any, materials to prepare, and your students will look forward to their word play *by ear*. Yopp (1993) provides us with recommendations for teaching phonological and phonemic awareness. These are listed below, and we have included some of our own recommendations as well.

- Begin teaching phonological awareness through *rhymes* (e.g., *cat*, *fat*, *sat*). This is the easiest of the phonological awareness tasks.
- Plan deliberate lessons and teach the sounds through explicit instruction.

Although some students may pick up phonemic awareness later through inter-action with print, most need direct instruction. *This instruction needs to be carried out in the form of oral activities.*

- Plan child-appropriate and playful activities to teach and provide practice. We use italics below to stress the *oral* or other *sound-based* aspects of these activities.
  - Teach students to *sing* new songs, leaving out some of the rhyming words and encouraging the children to *guess* at the words.
  - *Recite* short poems and nursery rhymes.
  - *Clap out* words in lines of poems, songs, or sentences as you *recite* them or *sing* them.
  - *Tap out* syllables in words, using musical instruments such as drumsticks, bongo drums, or tambourines.
  - Practice *orally* taking words apart and putting them together. These can include nonsense words. Use your hands to show them how to s-t-r-e-t-c-h the words, then watch them use their hands.
- Help parents understand their roles in promoting phonological and phonemic awareness by showing them how to play word games, reading rhyming stories, and reciting traditional nursery rhymes and singing songs. (See Chapter 10 for more discussion of inviting parents to engage in family literacy.)

Figure 3.1 is a chart of the tasks that Yopp (1993) suggests children should know and be able to do in order to develop phonological and phonemic awareness. Again, the most important thing to remember is that these tasks are *oral*. By training your students' ears to hear and distinguish between sounds, you can help your students to identify the sounds in print. You can use Figure 3.1 as a way to help sequence your lessons from easiest to most difficult.

Also remember that your lessons in phonological and phonemic awareness should (1) have consistent formats from day to day, (2) be integrated into your literacy cur-riculum, (3) have clear objectives, (4) be cumulative (you should add more tasks as the students learn them), and (5) be playful and fun. Your students will reap many benefits

---

1. **Rhyming words:** Being able to tell that two words rhyme: *cat–bat, dog–hog.*

2. **Counting words in a sentence:** Being able to tell that the following is a five-word sentence: *I have a new puppy.*

3. **Counting syllables in words:** Being able to tell that *horse* has one syllable, while *hamster* has two.

4. **Segmenting and blending syllables:** Hearing the word *barking* and giving it two syllables; hearing *trot-ting* and blending it together.

5. **Segmenting and blending onset and rime:** Hearing the word *skunk* and segmenting it into *sk-unk*; hearing *sk-unk* and being able to make the word *skunk.*

6. **Counting phonemes in words:** Knowing that *pig* has three sounds—/p/ /i/ /g/.

7. **Segmenting and blending phonemes:** Hearing the word *bat* and giving it three phonemes; hearing *b-a-t* and saying the word *bat.*

8. **Substitution of sounds:** Taking the word *dog*, substituting a *d* for the *h*, and saying *hog.*

FIGURE 3.1. Phonological and phonemic awareness tasks. Based on Yopp (1993).

from your diligence in teaching phonological and phonemic awareness when they are learning the phonetic elements needed to read print.

TRY THIS

Choose *one* of the phonological or phonemic awareness tasks from the chart in Figure 3.1. Then design a child-appropriate lesson in which you teach the skill and let them practice. Write your plan in the box below.

TEACHING PHONICS

What Is Phonics?

Beck (2006) describes *phonics* as the "relationship between letters and their sounds" (p. 25). In order to read words, she states, children need "to know the speech sounds associated with written words; they need to know how to put those sounds together to form a pronounceable word; they need to have a string sense of English orthography; and they need to recognize words rapidly" (p. 25).

What Knowledge Do You Need before You Can Teach Phonics?

We believe that in order to teach phonics well, you have to have a good knowledge of the terminology and concepts surrounding *phonology*—the study of the sounds in language—and *phonetic elements*. There has been some concern about the amount of deep knowledge that teachers of reading need to possess about the subject matter they teach (Pearson, 2007). We strongly urge you to learn as much as you can about the features of phonology, so you can make thoughtful and intelligent decisions about how best to teach your developing readers the sound–print code. To get a sense of what you must learn (or relearn) in order to be successful in teaching phonics, see Figure 3.2, which summarizes Beck's (2006) definitions of various phonetic elements. It is important for new teachers of reading to familiarize themselves with these elements before attempting to teach phonics.

In Appendix A, we again offer you the most common phonetics elements and the most common onsets and rimes, to get you started on developing the knowledge you need to be able to teach phonics. We also suggest you consult texts that deal specifically with phonics instruction, such as Beck's (2006) *Making Sense of Phonics: The Hows and Whys*. In this book, Beck walks teachers of reading through step-by-step, focused procedures to teach letter–sound relationships, blending, and word building.

So what is the best type of phonics instruction for beginning readers? The answer may seem paradoxical: "None is best; all are best." Although some instructors may promote one method over another, teachers of reading know that phonics can be taught in every possible way. There are many approaches and contexts for teaching phonics, and there are many published programs to help teach it. You can see that here (and throughout the text), we do not advocate any particular program. If your school or district uses a published phonics program, your job is to learn as much as you can about phonology and the teaching of phonics, so you can understand the components of the published program and the reasons why they are included there. We advocate excellent *teaching*, because teachers teach phonics; programs do not.

Term	Meaning	Example
Consonant blend	Two or three contiguous consonant letters. Each consonant maintains its sound. Sometimes called a *consonant cluster*.	*br = brush* *spl = split*
Consonant digraph	Two consonants representing a unique sound. Individual letters do not maintain their phonemes.	*sh = ship* *th = that* *ch = chat*
Vowel digraph	Long vowel sounds represented by two or more adjacent letters.	*ee = meet* *ea = meat* *oa = boat*
Vowel diphthong	A single speech sound that begins with one vowel sound and moves to another.	*ow = cow* *ew = few* *oi = soil*
R-controlled vowels	A word or syllable in which the letter *r* influences how the preceding vowel is pronounced.	*ar = car* *ir = fir* *ur = fur*
Phoneme	Smallest speech sound into which a spoken word can be divided.	/ch/ai/n/ = *chain* /j/u/m/p/ = *jump*
Grapheme	Smallest written representation of speech sounds.	*ch-ai-n = chain* (three graphemes) *j-u-m-p = jump* (four graphemes)

FIGURE 3.2. Explanations for phonetic elements. Based on Beck (2006).

Planning Your Phonics Instruction

If you teach grades K–2, or you are working with developing readers in any grade, you no doubt have to teach phonics to your whole class, in small groups, or both. Effective teachers integrate phonics instruction throughout the reading program, but they also know that it is only a part of an overall reading program. Research strongly suggests that phonics needs to be explicitly taught in a systematic way (Armbruster et al., 2001). That means that your lessons need to be preplanned and focused with a consistent design. To help you plan well-designed lessons, we have included the most frequently asked questions we hear in our graduate classes regarding the teaching of phonics. We follow the questions and answers with three examples of well-planned phonics lessons.

Question 1: What aspects of phonics do I teach, and in what order do I teach them?

To help you decide what to teach and in what order, you can refer to one of the many professional texts entirely devoted to teaching phonics, or you can consult a commercially designed phonics program. Fortunately, there are plenty of both. Commercially designed phonics programs and professional texts dedicated to the teaching of phonics usually offer a suggested sequence for teaching the phonetic elements.

Although the methods for teaching the elements may vary from program to program or from book to book, they typically begin with teaching single-consonant sounds that correspond well with the letter names. For example, the suggested instructional sequence might begin with teaching such single consonants and sounds as $T = $ /t/; $M = $ /m/; $S = $ /s/; and $B = $ /b/, because as you pronounce those letters, you can actually *hear* the sounds of the letters. Approximately two-thirds of the consonant letter names in the English language correspond closely with their sounds, so planning your instruction to begin with these consonants makes sense.

A typical instructional sequence that follows teaching the sounds of single consonants might look like this (again, see Figure 3.2 for definitions and more examples for each term):

1. The short sounds of vowels—for example, /a/ as in the word *hat*.
2. Consonant blends—for example, /st/ as in the word *stop*.
3. Consonant digraphs—for example, /sh/ as in the word *ship*.
4. Vowel digraphs—for example, /oa/ as in the word *boat*.
5. Vowel diphthongs—for example, /oi/ as in the word *boil*.
6. *R*-controlled vowels—for example, /ar/ as in the word *car*.

By using a systematic sequence for teaching the phonetic elements, you can be sure that all the elements are taught to the children who need them. Eventually your instruction will include teaching all the phonetic elements that correspond with what the students have learned *by ear* during their instruction in phonological and phonemic awareness. Effective phonics instruction will reinforce their phonological and phonemic awareness; effective phonological/phonemic awareness instruction will prepare them for learning more phonetic elements.

Question 2: When and where do I teach phonics?

Another important decision you need to make is when and where to teach phonics. In other words, in what setting or under what circumstances should phonics be taught? The answer to this question is twofold. Phonics can be taught during a reading lesson, when you are reading a real book to and with children. In this case, students use the real text to study the phonetic elements and to practice decoding. This is called *contextualized* phonics instruction because the instruction occurs *in the context of real reading*. This instruction can be carried out in whole-class or small-group formats.

The second part of the answer is that phonics can be taught *separately*, as a lesson itself, apart from reading a real text. This type of phonics instruction is called *decontextualized* phonics instruction, because it is *outside the context of real reading*. This instruction can also be implemented in whole-class or small-group formats.

Question 3: How do I choose between contextualized and decontextualized instruction?

The answer to the third question is simple: You do not *have* to choose. You can (and may have to) use both contextualized and decontextualized instruction for teaching the phonetic elements to your students. Your district or school may require that you devote a specific number of minutes per day to decontextualized phonics instruction. Or you may choose to teach phonics in separate, focused lessons, in order to ensure that all phonetic elements are taught to all your students. However, you can easily and effectively follow up that instruction by applying what your students have learned in a more contextualized setting.

Question 4: What does contextualized phonics instruction look like?

A common strategy for teaching a contextualized phonics lesson is the use of *big books*. A big book is an oversized picture storybook or expository text that introduces children to the concept of books, print, and meaning (Morrow, 2005). Big books can be used in a variety of ways to teach students about book handling (left to right, top to bottom), turning pages (left to right), and meaning-bearing print (the letters and words that convey the message). Many teachers of kindergartners and first graders teach phonics when they show their students how our language works while reading and rereading the stories and information in the big books.

A phonics lesson can begin with a reading of a big book, followed by a discussion of the story. Whenever we are using books to teach phonetic elements, the first reading should always be accompanied by a discussion that focuses on the comprehension of the text. Otherwise, we would switch the focus of reading for meaning to reading a collection of words. We do not want to do that for any readers, especially our developing readers.

The best way to answer the question is to give you an example. We observed a kindergarten teacher named Patrick as he used a big-book version of *Brown Bear, Brown*

Bear, What Do You See? (Martin, 1967) to teach initial-consonant blends such as *br*. After reading the book twice and talking about the playful language, Patrick guided the kindergartners to be "detectives" and use a (paper) magnifying glass to point out the words with the *br* consonant blend. They had to look very carefully, he explained, so they could find all of them. When the students picked up their smaller copies of *Brown Bear, Brown Bear*, they recalled the phonics lesson, but also associated the text with pleasure and having fun.

Question 5: What does decontextualized phonics instruction look like?

Decontextualized phonics instruction is referred to in many classrooms as *word study*. Good word study always begins with the reading of real texts, but the actual teaching of phonics is explicit and takes place in a separate, focused lesson that typically lasts 20–30 minutes. For example, in a decontextualized word study activity, the teacher does the following:

1. Introduce a phonetic element.
2. Model how to read the sound in isolation, then in a word or list of words.
3. Engage the students in hands-on activities to practice using the phonetic element. Hands-on activities can include using letter tiles to make words, or using word cards to sort words by different phonetic elements.
4. Reinforce the new skill by asking the students to write words using the new sound.

The instruction can begin with a whole-class activity; move to small, focused groups based on need; and then progress further to a dedicated word study center where students can continue their practice. In the word study center, the students can continue to do the things that were modeled by the teacher, such as sorting words on cards according to phonetic elements, reading more words, and writing words having similar patterns. Graves, Juel, and Graves (2001) offer a set of principles guiding the implementation of word study:

- Start where each child is.
- Make word study an active decision-making process, in which children classify words according to the similarity of their sounds and spelling pattern.
- Base word study on contrasting words with different sounds or spelling patterns.
- Help children understand how the writing system works.
- Keep comprehension as the goal.

There are many excellent texts written specifically about word study. We recommend using the comprehensive suggestions made by Bear, Invernizzi, Templeton, and Johnston (2008) in their text *Words Their Way: Word Study for Phonics, Vocabulary, and Spelling*.

Question 6: Can I combine contextualized and decontextualized phonics instruction?

Although you can and may want to keep the two different settings for teaching phonics separate, we also advocate combining both contextualized and decontextualized phonics instruction in a reading lesson. While decontextualized phonics instruction provides early readers with focused instruction at decoding words, it does not always provide enough of a connection to real reading in most of the classrooms we have observed. On the other hand, contextualized phonics instruction is not often explicit enough for students and forces them to figure out rules and guidelines on their own— something that is not automatic for many of our developing readers.

Here is an example of a combined approach: A reading lesson may (1) start with the choral reading of a big book for enjoyment and simple understanding; (2) progress to a teacher-directed word study session with specific words or phonetic elements extracted from the big book; (3) involve the students in working with the teacher to put the words back into the book and then in rereading the text with more fluency; and (4) end with moving to a dedicated word study center in the classroom, where the students can engage in sustained practice on their own or with a small group of peers.

Question 7: We keep hearing about different approaches to teaching phonics. What are the approaches to teaching phonics?

There are three major approaches to teaching phonics: a *synthetic* approach, an *analytic* approach, and an *analogy-based* approach. These *approaches* to teaching phonics should not be confused with the *settings* for teaching phonics. Approaches are specific methods for teaching the phonetic elements; the three approaches vary.

In a *synthetic* approach, students first learn the sounds represented by letters or letter combinations. Then they are taught to blend those sounds together to produce words. A synthetic phonics approach is also called *inductive* phonics. For example, in a synthetic approach to teach the word *street*, the students would use what they know about the consonant blend *str*, then use the sounds of the vowel digraph *ee*, then use the sound of the final consonant *t* to read the word: *str-ee-t* = *street*. This is an example of why phonemic awareness is so critical to the task of reading. You can see that if students cannot break words apart by ear, they have a difficult time taking words apart when they see them in print.

A synthetic approach is most effective when we are teaching students to take words apart by listening to the phonemes to read and spell them, and then putting them back together. The major drawback to *exclusively* using a synthetic approach is that not all words can be taken apart phoneme by phoneme and put back together to make a word. Take a look at the word *clothes*. This is a very difficult word to teach by using a synthetic approach. Many developing readers who are taught primarily by using this approach overuse it and attempt to decode every unknown word they encounter. That is why we have two other approaches to teaching phonics: analytic and analogy-based phonics.

In an *analytic* approach, students are first taught a number of high-frequency words and then learn phonics generalizations and rules, which they can then apply to other words. Another word for analytic phonics is a *deductive* approach. An analytic approach is most effective when used with phonics rules and generalizations that have high applicability. To that end, in order to teach analytic phonics, you have to learn another body of knowledge: knowledge about vowel generalizations, so that you can be prepared when you ask your students to "deduce" a rule.

For example, most words that have a single medial vowel in the middle take the "short" sound, such as the words *fox*, *pig*, and *cat*. One vowel generalization or rule you must know is that when a vowel is found in the beginning or middle of a word or syllable, it *usually* takes the short sound. We have placed the vowel generalizations in Figure 3.3 for your memorization and use.

A drawback to *exclusively* using the analytic approach is that not all words follow a rule or generalization that has high applicability. For example, if you teach students that when they see two vowels together, such as in the word *boat*, they should use the long sound of the first vowel, you will actually mislead them much of the time. (We have seen this sign in classrooms: "When two vowels go walking, the first one does the talking.") This rule does not work for the words *yield* or *found*, for instance. This generalization has very low applicability (approximately 50%) when it refers to two different vowels together, so it is not a very good rule to teach if half the time you have to say to your students, "But that's an exception to the rule."

In an *analogy-based* approach, students are taught to notice patterns in words and to use the words they know to figure out other words. An example of an analogy-based approach is teaching words that are consistent with word families or *phonograms*—the *rimes* in printed words. Words such as *cat*, *boat*, and *ball* can be applied to many other words having the same phonograms; for example, the word *cat* has the same phonogram as the words *bat*, *flat*, and *sat*. As Gaskins, Gensemer, and Six (2005) explain, "our brains are pattern seekers" (p. 152). In other words, our brains recognize patterns, which makes it easier to learn new words.

We see a drawback to this approach if the instruction is not systematic and explicit. It is not enough to tell students to notice the patterns in words. Rather, they need sufficient practice in reading and writing the words. As Gaskins et al. (2005) also note, "our brains remember better the more time we spend on task, being persistent, and practicing decoding and reading words" (p. 152).

---

1. One vowel at the beginning or middle of a word or syllable usually takes the short sound. Examples: *at*, *sat*, *mat*, *cat*.
2. One vowel at the end of a word or syllable usually takes the long sound. Examples: *so*, *ro-tate*.
3. When the vowels *ai*, *ee*, *ea*, *oa*, and *oe* come together, the first vowel is usually long and the second is not sounded.
   Note: There are many exceptions to this rule. For example, *ea* has three sounds: long *e* as in *eat*; short *e* as in *bread*; long *a* as in *steak*. However, the digraph *ee* follows this rule 99% of the time.
4. When there are two vowels in a word or syllable, the second of which is an *e*, the first vowel is usually long and the *e* is not sounded. Examples: *bake*, *make*, *cake*.
5. When the vowels *oi*, *oy*, *oo*, *ou*, *ow*, *eu*, *au*, and *oe* come together, they make a whole new sound.

FIGURE 3.3. Vowel generalizations.

Question 8: What does a specific phonics lesson look like?

To answer the final question, we show you three different phonics lesson plans. You will see that each lesson is similar to the others in some ways, and very different in other ways.

The three lessons are alike in the following ways:

- They share the same objective: to teach students to identify and read the phonetic element /ee/ = E.
- The phonetic element is derived from the same book: *Sheep in a Jeep* (Shaw, 1986).
- Each lesson plan combines contextualized and decontextualized phonics instruction.
- Each lesson begins and ends with the reading, discussing, and rereading of a real text.
- There is a focused phonics lesson embedded within the reading lesson.
- There are suggestions for following up the lesson with a word study lesson and a word study center activity.

However, each of the three lessons is different in one important way: Each lesson uses a different *approach* to teaching the phonetic element. We have decided to demonstrate the teaching of phonics in this way so you can understand that you can often teach the same phonetic elements in different ways, depending on the *approach* (or combination of approaches) you want to use.

We followed a consistent design as we planned our sample lessons for you. First, we selected a phonetic element to teach (vowel digraph *ee*). Next, we chose an appropriate book for grades K–2 that has many occurrences of the digraph we wanted to teach. For our sample lessons, we chose Shaw's (1986) book *Sheep in a Jeep*. We then extracted all the words that use the vowel digraph *ee*. Next, we planned how to introduce and use the story. Finally, we decided how and when to teach the vowel digraph, and how and when the children would practice their new knowledge of the phonetic element. The three lessons are presented below.

LESSON 1: A SYNTHETIC PHONICS LESSON

Lesson: Phonetic element—vowel digraph *ee*

Context: Combination of contextualized and decontextualized

Text: *Sheep in a Jeep* (Shaw, 1986)

Phonics Approach: Synthetic phonics

Lesson Grade Levels: K–2

Lesson Objective: Students will demonstrate an understanding of the sound of the vowel digraph *ee* when they encounter it in words in a text.

Procedure:

- **Step 1**: Introduce the story in a big-book version, and ask the children to read the title and examine the illustrations on the cover. Your students will mention the grass, the sheep in a jeep, and other interesting visual information. Ask the children to predict what they think might happen.

- **Step 2**: Read through the text for enjoyment. This can be done as a teacher read-aloud as the students follow along, or you can ask your students to join in.

- **Step 3**: Ask the children to respond to the story in a simple way: "What did you like about the story? What was the problem in the story? What made the story funny?"

- **Step 4**: (This is the explicit phonics lesson embedded in the plan.) First, introduce the vowel digraph by telling students that they will be learning about the digraph *ee*, as in the word *sheep*. As you tell them, put the following on the board:

    sh<u>ee</u>p

    sh-<u>ee</u>-p

Then, using the second word above and using a pointer, ask the children to follow along as you slowly pronounce the word: "sh-ee-p" (move your pointer along the individual phonemes as you speak them aloud). Next, ask the children to close their eyes and just listen to the sounds that they hear in the middle of the word as you slowly pronounce it: "sh-*ee*-p." Help students realize that the *ee* sound they hear in the middle of the word *sheep* makes the long *e* sound.

- **Step 5**: Now reread the text aloud, asking children to help you identify words that use the *ee* combination. When you complete this task, your board will look like this:

    sheep

    beep

    jeep

    steep

    keep

Finally, ask students to pronounce each word with you. Be sure to segment and blend the phonemes slowly: "sh-ee-p, b-ee-p, j-ee-p, st-ee-p, k-ee-p."

- **Step 6**: Now that students have had direct instruction in the vowel digraph *ee*, you can have them engage in *buddy reading* (see below), using smaller versions of *Sheep in a Jeep*.

- **Step 7**: Use this phonetic element in a word study lesson with your whole class or with a small group of students. This new phonetic element can also be added to a word study center where the students can practice reading, sorting, and writing words with similar elements.

LESSON 2: AN ANALYTIC PHONICS LESSON

Lesson: Phonetic element—vowel digraph *ee*

Context: Combination of Contextualized and Decontextualized

Text: *Sheep in a Jeep* (Shaw, 1986)

Phonics Approach: Analytic phonics

Lesson Grade Levels: K–2

Lesson Objective: Students will demonstrate understanding of the sound of the vowel digraph *ee* when they encounter it in words in a text.

Procedure:

- **Step 1**: Introduce the story in a big-book version, and ask the children to read the title and examine the illustrations on the cover. Your students will mention the grass, the sheep in a jeep, and other interesting visual information. Ask the children to predict what they think might happen.

- **Step 2**: Read through the text for enjoyment. This can be done as a teacher read-aloud as the students follow along, or you can ask your students to join in.

- **Step 3**: Ask the children to respond to the story in a simple way: "What did you like about the story? What was the problem in the story? What made the story funny?"

- **Step 4**: (This is the explicit phonics lesson embedded in the plan.) First you must introduce the vowel digraph by telling students that they will be learning about the digraph *ee*, as in the word, *sheep*. As you tell them, put the following on the board:
    sh<u>ee</u>p

- **Step 5**: Now ask the children to reread the text with you and identify words that use the *ee* combination. When you complete this task, your board will look like this:
    sheep
    beep
    jeep
    steep
    keep

- **Step 6**: Ask the children to read the list of words out loud with you. Then ask them: "When you hear each word, what do you notice about the sound of the vowels *ee* in the middle of the word?" Students will respond accordingly and will notice that all the words have the same long *e* sound. Then ask, "If all the words have the same long *e* sound, can you think of a rule that will help us remember how to read words that have the letters *ee* together?"

- **Step 7**: Lead students to write a rule adapted from the third generalization in Figure 3.3: "When the vowels *ee* come together, the first vowel is usually long and the second is not sounded."

- **Step 8**: Now that students have had direct instruction in the vowel digraph *ee*, you can have them engage in buddy reading, using smaller versions of *Sheep in a Jeep* to practice their application.

- **Step 9**: Use this phonetic element in a word study lesson with your whole class or with a small group of students. This new phonetic element can also be added to a word study center where the students can practice reading, sorting, and writing words with similar elements.

LESSON 3: AN ANALOGY-BASED PHONICS LESSON

You will notice that this lesson looks like a combination of the synthetic and analytic approaches. What is really different about the analogy-based approach is that the vowel sound is always taught embedded within a phonogram.

Lesson: Phonetic element—phonogram *eep*

Context: Combination of contextualized and decontextualized

Text: *Sheep in a Jeep* (Shaw, 1986)

Phonics Approach: Analogy-based phonics

Lesson Grade Levels: K–2

Lesson Objective: Students will demonstrate understanding of the sound of the phonogram *eep* when they encounter it in words in a text.

Procedure:

- **Step 1**: Introduce the story in a big-book version, and ask the children to read the title and examine the illustrations on the cover. Your students will mention the grass, the sheep in a jeep, and other interesting visual information. Ask the children to predict what they think might happen.

- **Step 2**: Read through the text for enjoyment. This can be done as a teacher read-aloud as the students follow along, or you can ask your students to join in.

- **Step 3**: Ask the children to respond to the story in a simple way: "What did you like about the story? What was the problem in the story? What made the story funny?"

- **Step 4**: (This is the explicit phonics lesson embedded in the plan.) First you must introduce the vowel digraph by telling students that they will be learning about the phonogram *eep*, as in the word, *sheep*. As you tell them, put the following on the board.

     sheep
     sh-eep

  Then, using the second word above and using a pointer, ask the children to follow along as you slowly pronounce the word: *sh-eep* (move your pointer along as you speak, but remember to keep the vowel sound within the rime!). Next, ask the children to close their eyes and just listen to the sounds that they hear as you slowly separate the onset from the rime: "sh-*eep*."

- **Step 5**: Now ask the children to reread the big book with you and identify words that use the phonogram *eep*. When you complete this task, your board will look like this:

     sheep
     beep
     jeep
     steep
     keep

  Finally, ask students to pronounce each word with you. Be sure to segment and blend the onset and rime slowly: "sh-eep, b-eep, j-eep, st-eep, k-eep."

- **Step 6**: Now that students have had direct instruction in the word family *eep*, you can have them engage in buddy reading, using smaller versions of *Sheep in a Jeep*.

- **Step 7**: Use this new phonogram (*eep*) in a word study lesson with your whole class or with a small group of students. This new phonetic element can also be added to a word wall and a word study center where the students can practice reading, sorting, and writing words with similar elements.

TRY THIS

Now that you have had a look at the three types of phonics instruction, you can try one out on your own. Use Figure 3.4 (page 52) to conceptualize the decisions you have to make as you design your phonics lesson. Refer back to the three lessons you have just read. We have provided a template for you here.

PHONICS LESSON PLAN

Lesson:

Context:

Text:

Phonics Approach:

Lesson Grade Levels:

Lesson Objective:

Procedure:

In the next section, we present another component of the phonics curriculum, which is essential for students to develop as proficient readers.

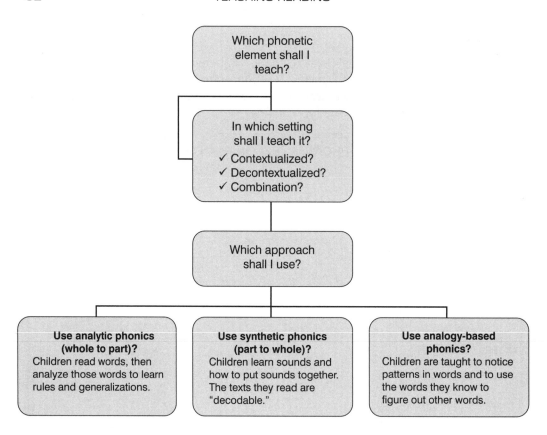

FIGURE 3.4. Decisions to make for teaching phonics.

TEACHING HIGH-FREQUENCY WORDS

High-frequency words are the words that appear most often in print. They are also called *sight words*. Because of their frequency, our brains recognize them as patterns of letters, and we "call up" the words on sight. High-frequency words can be recognized instantly by good readers because they are in their *sight vocabularies*.

High-frequency words include such words as *the, and, with, because, mother, cat, under, friend, very,* and *again.* Cunningham (2005), reporting the work of Fry, Polk, and Fountoukidis (1984), explains that 100 words account for nearly half of the words we encounter in print. So, you can see that teaching sight words is a high priority if we want our developing readers to succeed. Using books that have many high-frequency words helps early readers to develop their sight vocabularies more easily.

We have found that the books in Lobel's *Frog and Toad* series have many high-frequency words, and we highly recommend them for exposing students to these words. For example, the following is an excerpt from "The Garden," a chapter in *Frog and Toad Together* (Lobel, 1972, pp. 18–19). According to two high-frequency word lists—those prepared by Fry and Kress (2006) and by Dolch (1950)—the text shown below has a high percentage of sight words. We have italicized them for you.

Frog *was in his* garden.
Toad *came walking by.*
"*What a fine* garden *you have,* Frog," *he said.*
"Yes," *said* Frog. "*It is very* nice, *but it was hard work.*"
"*I wish I had a* garden," *said* Toad.
"*Here are some* flower seeds. Plant *them in the* ground," *said* Frog,
"*and soon you will have a* garden."
"*How soon?*" *asked* Toad.
"Quite *soon,*" *said* Frog.

As you can see, two of the words in this excerpt are the characters' names (*Frog,* *Toad*), which are repeated throughout the series. They are the only main characters throughout the series. Other words—*plant, quite,* and *nice*—follow regular phonetic patterns.

Rather than exposing students to word lists and flash cards, having them read books that are both engaging and have a great percentage of high-frequency words will increase their exposure to those words in a meaningful and authentic way. To teach high-frequency words, we recommend that you combine reading real books with word study events, as described below.

Activities for Teaching High-Frequency Words

Word Walls and Word Study

Cunningham (2005) has suggested a number of ways to teach high-frequency words, including using word walls as described in Chapter 2. She has developed many activities and learning events for developing knowledge of high-frequency words. For a full explanation of these activities, see *Phonics They Use* (Cunningham, 2005).

Cunningham's suggestions are part of a comprehensive word study curriculum, which includes phonemic awareness, phonics, and spelling as well as *structural analysis.* When students are taught to analyze the structure of words, they can recognize the root words, prefixes, and suffixes, and they know how to divide words into syllables. Combined with excellent instruction in reading comprehension (described in Chapters 5–9), students can gain the knowledge and skills to be strategic readers.

Reading Real Books

We highly recommend helping students develop their knowledge of high-frequency words by reading them *in context*—that is, in real books. Because high-frequency words occur naturally in our speech, writing, and texts, reading many books and other texts increases the chances of seeing them.

Books labeled as *easy readers* often have a great number of high-frequency words. However, some books are not specifically labeled as such, so you may have to scout out books that offer your students many opportunities to read many high-frequency words in engaging narrative and expository formats. To select books useful for teaching high-frequency words, try this exercise:

1. Choose any page.
2. Count the number of high-frequency words. Chances are that any page you choose will have a great proportion of these words.
3. Identify the words that are not considered high frequency. Ask yourself: Can the students decode the text by using the strategies you taught in your phonics lessons? If not, will the sentence context provide a meaningful clue?
4. When choosing narrative text, ask yourself: Does the story have an easily identified plot structure? Are the characters well rounded?
5. When choosing expository text, ask yourself: Is the information accurate? Is the text engaging?

In the next section of this chapter, you will see that students' development of learning strategies for decoding words and for identifying high-frequency words will aid their progress toward becoming fluent readers.

TEACHING FLUENCY

Fluency is a vital component of the reading curriculum and needs to be modeled and routinely assessed. Rasinski (2003) describes a fluent reader as one whose reading demonstrates three important characteristics: *accuracy*, *automaticity*, and *prosody*. Each term is defined below.

- *Accuracy*: An accurate reader decodes and recognizes words correctly.
- *Automaticity*: A reader who demonstrates automaticity reads quickly, both orally and silently, and so spends more time making meaning than decoding words. A reader who possesses both accuracy and automaticity has a large sight vocabulary.
- *Prosody*: A reader who has prosody makes the reading sound like natural speech. Prosody includes appropriate expression and volume, good phrasing, smoothness, and pace.

So a *fluent reader* is a reader who is accurate, automatic, and prosodic.

Why Is Fluency Important?

Because being a fluent reader means reading accurately, automatically, and with good prosody, a fluent reader has the ability to read words in context quickly and without deliberate attention (Allington, 2006; LaBerge & Samuels, 1974). Our brains can carry out many automatic functions at the same time, but can only do a limited number of nonautomatic things at a time (Cunningham, 2005). An example of a function that is not automatic is constructing meaning from text. Text comprehension involves very deliberate actions, as you will read in Chapters 5–9. If we can teach our students to make the decoding part of the reading process automatic, they can spend their time more efficiently by focusing on the part that is nonautomatic: *comprehension* (Armbruster et al., 2001; Cunningham, 2005; Cunningham & Allington, 2007; Rasinski, 2003).

For example, when you are a very experienced driver, steering, accelerating, and braking are automatic. Things that are not automatic include finding your way in unfamiliar places, negotiating traffic, and watching traffic signals. That is why when you first learned to drive, your driving instructor probably took you to an empty parking lot where there was no traffic, and you could learn the parts of driving that would eventually become automatic. Once you demonstrated that you could steer, accelerate, and brake without too much conscious effort, your instructor probably felt less trepidation about letting you practice your skills under very different conditions: in traffic. We want our students to be fluent readers so that they can concentrate on the real work of reading—comprehending text—and not be hampered by the words they need to recognize automatically.

How to Build Fluency

To develop fluent readers, have them read, read, read. The time students spend in and out of school reading silently correlates with significant gains in reading achievement (Allington, 2001; Anderson et al., 1988). As described in Chapter 2, you can provide silent reading practice by dedicating time during the school day for your students to read books independently. We have described that practice as *on-your-own reading* or *sustained silent reading*. During those periods of time, the students can select their own books and choose their own purposes for reading them. The results may be independent readers who get lost in a book and choose to read on their own, like the boy illustrated in Figure 3.5.

As also described in Chapter 2, a print-rich classroom promotes literacy, because students rely on the walls and displays to give them information they may need to read and write accurately. Well-positioned print, as shown in Figure 3.6 (page 56), allows students to practice their independence in finding information strategically placed there by teachers.

Another way to foster independence is through oral reading practice that is enjoyable and engaging. The following discussion is a guide to productive reading that builds fluency.

FIGURE 3.5. An independent reader.

FIGURE 3.6. A print-rich classroom.

First, we urge you to eliminate round-robin reading. We begin many of our literacy classes by asking our students how they practiced reading in school. Most describe a type of reading where students take turns reading aloud, one at a time, in a whole-class or small-group setting. We put a name to it: *round-robin reading*. When we ask our students (many of whom are already teachers) whether they think it is a good practice, they hardly ever say, "Yes." In fact, they can usually enumerate quite easily the reasons why it is *not* a good practice, mirroring what Rasinski (2003) and Kuhn (2007) say about it:

- Students are not really paying attention.
- They skip down to where they think they will read.
- They always lose their places.
- Most importantly, round-robin reading simply does not give developing readers enough practice in reading words to build fluency, even in a small-group setting.

Why then is round-robin reading so prevalent? Rasinski (2003) describes it as "an embedded part of classroom culture in the United States" (p. 17). Yet, he explains further, this is not because teachers want to carry out ineffective practices in their classrooms. Rather, it is because they have not been given any viable alternatives for promoting fluency. We hope you will try some of the viable alternatives suggested below.

As we have stated above and in Chapter 1, we feel strongly that the oral reading done in many classrooms is not productive reading. Yet there is often not enough time for students to read extensively on their own. We know that there is a place for oral reading in schools, and that when it is done well, it provides a great deal of reading practice—and, quite simply, can be fun!

Many literacy experts promote oral reading practice in some form or another (Armbruster et al., 2001; Cunningham, 2005; Kuhn, 2007; Morrow, 2005; Moskal & Blachowicz, 2006; Rasinski, 2003; Reutzel & Morrow, 2007). Furthermore, research has consistently shown that repeated reading works (Allington, 1983; LaBerge & Samuels, 1974; Samuels, 1979). There are many suggestions for developing fluency in the context of real reading and in authentic and meaningful ways. We list some of them below, followed by a short explanation of each.

Choral Reading

What it is: During *choral reading*, students read together. You can conduct choral reading with a whole class or in groups. The idea is for all voices to combine as one.

Why it is beneficial: When children are choral reading a 200-word passage, every student gets the same amount of practice. The students are not listening or scrutinizing each other. If a student makes an error reading, no one really knows. Choral reading is also an excellent method to build *prosody*. As students listen to each other, those students who have natural expression and phrasing will model those characteristics for the others.

Echo Reading

What it is: *Echo reading* is similar to choral reading, but the students "echo" what the teacher reads after he or she reads it.

Why it is beneficial: Echo reading has the same benefits as choral reading. It is also beneficial because teachers can control how the text is read for different purposes. It is particularly good for teaching students to read with expression and helping them to phrase sentences into meaningful parts.

Seesaw Reading

What it is: *Seesaw reading* is similar to echo reading, but the teacher and the students alternate reading sentences. That is, the teacher reads a sentence, and then the students read a sentence. It can also be practiced between two students: Each student in the pair reads every other sentence.

Why it is beneficial: Seesaw reading has the same benefits as echo and choral reading. It helps students pay particular attention to end marks in sentences, thereby increasing *prosody* through proper phrasing.

Buddy Reading

What it is: *Buddy reading* is also referred to as *paired reading*. This kind of reading allows a less able student to read alongside a more able reader. The students take turns reading the selection, and the more able reader gives assistance to the buddy. Student pairs should be selected carefully by teachers and changed periodically, so that more able readers are able to work in turn with less able ones. Figure 3.7 is a photo of two students engaged in buddy reading.

Why it is beneficial: Buddy reading has many benefits. The main one is that because fluent readers can be paired with less fluent readers, the former can provide support for the latter. It is important for buddy reading to be explicitly demonstrated by the teacher with an able reader in the classroom, so that the students can make the most of this reading context.

Readers' Theatre

What it is: In *readers' theatre*, students rehearse and perform a play or script for their peers. Props and actions are not needed; it can take place in chairs in front of the classroom. As in a theatrical reading of a play, the focus is on the dialogue, not the action. The actions are derived through the rich dialogue and the information given by the narrator.

Why it is beneficial: Readers' theatre is an authentic way of doing repeated reading. Students know that they must practice their parts before they perform; therefore, they do not complain about rereading text to make it sound good. Readers' theatre is also an exemplary way to model and practice all aspects of prosody. As students repeat and practice their lines, they will improve their expression, volume, phrasing, and pace. In Figure 3.8, we provide suggestions for implementing readers' theatre with fables.

Child–Adult Reading

What it is: *Child–adult reading* is exactly what its name indicates: one child reading with one adult.

Why it is beneficial: Children get the benefit of having more than one adult as a model of fluent reading in the classroom.

FIGURE 3.7. Buddy reading.

GETTING READY FOR YOUR READERS' THEATRE PERFORMANCE

1. Read the script silently two or three times. Think:

    Who are the characters?

    What is the problem?

    How does the problem get solved?

    How does it end?

    What is the moral?

2. Talk about the story. Answer the questions together.

3. Choose roles. Be fair and polite to each other.

4. Highlight your part with a highlighting marker.

5. Reread it silently a few times to get more practice.

6. Think:

    How is that character feeling?

    How should I portray him or her?

    How would I feel if I were that character?

7. Practice reading the script with your whole group. Help each other.

8. Read, reread, and reread. You might need to read it many times. That's okay.

FIGURE 3.8. Student directions for readers' theatre with fables.

From *Teaching Reading: Strategies and Resources for Grades K–6* by Rachel L. McCormack and Susan Lee Pasquarelli. Copyright 2010 by The Guilford Press. Permission to photocopy this figure is granted to purchasers of this book for personal use only (see copyright page for details).

Integrating Oral Reading Practices into Your Literacy Plan

We suggest that you implement a variety of ways for your students to become fluent readers. We advise teachers with whom we work that they should never miss an opportunity to build fluency, and the reading routines described above can be integrated in every aspect of the curriculum in every grade. In Figure 3.9, you can see that even in sixth grade, students are encouraged to engage in the kinds of reading that helps make them more fluent readers.

TRY THIS: FLUENCY ACTIVITY 1

Take a look at the chart in Figure 3.10 (page 61). In the right-hand column, we have listed the above-described strategies for supporting the development of fluent readers. As you look at each strategy, record the kinds of texts you could use and the kinds of grouping options (as described in Chapter 2) you might use to effectively carry out each reading event.

FIGURE 3.9. Sixth-grade fluency chart.

The Fluency Development Lesson

We feel that the *fluency development lesson* (FDL) deserves a place in the classroom. The procedure for Rasinski, Padak, Linek, and Sturtevant's (1994) original FDL is described in Figure 3.11 (at the top of page 62). Here is Rasinski et al.'s explanation of the lesson:

> The [FDL] is a 10- [to] 15-minute instructional event that incorporates several key principles of effective fluency instruction. To implement the FDL, each student is provided with a copy of a 50- [to] 150-word text for reading. Although a different text is used each day, teachers are encouraged to cycle back to previously practiced texts as the class develops a corpus of practiced texts. Texts are selected for content, predictability, and rhythm. Rhyming poems and song lyrics for children work well as tests for the FDL. (1994, p. 312)

Rasinski (2003) has since developed different versions of the original. We think that the FDL has a "value-added" aspect if you use it in your classrooms every day. In addition to building fluency, it exposes your students to a wide variety of topics, genres, syntactic structures, and rich language that can only help increase your students' language abilities, knowledge, literary elements, and background knowledge on a wide range of topics.

TRY THIS: FLUENCY ACTIVITY 2

Find a text that you think would be good for conducting an FDL as described by Rasinski and colleagues. Follow the plan that Rasinski et al. describe for carrying out your lesson. (See the box at the bottom of page 62.)

Event	Type of text	Kind of grouping
Choral reading		
Echo reading		
Seesaw reading		
Buddy reading		
Readers' theatre		
Child–adult reading		

FIGURE 3.10. Oral reading strategies for building fluency.

1. Teacher introduces the text and invites predictions.
2. Teacher models fluent reading by orally reading text to whole class.
3. Teacher leads discussion of the text content and the teacher's oral reading of the text. Particular attention is given to the teacher's rate, phrasing, expression, and intonation during reading.
4. Teacher leads whole class in several choral readings of the text.
5. Teacher divides class into pairs, and directs each pair to find a reasonably quiet and distraction-free place. Each student reads the text to his or her partner three times, and then the roles are reversed. The listening partner's role is to provide positive feedback to and support for the reader.
6. Teacher calls students back to their places after the paired reading practice, and invites individuals, pairs, or small groups to perform the text for the class.
7. Students place the text in a folder, and are encouraged to practice reading on their own and to read the text for their parents.

FIGURE 3.11. Procedure for the fluency development lesson (FDL). Based on Rasinski, Padak, Linek, and Sturtevant (1994).

Record your notes here:

Text:

Plan:

Choosing Books to Build Fluency

Choosing books to build accuracy and fluency should not be haphazard. The following are some guidelines.

Easy Readers

When children are learning to read, they should experience success quickly to keep their motivation high. However, the texts should not be contrived; they should be highly engaging while using a limited amount of words accessible to beginning readers. Books nominated and chosen for the American Library Association's Theodor Geisel Award give beginning readers a real sense of what it takes to be able to read good books and experience success. Recent nominees for this award include *There Is a Bird on Your Head!* (Willems, 2007), *Hello Bumblebee Bat* (Lunde, 2007), and *Jazz Baby* (Wheeler, 2007). (See Chapter 13 for a description of other book awards for which nominees and winners are posted on *www.ala.org.*)

Predictable Texts

Books in which the pictures, formats, test structures, and words are highly predictable help students take risks when they encounter words they may not know. Predictable texts include rhyming books, such as *Llama, Llama, Red Pajama* (Dewdney, 2005); stories with repetitive text, such as *We're Going on a Bear Hunt* (Rosen, 1989); and stories with cumulative rhyme, such as *The Napping House* (Woods, 1984) or *Why Mosquitoes Buzz in People's Ears* (Aardema, 1975).

Several years ago, using predictable texts was routine practice in elementary classrooms for teaching reading. Replaced by highly decodable texts for a time, they have made a comeback in classrooms as effective texts to use with developing readers, to teach them to read and enjoy literature. We have never abandoned these texts, and we are happy to see them appreciated again. These are the books that children pick up and read over and over. Each reading increases exposure to the rich language of well-written literature for children.

High-Quality Texts

Remember that *all* the books that effective teachers of reading use with developing readers should meet high standards, or why would any child learning to read keep trying? As you have seen in the *Frog and Toad* series, Lobel has carefully crafted engaging stories for developing readers, using a combination of high-frequency words and words that are decipherable through decoding or sentence context. But that is not all. He has been able to do it all with humor and provide his readers with worthwhile themes and excellent characterization.

You can use the chart in Figure 3.12 (page 64) to review your bookshelves at home or in your classrooms. Look particularly at the books you use for early readers. Choose a few books, and then use the criteria in the chart to assess them. If the books satisfy all the criteria, they are probably great books to use for developing readers.

Title of book	Engaging theme for children?	Predictable format?	Strong characterization?	Percentage of high-frequency words?	Easily identifiable plot structure?

FIGURE 3.12. Evaluating books for developing readers.

Now take a few moments to assess your comprehension of this chapter by referring to the Key Terms Chart in Figure 3.13 (page 66). Try to write definitions to these terms in your own words.

REFLECTION ON ARTIFACTS FOR YOUR SELF-STUDY

For your self-study, record on Figure 3.14 (page 67) the artifacts you created while you read this chapter.

KEY TERMS FOR CHAPTER 3

In this chapter, the following key terms are essential to your understanding of reading instruction. Think about what they mean, and try to define them in your own words.

phonological awareness

phonemic awareness

phonics

phonetic elements

settings for teaching phonics

approaches to teaching phonics

high-frequency words

fluency

oral reading strategies

fluency development lesson (FDL)

FIGURE 3.13. Key Terms Chart for Chapter 3.

SELF-STUDY REVIEW CHART FOR CHAPTER 3

Name of Artifact	Teacher Instructional Actions and Language	Provisions for Individual Differences	Variety of Modes of Communication	Critical Thinking and Active Engagement	Opportunities for Assessment

FIGURE 3.14. Self-Study Review Chart for Chapter 3.

From *Teaching Reading: Strategies and Resources for Grades K–6* by Rachel L. McCormack and Susan Lee Pasquarelli. Copyright 2010 by The Guilford Press. Permission to photocopy this figure is granted to purchasers of this book for personal use only (see copyright page for details).

CHAPTER 4

Cultivating Children's Curiosity for Words

Teaching Vocabulary

ALBERTO'S CLASSROOM

Alberto is beginning to teach a reading lesson to his fifth graders, using the social studies textbook. In social studies, they are learning about the westward expansion in the United States—the migration of early settlers from the East to the West from 1832 to 1860. Alberto has chosen to use the social studies text to teach both reading strategies and history. All the students have access to the social studies text, and they read it with support if they need it.

Alberto begins the lesson by preteaching the vocabulary. The teacher's manual for the social studies text has selected words for Alberto to teach the students. However, Alberto has added a few words to the list, because he has reason to believe that they do not have sufficient background knowledge about the words *migration* and *resettlement*.

In addition to the social studies text, the students in Alberto's class have many other texts to support their reading and understanding of migration in the 1800s. The classroom library showcases books—both narrative and expository—about the westward expansion. Alberto has included magazines and journals on this topic, and he has set the four classroom computers on websites that help the students navigate the routes of the travelers during that time.

Alberto is an example of an expert teacher who knows that multiple encounters with new words and concepts, in a variety of contexts, facilitate students' understanding of those words. We will hear more about Alberto and other excellent teachers in this chapter on teaching vocabulary.

BEST PRACTICES YOU WILL SEE IN THIS CHAPTER

✓ Promoting wide reading.
✓ Choosing vocabulary words to teach.
✓ Teaching vocabulary in the context of teaching reading.

WHAT WE KNOW
ABOUT EFFECTIVE VOCABULARY INSTRUCTION

We know of no teacher who would argue with the fact that teaching vocabulary is a great responsibility and should be carried out well. Teachers understand the implications of having a rich vocabulary: They know that understanding the meanings of words affects their students' comprehension of the texts they read; they also know that if their students have a large fund of words that they can use accurately, it affects their writing; and they realize that precise knowledge and use of terminology can improve their students' ability to express themselves orally. We would argue that every teacher wants to do a great job of teaching vocabulary. The problem is that traditional methods of teaching vocabulary are not consistent with best practices.

Nagy (1988) offers what he believes are reasons for our failure to teach vocabulary well. First, he explains, we are not teaching our students in-depth word knowledge—the rich and deep understanding that is necessary to truly comprehend difficult text. Second, he believes that our efforts to teach individual words do not always pay off, if not knowing those words does not hinder the comprehension of the text. Our students need to encounter those words over and over in text in order to remember them. The way to increase multiple encounters with those words is not hard to figure out. As Nagy states, the implication is that "what is needed to produce more vocabulary growth is not more vocabulary instruction, but more reading" (p. 3).

WHAT IS A VOCABULARY PROGRAM?

Wide Reading

There is no doubt that Nagy puts the greatest emphasis on the amount of reading our students should do. This idea of *wide reading* as an important way of building vocabulary is well supported (Anderson, Hiebert, Scott, & Wilkinson, 1985; Blachowicz & Fisher, 2002). Recall our reference in Chapter 1 to the study by Anderson et al. (1988) and their findings about the connection among achievement, the amount of time spent reading, and the number of words read in a year. Surely students who read 4½ million words a year, as described in their study, are encountering new words in multiple contexts.

Many kindergarten teachers have told us that they notice that their students enter school with relatively small reading vocabularies, but a much greater knowledge of words. This is fortunate, but they will need to increase the number of words they know in leaps and bounds in order to understand what they are expected to read. They may have a general knowledge or vague idea of many of the words they encounter, but word knowledge is far more complex. Knowing words involves understanding that (1) knowing words is incremental; (2) words often have more than one meaning; (3) word knowledge consists of multiple dimensions; (4) knowledge of one word is often dependent upon the knowledge of another word; and (5) knowing what a word means depends greatly on the kind of word it is (Nagy & Scott, 2000).

According to Graves et al. (2001), if we want our students to understand the texts they are expected to read, their knowledge of the words must be at the *established* level. That is, the words must be easily, rapidly, and automatically recognized.

> Students need to know most of the words they encounter at the established level because words that are not recognized automatically will thwart the process of comprehending text. Unless words are understood at the established level, students are not likely to use them in writing and speaking. (pp. 204–205)

Graves et al. (2001) recommend wide reading as part of a comprehensive vocabulary program (see Figure 4.1). They follow this recommendation with suggestions for teaching individual words, teaching strategies, and promoting word consciousness. We continue our discussion with the research-based qualities of that instruction.

Effective Vocabulary Instruction

Nagy (1988) describes three qualities of effective vocabulary instruction: *integration, repetition*, and *meaningful use*. These are summarized in Figure 4.2, and we provide a fuller explanation of each quality below.

Integration

Integration is critical to the task of learning new words. Acquiring new words requires students to assimilate them into their background knowledge or *schemas* (a detailed discussion of schemas and schema theory is presented in Chapter 5). In order for new

---

- Emphasizes the importance of *wide reading*, because students learn much of their vocabulary from reading.

- Includes instruction on *individual words*, because such instruction can assist students in learning some words, improve comprehension of selections from which the words are taken, and show students the value we place on words.

- Provides instruction in learning words *independently*, because students must learn much of the vocabulary on their own.

- Promotes activities leading to *word consciousness*, because only if students are interested in words, value them, and find them intriguing are they likely to develop full and rich vocabularies.

FIGURE 4.1. Components of a comprehensive vocabulary program. Based on Graves, Juel, and Graves (2001).

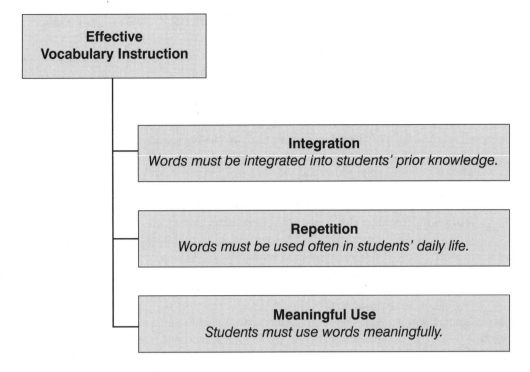

FIGURE 4.2. Principles of effective vocabulary instruction. Based on Nagy (1988).

words to make any sense for our students, we have to remind them of the things they already know and help them make analogies between what they already know and what they are about to learn.

Repetition

Providing multiple encounters with new words is essential to vocabulary growth. It is through these multiple encounters and through the repetition of each word or term (using the word often) that students come to understand the meanings of words at the established level.

Meaningful Use

It is not enough for students to be able to define words. Being able to define words is not really what it means to *know* words. Students who memorize definitions are not necessarily using them in their writing and speaking. In fact, when they encounter those words in text, they may not even recognize them, especially if they have memorized a definition that does not match the context. Asking students to demonstrate their knowledge of words in a *meaningful* way helps to drive them to a deeper understanding of the words.

GUIDELINES FOR EFFECTIVE VOCABULARY INSTRUCTION

Many vocabulary scholars have suggested guidelines for teaching vocabulary to our students. From his own work and review of the research on vocabulary instruction, Johnson (2000) offers these guidelines for teaching vocabulary effectively:

- Involve students in rich oral language activities, including conversations, discussions, debates, participating in/listening to speeches, and watching high-quality films and TV programs.
- Promote and enable wide reading of many genres of print on a daily basis, and have students engage in discussions of their current and previous readings.
- Provide direct instruction with important words that might otherwise become stumbling blocks to students' understanding. Use strategies that integrate the words into students' prior knowledge. In addition, have students use the words meaningfully and often in your classes.
- Teach students why, when, and how to use a thesaurus.

As we describe the practices in the rest of this chapter, we use the work of Johnson (2000), Nagy (1988), and others to present learning events that are consistent with best-practice research. We include our own belief that effective instruction in vocabulary should embrace a great deal of *fervor* for learning new words.

PROMOTING WIDE READING

We hope you have discovered that increasing the amount of reading our students do is a high priority, and it should be foremost in our minds as we develop a curriculum that includes learning new words.

In kindergarten, it is common practice to immerse the students in good literature through read-alouds, repeated reading, poetry, chanting, and singing. In Chapter 3, we have elaborated on those methods. We applaud kindergarten teachers who do these things, and we say to them, "Please don't stop!" Read-alouds can provide excellent models of rich vocabulary in any grade. Promoting rich vocabulary through listening and oral language can only result in better use of vocabulary in writing and better comprehension in reading.

Recall that in Chapter 2 we have described the importance of the classroom library. Your library will be the first place your students choose books; it should be the best place for them to find books on a variety of topics and genres. To experience the amount of wide reading your students need, they should not have to go any further than your classroom. We have seen an excellent example of this in Alberto's classroom.

In fourth, fifth, and sixth grades, you can further facilitate wide reading by encouraging your students to move beyond the classroom library and into your school's resource center. If your school has a media center, you can teach your students ways in which they can research their topics through various media. That way, they will see the key terms and concepts presented repeatedly in a variety of contexts and texts: journals, newspapers, textbooks, and expository texts. The slight differences in usage among contexts, as well as the repeated exposure to the words, will help the students grab onto the words.

CHOOSING WORDS TO TEACH

Limit the Words You Teach

One mistake we teachers sometimes make is spending too much time teaching vocabulary and diminishing the amount of time allotted for actual reading. Because we all develop much of our vocabulary through text reading, the best idea is for students to do a great deal of reading. This way, the probability of their encountering new words increases. It is through repetition, integration, and use of new vocabulary that we gain understanding. Recall that it takes quite a number of encounters with words before we truly use the words accurately and meaningfully. We cannot expect our students to grasp the meanings after one encounter.

Graves et al. (2001) have suggested a useful protocol to follow when choosing the words to teach. Our version of this is shown in Figure 4.3. This figure guides you to select vocabulary by category. Category 1 consists of words that are essential for understanding the day's reading. Category 2 consists of words that can be used to teach a particular strategy. Category 3 consists of words in the selection that are otherwise important for students to know. We discuss each of these categories in more detail below. We know that many words fall into more than one category, but we have found that asking ourselves category-related questions serves as a good guide in making our selections.

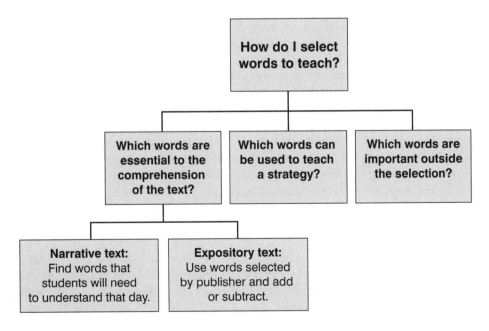

FIGURE 4.3. Selecting words to teach. Based on Graves et al. (2001).

Category 1: Words That Are Essential to the Meaning of the Text

Is understanding a word important to that day's text reading?

EXPOSITORY TEXTBOOKS

Authors of content-area textbooks often identify and reinforce the key terms and concepts in their texts. For example, most science textbooks are divided into units and chapters, and if the text is read in order, the vocabulary words build on each other. At the beginning of each chapter, the authors typically select three to five words as the key vocabulary for that chapter. Limiting the number, especially in the content areas, is important: The key vocabulary words are often the *concepts* that need to be taught, and they need to be well developed.

The words can very often be found enclosed in a box or in a sidebar at the beginning of the chapter. Then, as the words are introduced, they are presented in bold print or highlighted. The authors may explicitly define each key term within the first or second sentence containing that new word. The word is then repeated throughout that section of the text and is included in the questions at the end of the chapter. For further help, or to serve as a reference, the vocabulary words are included in the glossary at the end of the text.

To illustrate, we have chosen the chapter "We Have One President" from *Some People I Know*, a Houghton Mifflin second-grade social studies text (Armento, Nash, Salter, & Wixson, 1991). The words selected are set in the margins as key words: *president, vote, ballot*. The first occurrence of each word is presented in bold, and the word is defined in the sentence:

> Every four years, grown-up citizens in our country vote on who should be **president**. They vote by going to places such as schools in their neighborhoods. There they get a card or piece of paper called a **ballot**. They mark the ballot next to the name of the person they want for president. (p. 115)

The question at the end of the chapter, "How do we decide who should be president?", gives the students opportunities to use all the key words repeatedly in their discussions and to hear each other use them. The key words are also defined in a picture glossary at the end of the text. Using the words selected by the authors of expository textbooks is one way that you can select words to teach in content-area classes. The program authors make predictions based on the students' grade level, but they do not have the benefit of knowing how much background knowledge your students have. So words chosen by the authors should be adjusted according to what your students know.

EXPOSITORY TRADE BOOKS

You may also use one of the many available trade books when teaching social studies or science. Expository trade books offer the reader similar tools for deciphering the meanings of new words, but they are not as conspicuous as textbook tools. In a delightful expository trade book from National Geographic Children's Books, *Sea Critters* (Earle, 2000), the author and the illustrator combine efforts to define and illustrate the many kinds of underwater creatures. For example, in a chapter called "Animals with Holes," the word *Porifera* is introduced and defined within the context.

Imagine sitting in one place most of your life with tasty morsels brought to you by the surrounding sea. That's what sponges do. Sponges—the animals with holes—are called **PORIFERA**. Water flows through hundreds of tiny holes all over the sponge's body, then squirts out through a big hole—or lots of big holes—at the top. Sponges come in many colors, from red to bright blue to gold to clear like glass. (p. 7)

From this paragraph, we learn quite a bit about sponges, and we also learn the scientific name *Porifera*. However, the author does not repeat the word in the next sections or chapters, and there is no glossary for further reference. Nonetheless, it is an engaging text whose purpose is to delight children and teach them the names of underwater sea creatures. If you were using this text to teach about the ocean, you could easily choose words to develop with your students.

NARRATIVE TEXT IN PUBLISHED ANTHOLOGIES

If a narrative text is part of a published anthology and is accompanied by a teacher's manual, the authors select key terms, and they may give suggestions for ways to teach them. As in content-area text, these are most likely to be the words that students must know to understand the plot. Once again, you should adjust the words chosen by the authors according to what your students know.

NARRATIVE TRADE BOOKS

Narrative trade books do not provide guidance in which words are absolutely essential to understanding the text that day. Instead, you must rely on your knowledge of your students' needs in selecting these words. For example, in the chapter "Graffiti," from *The Higher Power of Lucky* (Patron, 2006), the main characters, Lucky and Lincoln, revise a street sign that originally says

SLOW
CHILDREN
AT
PLAY

so that it says

SLOW:
CHILDREN
AT
PLAY

That is, the children add a colon with a black marker. Lucky argues that it is *illegal* to draw on a traffic sign, but never once mentions or uses the word *graffiti*. The reader has to draw conclusions about the meaning of the chapter title—and can do so as the chapter progresses—but a quick preview and short discussion of the word could help to set up the reader for the chapter.

HOW TO TEACH WORDS IN CATEGORY 1

After you have chosen the words you want to teach, the next step is choosing an efficient way to teach it. We offer some practical suggestions below for introducing words before reading.

1. *Using a visual aid.* Many times the easiest and most effective way of introducing a new word is through a visual aid. For example, in the text *A Single Shard* (Park, 2001), the reader encounters the word *pottery* early in the text. Understanding the meaning of the word *pottery* is critical to understanding the context of the novel. As students read, they will gain understanding of it, but a visual aid—a piece of pottery similar to the celadon pottery in the text—would be the most efficient way of introducing the word. It is not necessary to elaborate on the process of making porcelain pottery; in fact, that would not be a good use of instructional time. The text does an excellent job of weaving the process into the plot.

2. *Making an analogy.* Whenever you can introduce a word by using an analogy, you should. For example, when reading the text *Joseph Had a Little Overcoat* (Taback, 1999) with kindergartners, you can help them understand the term *overcoat* (a word they might not normally use) by showing them one of the pictures and saying, "An overcoat is like a _____." They will answer *coat* or *jacket*. The picture book provides the repetition as they see the transformation of the overcoat into other items of clothing. Then it can be further reinforced if they read or reread *Grandfather's Journey* (Say, 1993). The students will recognize a word they have learned: The illustration on the cover shows a person on a ship wearing an *overcoat*.

3. *Brainstorming through webbing.* Another quick and easy way to introduce new terms is brainstorming through webbing. Webbing words is a high-utility strategy— one that has a wide range of applicability. Blachowicz and Fisher (2002) define a *web* or a *brainstorming map* as "any form of graphic representation that shows the relationship among words or concepts" (p. 96). Webbing gets students thinking and talking about words, requires little preparation, and can be tied to other parts of the curriculum. When you use webbing, remember that your lesson needs to be focused on what the students are reading on that day or soon after. You need not worry about teaching them everything about the word or concept.

Say, for example, that you are reading the story *Stone Soup* (Brown, 1947) with second graders. You want to build background knowledge about the story before you begin, and you can do it efficiently while introducing some of the vocabulary words. In first and second grades, many of the words you introduce will be words for which the students may already have a concept, but they may need a preview to decode them. Let us follow Taylor, a second-grade teacher, as she leads the students in a prereading vocabulary exercise before asking her students to read Brown's (1947) version of *Stone Soup*.

Taylor begins by telling the students that they will be reading a story about a very special kind of soup. She then asks the students whether they know the ingredients that might go into a vegetable soup. The students begin offering her words, and she records them on the web. As you can see in Figure 4.4, the students volunteer the following words: *chicken, beef, onions, carrots, celery, broth, potatoes, salt,* and *pepper*. Taylor records each one. Because she predicts that most of the students know the meanings of these

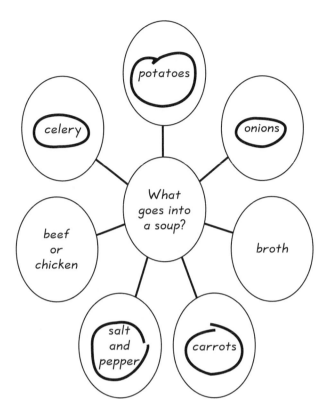

FIGURE 4.4. Brainstorming web for *Stone Soup*.

words, she does not take the time to explain what each one is. Instead, she simply has the children practice reading them. She circles the words that will be in the text, saying, "Good job! These are all ingredients for soup. The ones I have circled are in the soup in the story we will read."

No one has mentioned *barley*, another ingredient in the soup. Taylor has also predicted this. From experience, Taylor knows that her students hardly ever suggest barley, and most of them do not know what barley is. So Taylor is prepared. She shows the students a glass baby food jar filled with barley. "Do you know what this is?" she asks. "Rice," everyone yells. She says that it *looks like* rice, but directs them to look more closely; then she gives them the word *barley*. She asks them, "How is barley similar to rice? How is barley different?"

Taylor has introduced the only word in the story that she thinks her students might not know. But she has also helped her students to preread the other words—the ingredients—they will encounter in the story.

Find a narrative text or chapter of a trade book. As you look through the text, select five words, preferably ones that are used throughout the selection, that fall into Category 1: ones that are critical to the understanding of the text. Then plan a procedure for introducing those words *efficiently*. Remember to integrate the words into the students' prior knowledge. The text, and the discussions you have about the text, will provide the repetition and meaningful usage. (See the box on page 78.)

Choose a text or section of text you could use to teach reading on one day. Text:	
Word	How can I teach this word efficiently?

Category 2: Words That Present Opportunities to Teach a Strategy

Can you teach a strategy to help your students use context or structural analysis skills to discover the word's meaning?

USING CONTEXT

There is no better time to teach a strategy than before or while students are actually reading a text. We are strong advocates of contextualized vocabulary instruction, and we think that this high-utility strategy is one from which students profit the most. Teaching words in context usually involves more work for you. It would be far easier to define the words for your students—but in the end, they would have a meaning, but not a strategy.

We provide two examples below.

Example 1. In the novel, *The House of Dies Drear* (Hamilton, 1968), abolitionist Dies Drear owned a house that was part of the Underground Railroad in the 19th century. He is described as *eccentric*. Knowing what *eccentric* means is critical to understanding the novel. This word presents an excellent opportunity to show the students the importance of using a dictionary *only after* the students have made a prediction about the meaning of the word.

The novel introduces the character of Drear and the word in the following sentence:

> "He was a New Englander," Mr. Small said, "so independent and eccentric, most Ohio abolitionists thought him crazy." (p. 18)

Like all outstanding authors for children, Hamilton introduces a word that might be unfamiliar to many readers, *eccentric*, but she respects the reader's ability to decipher the words in context. She gives the readers a hint about the word's meaning within the sentence by using the word *crazy*. For some students, that might be enough, but she provides more clues as they read. We could guide the students to confirm the meaning in a dictionary at this point, but stopping to look up a word in a dictionary is not always an efficient strategy, and it detracts from the joy of reading. In addition, reading ahead gives more clues.

> "He came from an enormously wealthy family of shipbuilders, and yet his house in Ohio was fairly modest. To give you an idea how odd he was," said Mr. Small, "his house was overflowing with fine antiques, which he took neither any interest in nor sold for profit. All the furniture remained in great piles, with just enough space to get through from room to room, until the house was plundered and Drear was killed." (pp. 18–19)

Showing the students the ways to gather the clues—to be word detectives—is a useful strategy for deciphering the meaning of this word and many others. This is one example of teaching students to be strategic and independent when reading on their own.

We observed Julie teaching the above-described strategy to her fifth graders and producing the word web shown in Figure 4.5. She began by reading the sentence introducing Drear from the novel and then asking, "Do we know what *eccentric* means from this sentence?" It was likely that most of Julie's fifth graders were unaware of the exact

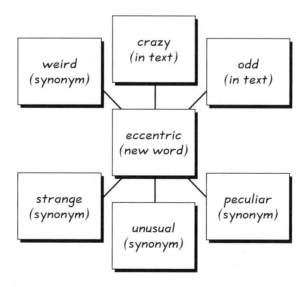

FIGURE 4.5. Webbing the word *eccentric*.

meaning, but they offered the word *crazy* because it is contained in the sentence. So she began making a web and said, "Let's read on and see if Hamilton gives us any more clues." The students read on and stated that maybe eccentric means *odd*, so Julie recorded that word on the web. As they continued reading, Julie helped the students tap into their own prior knowledge to find other words that are synonyms for *odd*, and then she recorded them on the web.

At the end, Julie guided the students to look at the word web, and she explained that by being word detectives, they could figure out the meanings of new words while they read. As a reinforcement of their effective use of the strategy, Julie then guided her students to confirm their predicted definition by looking up the word *eccentric* in their student dictionaries.

This webbing strategy, though initially conducted on the whiteboard for Julie's demonstration, could move temporarily into the notebooks of the students as they practiced the strategy. But, ultimately, this strategy would need to be *in their heads*, as they read on and gathered cues from other sentences.

Example 2. You can teach the word detective strategy to younger children and eliminate the dictionary portion of the lesson if the text purposefully gives more clues. In the classic novel *Charlotte's Web* (White, 1952), White introduces and defines several sophisticated words for the reader through interactions between Charlotte and Wilbur, the main characters. For example, when Wilbur meets Charlotte in Chapter 5, she greets him with the word *salutations*. Here is the exchange:

> Wilbur jumped to his feet. "Salu-*what*?" he cried.
>   "Salutations!" repeated the voice.
>   "What are *they*, and what are *you*?" screamed Wilbur. "Please, *please*, tell me where you are. And what are salutations?"
>   "Salutations are greetings," said the voice. "When I say 'salutations,' it's just my fancy way of saying hello or good morning." (p. 35)

White repeats similar exchanges throughout the book to purposefully define other words and terms, such as *sedentary*, *versatile*, and *magnum opus*. Through these playful interactions between characters, the readers benefit from White's unmistakable passion for words, and they learn the meanings of new words in an authentic and meaningful way. There is usually no need to develop those words any further, because White has masterfully guided the reader through the meanings.

TEACHING THE STRATEGY OF STRUCTURAL ANALYSIS

Using a similar strategy, students may also predict meanings of words from their knowledge of word parts: Greek and Latin roots, prefixes, and suffixes. For example, they can determine the meaning of the word *unfortunate* by separating the prefix from the root and determining the meanings of both parts.

Or you can teach students to recognize one part of a term, and then make analogies to guide their predictions of the word meanings. For example, most students know that *unhappy* means *not* happy. Therefore, if they encounter the word *untied*, they will be able to make an analogy and determine that *untied* means *not* tied.

Finally, the students can consult their dictionaries. In this way they have already done the hard work, and they can confirm what they thought by finding the definition that best matches the usage in the text that they are reading. This strategy serves as a good tool to practice predicting and confirming the meanings of words.

Graves et al. (2001) suggest a three-step process for teaching students new words by using word parts: (1) identify the specific word parts to teach; (2) teach the meanings of the word parts; and (3) repeat and review the process often, gradually adding new word parts.

Below is a passage from the second text page of the award-winning picture book *Rosa* (Giovanni, 2005). Read this excerpt and think about how you could teach *alterations*—the word Giovanni uses as she gives the reader some background about Rosa Parks. Pay close attention to the word parts and the context clues Giovanni has woven throughout the passage to help young readers craft the meaning of the word.

> Everyone knew the alterations department would be very, very busy. Mrs. Parks would laugh each year with the other seamstresses and say that "those elves in the North Pole have nothing on us!"
>
> The women of Montgomery, both young and older, would come in with their fancy holiday dresses that needed adjustments or their Sunday suits and blouses that needed just a touch—a flower or some velvet trimming or something to make the ladies look festive.
>
> Rosa Parks was the best seamstress. The needle and thread flew through her hands like the gold spinning from Rumpelstiltskin's loom. The other seamstresses would tease Rosa Parks and say she used magic. Rosa would laugh. "Not magic. Just concentration," she would say. Some days she would skip lunch to be finished on time. (p. 2)

Now record your notes below. How can you teach the meaning of the word *alterations* by teaching your students a strategy for both decoding the prefix, suffix, or root and using the context of the excerpt? We will leave it up to you to decide what meaningful parts are in the word *alterations*.

Category 3: Words That Are Important Any Time

How useful is this word outside the current reading selection? What are the chances that the students will see this word again soon?

Time spent teaching students words that they will rarely encounter is not time well spent, because the task of teaching vocabulary is enormous. However, if you see a word in a text that does not fit either Category 1 or Category 2, but that you feel is an important word to teach or review, you should teach it because (1) it is presented in context, and (2) it is a word your students should know. Many encounters with words help ensure the success of learning new words. Frequently students will encounter words they have seen in previous texts. Making a point of reviewing words they may have encountered before helps the students gain the repeated exposures they need to learn them.

For example, suppose you are using the book *Hoot* (Hiaasen, 2002) while teaching your fourth graders a reading lesson. In the seventh chapter, there is a passage that contains the word *twilight*.

> Beatrice parked the bike and motioned for Roy to follow her through the hole in the fence. They entered a junkyard full of wrecked automobiles, acres of them. In the twilight Roy and Beatrice crept along, darting from one rusted hulk to the next. From the way Beatrice was acting, Roy assumed they weren't alone on the property. (p. 72)

In this chapter, it is not absolutely necessary to understand the meaning of the word *twilight*, but it is a word that the students will see again, and it will be useful for them to know that twilight is the time right before darkness. There is no need to go into great detail, but teaching the meanings of words as they are encountered—in an informal way—increases the number of exposures for your students.

Other Ways to Build Vocabulary: Strategies That Work in All Categories

DEVELOPING KNOWLEDGE ABOUT GRADABLE ANTONYMS

You can use a teacher-directed learning event for teaching *gradable antonyms*. These are words that differ in degree and that occur between two ends of a spectrum, such as between *slow* and *fast*. In addition to helping your students to understand the new word or words, this activity leads to a kind of *wordsmithing*, and it helps your students use words more precisely both in speaking and in writing.

We observed Gail while she was teaching a second-grade science lesson. The lesson required the students to mix sugar with *tepid* water, so she took the opportunity to involve the class in figuring out what the word *tepid* meant. In Figure 4.6, you can see that the students brainstormed words between *hot* and *cold*. As each word was offered, Gail asked, "Do you think your word is closer to *hot* or to *cold*? Where shall we put the word?" Then she placed the word in the spot indicated by the students. When the students were finished and she wrote the word *tepid*, she helped the students in discovering that tepid water is similar to lukewarm water.

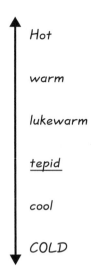

FIGURE 4.6. Gradable antonyms.

USING A FEATURE MATRIX

A *feature matrix* is a chart that shows how concepts are related to each other (Johnson & Pearson, 1984). Making a feature matrix with students is another teacher-directed event that results in students' understanding of a concept. The matrix is also an excellent example of the kind of purposeful and meaningful print on walls we have described in Chapter 2, because the display is interactive and dynamic. For example, in Figure 4.7, we see the results of a lesson in which first-grade students were learning about mammals. After reading the text *Animals Born Alive and Well* (Heller, 1982) with his students, Jake recorded the characteristics of mammals. Then Jake provided many more books about animals, and he directed the students to look through their books and find pictures of mammals. Together, they listed the mammals, and they checked off the characteristics of the mammals they read about. As the children read or talked about more mammals in school or at home, they added mammals to the matrix and checked off the characteristics. They were able to use the terms associated with mammals often, and the activity increased their ability to talk about mammals in a more scientific way.

Mammal	Fur or hair	Plates	Wings	Legs	Live birth	Eggs
dog	✓			✓	✓	
whale	✓				✓	
platypus	✓					✓
bat	✓		✓	✓	✓	
armadillo		✓		✓	✓	

FIGURE 4.7. Feature matrix: What is a mammal?

Look through some of the published anthologies and programs you can use when teaching reading to children. Choose one narrative selection. Consult the teacher's manual, and record the words the program authors chose as key words or terms. Ask yourself these questions: Which words did they choose? Why were these words selected? How is the instruction suggested for the words consistent with best practice in teaching vocabulary?

Selection:		
Words to Teach	Why?	How?
1.		
2.		
3.		
4.		
5.		

Peer Talk

The Talk around the Task

In Chapter 2, we have described the benefits of peer talk. We cannot overstate the importance of classroom discussion and peer talk for students in learning to be competent language users, in developing and using vocabulary, and in understanding and responding to text. Giving students opportunities to use the words they are learning in school is critical. Children know that there is "school language" and "play language." If we do not give our students many opportunities in school to practice "school language," we cannot expect newly acquired words to spill into their everyday speech outside the school context.

We sat in on Nina's first-grade classroom during a lively discussion of fairy tales. In this class, Nina was immersing her students in fairy tales. She read many of them aloud, and the students read many on their own. After they read several of them, Nina put the students into groups to discuss them, and asked them what they noticed about the fairy tales they read. They were clever at extracting the elements of fairy tales, such as *things happening in threes, magic,* and *mean people.*

Nina began to make a feature matrix, using the elements of fairy tales the students had discovered on their own; she supplied others for them. Then she recorded some of the fairy tales they had read on the matrix (see Figure 4.8), saying, "Let's check off the elements of the fairy tales we have read so far. We can add more fairy tales later." Some of the words on the matrix were new words—*royalty, conflict,* and *evil*—and it was important to Nina that the first graders use these words when discussing the fairy tales and completing the chart. In this way, the *talk around the task* became more important than the task itself. The students had to use the words over and over as they participated in the activity. In the end, the students had categorized the fairy tales according to their features on the matrix. More importantly, they were able to practice using the words in a meaningful way.

Let us return to Alberto's fifth-grade classroom, the one we have showcased at the beginning of this chapter. Recall that Alberto's students are learning about the westward expansion of the 1800s. Alberto has begun the lesson by preteaching the essential vocabulary, including the words *migration* and *resettlement*. He has provided his students with many texts about the westward expansion, including websites on the classroom computers.

Several days later, Alberto guides his students in a discussion about the courageous women who journeyed to California during the California gold rush. Alberto's students

Text	Magic	Things in threes	Animals	Royalty	Conflict with evil	Special phrases
Cinderella	✓	✓	✓	✓	✓	✓
The Three Wishes	✓	✓			✓	✓
Rapunzel	✓	✓		✓	✓	✓
Rumpelstiltskin	✓	✓	✓	✓	✓	✓

FIGURE 4.8. Feature matrix: Elements of a fairy tale.

have been researching women such as Elizabeth Gunn and Luzena Stanley Wilson, and they are learning about the kind of character it took to withstand the hardships these women endured traveling by land and by sea from the East to California. As the students learn about the women, they add attributes to a word bank displayed on a wall in the classroom.

tenacious	arduous		*determined*
strenuous	**laborious**	indomitable	*unwavering*
feisty	**persistent**	resolute	*painstaking* **spirited**
demanding	resilient	hardy	**risk takers** vigorous

Alberto directs the students to talk in groups of four about the women they have researched, and he advises them to use the new words they have learned in their discussions. "Yes, we know they were *brave*," Alberto says, "but they were much more. Refer to the word bank we developed when learning about these women, and use them in your discussion." In this way, Alberto is encouraging his students to be conscious users of these words; also, through repetition, they are more likely to integrate the words into their speaking and writing vocabularies.

Talk around the Edges

One sign that our rigorous efforts in teaching vocabulary are paying off is hearing our students use the words meaningfully outside the instructional context. Dudley-Marling and Searle (1991) describe this as *talk around the edges*. Talk around the edges, Dudley-Marling and Searle suggest, is a context in which students stretch their language. These times occur before and after lessons, outside school, during field trips—whenever our students see us, their teachers, in a less evaluative role (see Figure 4.9). Rather, we are

- It occurs before or after school or lessons.
- Teachers establish themselves as listeners.
- Teachers are more apt to respond like an authentic audience.
- Teachers focus on the meaning.
- Students take risks.
  They stretch their vocabulary.
  They ask questions.
  They organize events.
  They make meaning explicit.
  They learn to handle the give and take of conversation.

FIGURE 4.9. Talk around the edges. Based on Dudley-Marling and Searle (1991).

listening to *what* they are saying, not *how* they are saying it. The students may choose to "show off" what they have learned, and they may take risks using the new words. Similarly, we may take the opportunity to use new words in this context ourselves, and to observe the ways in which each student demonstrates understanding. These "edges" are important instructional moments, and we feel that they should be as valued as the scheduled instructional times when we are "teaching" vocabulary.

SATISFYING CHILDREN'S NATURAL CURIOSITY ABOUT WORDS

Children are naturally curious about words. Observe them after you have shown them how excited you are about the new words you encounter. Recall that in Chapter 2 we have discussed the importance of providing a motivating environment by showing your own enthusiasm for reading. The same is true when creating an environment in which learning new words is given high priority.

There are many books about words to satisfy your own interest, and there are books to share with your students during read-alouds and during sustained silent reading. Include these books in your weekly book previews, and showcase them in a prominent place in your classroom library. Some examples of books that quench children's thirst for learning words are offered in Figure 4.10.

Your excitement at learning new words is contagious to your students; your enthusiasm has an effect on your teaching. Good teaching usually involves very deliberate actions (you will learn more about these in the next chapter), so modeling enthusiasm is usually *not* sufficient. If demonstrating zeal were enough, our students would have far more extensive vocabularies to use in their speech and their writing, and their reading comprehension would be substantially better. It is the instruction of those words, explicitly and through the teaching of strategies, that brings those words alive for students and makes them their own.

In this chapter, you have learned the value of teaching explicitly the words your students need to learn for effective comprehension of the texts and books they will read.

Max's Words by Kate Banks

The Boy Who Loved Words by Roni Schotter

Mom and Dad Are Palindromes by Mark Shulman

Many Luscious Lollipops by Ruth Heller

A sample of books by Brian Cleary:

A Mink, a Fink, a Skating Rink: What Is a Noun?
Quirky, Jerky, Extra-Perky: More about Adjectives
Slide and Slurp, Scratch and Burp: More about Verbs
Stop and Go, Yes and No: What Is an Antonym?

FIGURE 4.10. Examples of picture books about words.

Although *teaching* vocabulary and *assessing* vocabulary often go hand in hand, they are really very different. We describe strategies for assessing vocabulary in Chapter 12.

To demonstrate your own ability to learn new vocabulary, please refer to the Key Terms Chart in Figure 4.11, and attempt to put the terms in your own words.

In the next chapter, we describe the foundations of cognitive strategy instruction, which underlies all good pedagogy.

REFLECTION ON ARTIFACTS FOR YOUR SELF-STUDY

For your self-study, record on Figure 4.12 (page 90) the artifacts you created while you read this chapter.

KEY TERMS FOR THIS CHAPTER

In this chapter, the following key terms are essential to your understanding of reading instruction. Think about what they mean, and try to define them in your own words.

wide reading

integration

repetition

meaningful use

webbing

gradable antonyms

feature matrix

talk around the task

talk around the edges

FIGURE 4.11. Key Terms Chart for Chapter 4.

SELF-STUDY REVIEW CHART FOR CHAPTER 4

Name of Artifact	Teacher Instructional Actions and Language	Provisions for Individual Differences	Variety of Modes of Communication	Critical Thinking and Active Engagement	Opportunities for Assessment

FIGURE 4.12. Self-Study Review Chart for Chapter 4.

CHAPTER 5

Preparing Strategic Readers

Teaching Reading
through Cognitive Strategy Instruction

It is often beneficial for teachers of reading to consider their own informal learning and transfer what they know about those experiences to formal teaching and learning. To prepare for this chapter on the teaching of reading, we would like you to reflect on the process of learning basic skills when you were young. To that end, consider the following questions, and record your responses in the grid below.

Question	Who taught you and how?
How did you learn to tie your shoes?	
How did you learn to ride a two-wheeler bike?	
How did you learn to fit in with your peers?	

Now compare what you wrote to the responses listed below, which we have recorded from our work with teachers. We believe you may have recorded similar teaching methods.

Question	Who taught you and how?
How did you learn to tie your shoes?	• *Mom showed me how to make bunny ears with the laces.* • *My kindergarten teacher showed me how to loop and tie.* • *Dad had me practice while he talked me through the steps.* • *I practiced by myself.* • *I tried other ways when it was not working.*
How did you learn to ride a two-wheeler bike?	• *I learned to ride a tricycle first.* • *My friend got on her bike and showed me how she balanced the wheels.* • *My mom held the back of the bike until I told her to let go.* • *I fell a lot.* • *My friend showed me how she pedaled fast to stay upright.*
How did you learn to fit in with your peers?	• *My friends told me what to say and do.* • *I learned by reading books about teens.* • *During lunch period, I observed my peers fitting in.* • *I tried out some ways to be friendly and meet new friends.*

Let us consider what we have learned about teaching and learning from this activity. First, if you responded that someone "showed" you how to tie your shoes, then you are suggesting that *modeling* or *demonstration* is a valuable teaching step. Did you also suggest that someone *coached* you through the act of tying your shoes while repeating the steps of the activity? We all know the value of *coaching* in the act of learning something new. Another teaching method you may have identified was the act of breaking down a complex task into small manageable parts. This may have occurred when you learned each step of tying your shoelaces, or when someone held on to the back of your bicycle until you could balance on your own. This valuable teaching step is called *providing a scaffold* or *scaffolding*, and is explained in this chapter. Other valuable learning activities or teaching steps you may have identified include *repetition, guided practice (practice with an able adult or peer present), independent practice, trial and error,* and *observation*.

Not surprisingly, you will discover through this chapter that all of these informal teaching and learning methods are embedded in a model for teaching reading, called *cognitive strategy instruction*. This chapter provides a detailed description of this explicit, direct instruction model, which shows *how* to teach reading strategies. Chapters 6–9 focus on *what* specific comprehension strategies to teach. Before we present the cognitive strategy instructional model, however, it is necessary to consider the many research principles from which it has evolved.

BEST PRACTICES YOU WILL SEE IN THIS CHAPTER

✓ Teaching cognitive strategy instruction in the elementary curriculum.
✓ Scaffolding instruction for all learners through modeling, coaching, and practice.

WHAT IS COGNITIVE STRATEGY INSTRUCTION?

A well-known body of research evidence conducted from the 1980s to the mid-1990s supports *cognitive strategy instruction* (Pearson & Dole, 1987; Pressley & El-Dinary, 1993; Pressley et al., 1992; Pressley, Goodchild, Fleet, Zajchowski, & Evans, 1989). To arrive at a working definition for this type of instruction, let us examine the two key words: *cognitive* and *strategy*. *Cognitive*, as we know, refers to *thinking*, or the acquisition of knowledge by such processes as reasoning, recognizing, judging, and perceiving. The word *strategy* typically means a systematic plan of action to accomplish a goal. Thus a *cognitive strategy* is a thinking process whereby a reader employs a plan to accomplish a reading goal.

For example, let's consider the mind of an imaginary fourth-grade reader, Anthony, as he is attempting to read the following sentence in an expository textbook about elephants: "Both species of elephant, the African and the Asian, are endangered because deforestation threatens their habitat." If Anthony has no idea what the word *deforestation* means and has no strategy for attempting to unlock the meaning of this word, then his understanding of the text is compromised. However, if he has a clear strategy such as the one suggested below, his chance of success is increased.

Recall in Chapter 4 that we have described how important it is to teach students to decipher the meaning of unknown words in context. Here is a cognitive strategy you can teach students to apply when they come across an unknown word:

Strategy for Unlocking the Meaning of an Unknown Word

1. When you come to a word that you do not know, stop and ask yourself if you have heard of the word before. Where? If you have heard of it, think of another word or synonym you can insert in its place. Now does the sentence make sense to you?
2. If that doesn't work, go back to the word and break the word into smaller words. Are there word parts that you know? Can you identify prefixes, suffixes, and root words to help you assign meaning to the word?
3. If not, read to the end of the sentence to see if you can figure out the word from the surrounding words (the context).
4. Finally, try using your reference books to help you with the word in question. Or you can look up the word in an online dictionary or other reliable source.

This vocabulary strategy is an example of a cognitive strategy. You can see that "ways of thinking" or "thinking steps" are embedded in the strategy *heuristic*. A *heuristic* is simply a helpful procedure for arriving at a solution; it is not foolproof, but rather, provides ways of thinking to solve a problem. If Anthony knows this strategy, he may be able to arrive at a preliminary meaning of the word *deforestation* by identifying its root, *forest*, and its prefix, *de*, which usually means "down" or "away from."

Teaching a cognitive strategy, therefore, is a way to aid young and/or developing readers to think like older, more experienced readers by teaching strategy "thinking steps" that more able readers use.

GUIDING PRINCIPLES
OF COGNITIVE STRATEGY INSTRUCTION

The research on cognitive strategy instruction was comprehensive and thorough from the late 1970s through the 1990s (Pearson & Dole, 1987; Pressley & El-Dinary, 1993; Pressley et al., 1989, 1992).

Although much of this earlier research was conducted in the context of reading comprehension, cognitive strategy research has continued in other areas of literacy, especially vocabulary and writing instruction (Flower et al., 1990; Gaskins & Elliot, 1991; Lubliner & Smetana, 2005). Practitioners have begun to use the cognitive strategy approach to teach many thinking processes, even mathematics. However, Michael Pressley (2000), one of the more prolific researchers in this area, has suggested that although the research on cognitive strategy instruction has demonstrated positive results, the instruction has not been incorporated into the schools, perhaps due to difficulty in implementation.

The reason why cognitive strategy instruction is considered a best practice is clear. Comprehension is increased if practitioners (1) teach strategies as thinking processes, (2) give multiple opportunities to try out those strategies in different reading contexts, (3) teach readers to combine and manipulate strategies to each new reading situation, and (4) provide readers with practice combining strategies.

To better understand cognitive strategy instruction, it is important to look at two theories that have had a significant influence on our changing views about reading comprehension: *schema theory* (Anderson & Pearson, 1984) and theories about *metacognition* (Garner, 1987).

Schema Theory

Research on schema theory has had an important impact on reading comprehension instruction (Anderson, Spiro, & Anderson, 1978; Rumelhart, 1980). Researchers who investigated a "schema view" of reading suggested that a reader's prior knowledge, including experiences and attitudes, determines the ways in which new information is understood. Therefore, new information is learned more easily during reading when it can be integrated into a reader's preexisting knowledge (Anderson et al., 1978). In regard to teaching practice, numerous studies on schema theory have validated the importance of a teacher's activating students' prior knowledge before or during reading for a better understanding of what is being read (Anderson, 1985; Anderson & Pearson, 1984; Rumelhart, 1980).

Anderson (1985) has defined a schema as an organized knowledge of the world. He explains that comprehension occurs when a reader activates or constructs a schema that provides a framework for the message delivered in the text. He has proposed five ways in which a reader's schema affects learning and comprehension:

1. It allows for information to be filed in slots or niches.
2. It allows for selection of important material or main ideas, in situations where closer attention to detail is important.
3. It enables the reader to make inferences from implied text.
4. It allows the reader to determine relevance and irrelevance of information.
5. It allows the reader to activate knowledge and to reconstruct what is missing by combining the new material with what is previously stored.

Paris and Lindauer (1976) found that young and developing readers may not activate prior knowledge on their own and may need a teacher's help to do this before reading a text. Other researchers have stressed the need for teachers to build students' schemas through broad experiences (Afflerbach, 1990; Cross & Paris, 1988; Paris, Lipson, & Wixson, 1983). The following scenario illustrates why this research on schema theory is important for your teaching of reading comprehension.

Li-Ling is about to read a story about Groundhog Day to her second-grade class. She is unsure which children, if any, have had experiences with groundhogs, and predicts that groundhogs will be unfamiliar to most children in her urban classroom. Therefore, before reading, Li-Ling takes a few minutes to activate her students' schemas through asking various questions about what groundhogs look like, where they live, and the American legend about Groundhog Day. During this prior knowledge activation step, Li-Ling is careful to build the students' knowledge about groundhogs. This added teaching step prepares her students for understanding the reading in a significant way.

Metacognition of Comprehension Strategy Usage

An underlying principle of cognitive strategy instruction is the reader's development of *metacognitive knowledge* about reading strategies. *Metacognition* literally means "thinking about thinking." If readers have metacognitive knowledge about reading strategies, they know what strategy to apply while reading, and why and when to use certain strategies (Garner, 1987). For example, an intermediate reader who notices that he or she does not understand a text may deliberately use a "fix-up" strategy, such as rereading or summarizing.

Paris et al. (1983) have described three types of metacognitive knowledge: *declarative knowledge, procedural knowledge*, and *conditional knowledge*. This provides us with a useful framework for thinking about our cognitive strategy instruction. The three types are defined as follows:

1. *Declarative knowledge* represents what readers know about strategy usage (Brown, Armbruster, & Baker, 1986; Flavell, 1985; Garner, 1987).
2. *Procedural knowledge* represents the procedures readers use when applying a strategy (Cross & Paris, 1988).
3. *Conditional knowledge* represents the understanding readers have about when and where to apply a strategy, and how to evaluate the effectiveness of the strategy (Cross & Paris, 1988).

In simpler terms, metacognition refers to readers' awareness of and motivation to use their known strategies (*declarative knowledge*), their systematic plans for applying strategies in reading text (*procedural knowledge*), and their knowledge when and where to use them (*conditional knowledge*). If the goal of our reading program is to have students gain metacognition of reading strategies, then our task is to teach the three types in a concise and clear way. Later in this chapter, we describe how these three types of metacognitive knowledge can be used to structure your teaching. First, to better understand the three types of metacognitive knowledge, think about some activity or process in which you are an expert, and fill out the chart below. We have completed one entry for you as a model.

A metacognitive strategy	Declarative knowledge: What the strategy is and why it is important	Procedural knowledge: How to apply the strategy (the heuristic)	Conditional knowledge: When to use the strategy and the conditions of success
Crossover dribble while playing basketball	*The crossover dribble is a method of dribbling a basketball and keeping it away from your opponents at the same time. It is important because it is an essential part of the game.*	*1. To start the crossover, I dribble with my right hand.* *2. When the opposing player gets really close, I push the ball out in front of me and switch it over to my left side.* *3. Just as I change the ball to my left hand, I move past the opposing player.* *4. If the defense is close, I must remember to keep the ball low as I dribble.*	*The crossover dribbling technique is good to use when your defender is right on top of you. My strategy heuristic only works if there is only one defender in my vicinity. More steps must be added if there is more than one defender blocking me.*
A metacognitive strategy	Declarative knowledge: What the strategy is and why it is important	Procedural knowledge: How to apply the strategy (the heuristic)	Conditional knowledge: When to use the strategy and the conditions of success
The strategy I have metacognitive knowledge of is:			

There are many processes for which we, as adults, have clear metacognitive strategies. When we consider the many daily activities in which we engage, we can provide quite a list of strategies that we employ every day, from driving a car to carrying out a recipe to reading with purpose. In the next section, you will learn how to use a metacognitive instructional model to teach a reading strategy.

THE INSTRUCTIONAL MODEL

The informal learning steps we have identified at the beginning of this chapter include modeling, verbal explanation, guided and independent practice, and other teaching methods. You will soon understand that a strategic instructional model for *all grades* and for *all learners* includes (1) explaining what a strategy is and why one should learn it; (2) modeling the procedure by thinking aloud while applying the strategy; (3) providing a *heuristic* (a helpful procedure) of ways of thinking for applying the strategy; (4) providing both guided and independent practice of the strategy; and (5) giving students opportunities to evaluate the effectiveness of the strategy in multiple contexts (Paris & Winograd, 1990). Figure 5.1 (page 98) summarizes the cognitive strategy instructional model we are advocating for direct instruction (Pasquarelli, 1997).

A Lesson Using the Instructional Model

The simplest way for you to understand the cognitive strategy instructional model (Figure 5.1, page 98) is to experience an actual lesson plan for teaching one of the basic comprehension strategies: how to activate prior knowledge before reading. The lesson proceeds as follows.

Lesson: Strategy for activating prior knowledge

Text: *Hide and Seek Science #02: Where's That Reptile?* (Chardiet & Schwartz, 1995)

Lesson Grade Levels: 1–3

Lesson Objective: Students will demonstrate understanding of activating prior knowledge about a text topic before reading.

Declarative Knowledge: First, the teacher tells the students that they will be learning a new strategy. The declarative knowledge segment of the lesson may proceed as follows:

"Today, children, we are going to learn a new reading strategy called *activating our prior knowledge*. This strategy will help us understand how to remember what we know about the information we will read in the text. We know that as good readers, we always think about what we know about the text topic before and during reading. To do so helps us add new information to the information we already know.

"The reason why this strategy is important is that it will help us to understand the meaning of the text by bringing together what we already know with what we are going to learn in the book."

DECLARATIVE KNOWLEDGE:
What strategy are we learning?
Why are we learning this strategy?

- Tell students what they will be learning by providing the name of the strategy and a conceptual understanding of it.
- Tell students why they will be learning the strategy (authentic reason).

PROCEDURAL KNOWLEDGE:
How do we apply the strategy?

- Teach and model the use of the strategy through a think-aloud approach.
- Provide a heuristic of the cognitive processes (thinking steps) used to carry out the strategy.
- Provide students with both guided and independent practice in using the strategy.

CONDITIONAL KNOWLEDGE
When do we use the strategy?
How effective is the strategy when applied in different texts?
Under which conditions will I be successful?

- Help students to evaluate the effectiveness of the strategy (the heuristic).
- Guide students to an understanding of when to use the strategy again.
- Provide practice in a wide variety of texts (for reading instruction) and a wide variety of genres (for writing instruction).

FIGURE 5.1. Cognitive strategy instructional model. Based on Pasquarelli (1997).

From this script, you can see that the teacher is careful to (1) tell the students the name of the strategy, and (2) give an authentic reason for learning the strategy. In the case of more complex strategies, the declarative portion of the lesson plan may have to be longer. For example, if you are teaching students how to compare and contrast text information, you may have to spend a few minutes conceptualizing what it means to compare and what it means to contrast.

Procedural Knowledge: Consider that when you learned to tie your shoes or ride a bike, the person who taught you was able to *model* the task by *showing* you what to do. Likewise when you learned any other strategy that can be *seen* (such as dribbling a basketball), the person modeling the task had the benefit of your ability to watch him/ her perform the strategy. Unfortunately, learners cannot "see" your thinking while you read or write, so while you are providing procedural knowledge, you must carefully consider both your instructional language and your instructional actions.

Garner (1987) has suggested that explicit explanation is enhanced by the use of *think-alouds* during modeling of a specific strategy. She advocates a technique whereby a teacher models and thinks aloud simultaneously. Thus the procedural knowledge portion of the lesson plan requires teachers to be prepared to model the strategy for the students in an appropriate grade-level text. Perhaps the modeling and think-aloud portion of the lesson may sound like this:

"I am now going to model for you how to think about what you already know about the topic before reading. While I model, I want everyone to listen to my thinking. For this part of the lesson, I am going to ask you to be silent while I think out loud. After I think out loud, so you can see how I read, I am going to ask you to practice in the same way.

"[Think-aloud begins.] The first thing I am going to do is look at the pictures on the cover of the book and read the title. On the cover of the book, I see a crocodile, a turtle, a few snakes, and a very scary-looking lizard. Now I am going to read the title of the book. I can see that it is is called *Where's That Reptile?*

"Now that I have looked at the cover and read the title, I know the book is about reptiles, and some reptiles are pictured on the cover. So now I am going to think about all the things I know about reptiles. Hmmm. . . . Well, I don't know much about crocodiles. I do know that there are a few in Florida, where my uncle lives. Hmmm. I don't really know much about them . . . But . . . I know that a snake is a reptile, because there are many harmless snakes in my backyard, so I have seen them and asked my dad about them. He is the one who told me a snake is a reptile. I also know that snakes shed their skins every now and then, because I find old snake skins in my backyard and bring them in to scare my sister.

"I really don't know that much more about the snakes in my backyard, but if I think about what I have read about snakes, I can think of more facts. For example, once I read about a snake in the Amazon that is 15 feet long and can kill large mammals. I don't remember much about that kind of snake, other than it wraps itself around its prey and squeezes it. So I know that there are many different kinds of snakes and they are all reptiles because they are 'cold-blooded.' Hmmm. . . . I don't know what that really means, other than it is different from a human, which is 'warm-blooded,' so maybe I'll learn more about that in this text. [Think-aloud ends.]

"Now, children, let's record the steps of my strategy for activating prior knowledge on this easel paper [see Figure 5.2, page 100]. The first thing I did was look at the cover pictures and read the title of the book. The second thing I did was ask myself questions such as these: What do I know about this topic? What have I read about this topic? What have I seen concerning this topic? Has anyone ever told me anything about this topic? These questions helped me to identify everything I know about reptiles and got my mind ready to read more." [Verbal explanation ends.]

You can see from the example above that the think-aloud portion of the strategy instruction includes both explicitly stating the strategy steps and applying them to the text the teacher is using to model. The strategy demonstrated above is a simple one for grades 1–2, and requires that students only pay attention for a few minutes.

1. Look at the cover pictures.

2. Look at the title.

3. Ask yourself the following questions:
    - What do I know about this topic?
    - What have I read about this topic?
    - What have I seen concerning this topic?
    - Has anyone ever told me anything about this topic?

FIGURE 5.2. Strategy for activating prior knowledge before reading (grades K–3).

The next step of the process is for students to try out the strategy immediately in another text. This aspect of gaining procedural knowledge is called *guided practice*, and is initiated immediately after the modeling and think-aloud, to ensure that students remember these. The guided practice part of the lesson may sound like this:

"Now who is ready to try out this strategy with another book? I would like you to work with your buddies to try out the strategy with the new book I placed on your desk earlier. First, let us review our strategy steps. . . . "

As the teacher points to the easel chart (Figure 5.2) and reviews the strategy, he or she can then ask the students to apply the strategy, using the cover and title of a new book to activate their prior knowledge. As soon as the students are engaged in guided practice, it is important for the teacher to walk around the room, assisting students as needed. We call this assistance *coaching*; it is a valuable part of cognitive strategy instruction, because it provides opportunities for children who may not have grasped the strategy during the whole-group lesson to have the benefit of the teacher's assistance in learning the strategy during guided practice. (We discuss it further below.) When students have completed the guided practice task, the teacher can then proceed with the conditional knowledge section of the lesson plan.

Conditional Knowledge: The purpose of the conditional knowledge section of the instructional model is twofold: (1) to have young readers evaluate the effectiveness of the strategy, and (2) to be sure students know when and where to use the strategy again. These two aspects are discussed separately.

First, to have the students evaluate the effectiveness of the strategy, the teacher should immediately follow the guided practice with a *debriefing* of what the students have learned as a result of applying the strategy. The teacher can start by asking the students what prior knowledge they were able to activate with the book they used for guided practice. After being assured that the students were able to activate their prior knowledge, the teacher can then turn his/her attention to the strategy and ask the children how effective it was in the new book. This portion of the lesson may sound like this:

> "Okay, now, children, let's look once again at our easel chart [Figure 5.2] and review our strategy. How many of you felt that the questions you asked helped you to think of what you already know about the topic? Can anyone add a step to our strategy?"

Very often children will volunteer their own ways of thinking to add to the strategy. For example, a student may say, "Well, this book did not have as many pictures on the cover as the reptile book, so I decided to open the book and look at the pictures in the text to help me remember what I know." What actually occurred was that the child had to alter his or her strategy to accommodate the change in the text *condition*. This is a common practice during this stage of the lesson plan. Remember, conditional knowledge is the aspect of metacognitive knowledge that tells the reader under which conditions a procedure is useful.

The second step of the conditional knowledge portion of the lesson plan is to be sure students understand when to use the strategy again. This next step may sound like this:

> "Okay, children, so when can we use this strategy again? [Students respond.] Yes, that is correct; whenever we begin reading a new book, it is a good idea to think of everything we know *before* reading to get our minds ready to learn new information. Will we use this strategy with our social studies and science books? With our picture books? As we learn more and more strategies, you will see that we use this strategy often, both *before* reading and *while* we are reading." [End of lesson.]

The research tells us that students will not often transfer the strategy to different types of books and different contexts of reading, and teachers must provide multiple practice opportunities (Garner, 1987). Therefore, we suggest that students be given guided practice in all types of texts and reading contexts. Once students appear to grasp this strategy, teachers must be sure to give them independent practice and assess their progress in applying the strategy before and during reading.

Other Important Instructional Acts in the Model

As you think about the lesson presented above, you may have some questions as to why certain parts of the model are important. As indicated in the procedural knowledge section of the lesson plan, there are specific reasons why researchers have suggested the importance of modeling, think-alouds, and guided practice. There are equally important reasons why teachers are careful to provide debriefing and guidance for future use of the strategy during the conditional knowledge component of the lesson plan.

Roehler and Duffy (1991) have identified two further instructional acts that are associated with the success of direct instruction: (1) gradually releasing the responsibility for strategy use to students by first modeling and thinking aloud, and then grouping children with able peers during guided practice, and (2) coaching during both guided and independent practice. These instructional actions are described on the following page.

Gradual Release of Responsibility

Pearson and Gallagher's (1983) model of the *gradual release of responsibility* is an integral part of strategy teaching. Based on Vygotsky's (1978) concept of the zone of proximal development, the Pearson and Gallagher model suggests that teacher support should guide students from one level of understanding a new strategy to another, and that gradually shifting responsibility from teacher to student is the ultimate aim. Crucial to this process is grouping children with able peers for guided practice. In our lesson plan on the previous pages, you may have noticed that the teacher asks the students to listen quietly and be attentive as he or she demonstrates the strategy in a think-aloud format. Only after the teacher has modeled the entire strategy does he or she ask the students to try it out with an able peer. The teacher takes the whole responsibility for the task completion before asking students to try it out. His or her part in gradually releasing the strategy application is far from completed at this juncture, however. One of the most important parts of strategy instruction is coaching students to success.

Coaching

Coaching is an integral part of strategy instruction after the original modeling is accomplished. In order for students to learn new strategies, they must practice them often and in multiple contexts. Roehler and Duffy (1991) have defined *coaching* in this way: "Coaching requires teachers to observe students while they carry out the task and to offer feedback, modeling, reminders, explanations and clues designed to help them successfully complete the task" (p. 873).

Coaching also includes *scaffolding* students to success. Just as a construction site has structural scaffolds as a building is being built, a reader may need a scaffold or support from a more knowledgeable other—a teacher or an able peer (Bruner, 1975; Vygotsky, 1978).

As you can see, the demands of cognitive strategy instruction do not begin and end with the first teaching step. Research indicates that students need multiple exposures to strategies for ownership and continued usage (Garner, 1987). Pearson (1984) has suggested that students must have continued practice with strategy applications while the teacher provides constant coaching with verbal support and feedback.

TEACHING STUDENTS TO COMBINE STRATEGIES WHILE READING

Teaching isolated comprehension strategies is only a precursor to teaching students to apply multiple comprehension strategies while reading. Perhaps the most best-known model of combining reading comprehension strategies is Palincsar and Brown's (1989) *reciprocal teaching*. Reciprocal teaching requires a teacher, tutor, or other "expert" to be responsible for providing the scaffolding necessary for students to acquire reading comprehension strategies. The term *reciprocal* refers to the mutual or shared manner in which the teacher or other "expert" and students engage.

In Palincsar and Brown's original research, students were taught four reading comprehension strategies: how to predict, how to seek clarification, how to ask questions of the text, and how to summarize. Teachers modeled how to apply the strategies, and then had groups of students work on applying the multiple strategies while reading. Reciprocal teaching has been researched extensively, with positive findings for its effects on reading achievement.

Another model of cognitive strategy instruction that combines reading strategies is called *transactional strategies instruction* (TSI). The name was derived from Rosenblatt's (1978) reader response theory, which suggests that meaning is constructed through the reader's making a *transaction* with the text. TSI is also designed to group students together as they practice applying various transactional strategies in a wide variety of contexts.

Like reciprocal teaching, TSI has been widely researched (Bergman, 1992; Brown & Coy-Ogan, 1993; Pressley et al., 1992). One of the consistent findings is increased student motivation to (1) practice the comprehension strategies, and (2) consistently use the comprehension strategies while working alone.

In sum, as students accrue more and more comprehension strategies, it is essential that we give them multiple opportunities to combine strategies while reading for maximum effectiveness. Naturally, as we consider the cumulative process of acquiring comprehension strategies in grades K–6, we will need to consider instruction for the primary grades versus the intermediate grades. In the next section of this chapter, we discuss how to alter strategy instruction from grade to grade.

ALTERING THE COGNITIVE STRATEGIES ACROSS GRADE LEVELS

What to teach *when* is a question often asked by teachers who are learning to implement reading comprehension instruction. Although individual districts or schools most often decide the scope and sequence of the reading program, the cognitive strategy instructional model (Figure 5.1, p. 98) remains the same, no matter the grade level or expertise of the learner. Two changes that occur from grade to grade include (1) the use of increasingly demanding textbooks (change in text rigor), and (2) change in the strategy heuristic. Each is explained below.

Change in Text Rigor

As readers progress, they move from simple texts to more complex texts in school-based programs. First-grade texts, whether they are narrative or expository, present simple topics in simple ways. It stands to reason that as the rigor of a text grows, the comprehension strategy heuristic must become increasingly complex to meet the text's demands. In the next few chapters, you will see that the strategies for teaching comprehension remain the same from grade to grade, but that the strategy heuristic changes to match the demands of the text complexity or writing style.

Change in the Strategy Heuristic

The demands of strategy application increase from grade to grade. For example, let us consider how a sixth grader, as opposed to a kindergartner, performs the task of a reader's activating prior knowledge. First, the sixth grader probably has more prior knowledge of school-related reading materials than the kindergartner. The sixth grader has also had years of practice applying this strategy to increasingly difficult texts. By now, this older reader will have internalized the strategy for activating prior knowledge and will apply it as a matter of course while reading. Over time, too, the strategy has become increasingly complex to accommodate the rigors of more complex trade books or textbooks.

Of course, there is always a chance that you will receive a new class of sixth graders who have never been taught metacognitive reading strategies. If that is the case, we doubt you would use the same strategy heuristic as the one used during the lesson plan presented earlier in this chapter (Figure 5.2, page 100). Instead, you may use the one presented in Figure 5.3. As you examine the more advanced strategy heuristic in Figure 5.3, you will immediately notice that this heuristic is far more extensive than the one designed for the primary grades and less rigorous books.

---

1. Look at the cover pictures and read the title.

   Ask yourself the following questions:

   • Have I read a book about this topic before? If so, what do I remember about this topic?

   • Have I learned about this topic or a related topic at school? If so, what do I remember about this topic?

2. While reading the text, think about the chapter headings, the bold headings, and subheadings.

   Before you read each section, ask yourself the following questions:

   • What do I know about this topic or subtopic?

   • What have I read about this topic or subtopic?

3. Throughout the reading process, continue to remind yourself of what you know as topics emerge.

   REMEMBER! TO GET YOUR MIND READY TO LEARN NEW INFORMATION,
   IT IS IMPORTANT TO ACTIVATE YOUR PRIOR KNOWLEDGE!

FIGURE 5.3. Strategy for activating prior knowledge before and during reading (grades 4–6).

As we continue our work in the area of reading comprehension in the next few chapters, your conceptual understanding of strategy instruction will continue to improve.

FINAL THOUGHTS
ABOUT COGNITIVE STRATEGY INSTRUCTION

Learning to teach cognitive strategy instruction is not easy, and first-year "strategy" teachers may need hours to prepare their cognitive strategy instruction. We hear from our graduate students that they may spend a year understanding and implementing this practice, and another year perfecting their practice. They do, however, report that the payoff for their students is increased reading achievement. One graduate student recently remarked, "Once a cognitive strategy teacher, always a strategy teacher."

To assess your comprehension of this chapter, please refer to the Key Terms Chart in Figure 5.4 (page 106), and try to write definitions in your own words. The chances are great that you will find yourself using good-reader strategies, such as looking back to reread sections of this chapter, to complete the task.

In the next three chapters on comprehension instruction, you will see the cognitive strategy instructional model in use. When you finish reading and understanding Chapters 6, 7, and 8, the model will be more familiar, and you will have a deeper understanding of how and why it works for *all* learners.

REFLECTION ON ARTIFACTS FOR YOUR SELF-STUDY

For your self-study, record on Figure 5.5 (page 107) the artifacts you created while you read this chapter.

KEY TERMS FOR CHAPTER 5

In this chapter, the following key terms are essential to your understanding of reading instruction. Think about what they mean, and try to define them in your own words.

cognitive strategy

cognitive strategy instruction

strategy heuristic

schema theory

metacognition or metacognitive knowledge

declarative knowledge

procedural knowledge

conditional knowledge

modeling

think-aloud

guided practice

independent practice

gradual release of responsibility

coaching

scaffolding instruction

FIGURE 5.4. Key Terms Chart for Chapter 5.

SELF-STUDY REVIEW CHART FOR CHAPTER 5

Name of Artifact	Teacher Instructional Actions and Language	Provisions for Individual Differences	Variety of Modes of Communication	Critical Thinking and Active Engagement	Opportunities for Assessment

FIGURE 5.5. Self-Study Review Chart for Chapter 5.

CHAPTER 6

Helping Children to Construct Meaning

"Good-Reader" Comprehension Strategies

On a snowy day in January, Margo, an urban kindergarten teacher, was about to read aloud a story from a big book on an easel in the front of the room. The children were all seated on the floor, anticipating a storybook reading. Before Margo opened the book to read the story, she said:

> "Today we are going to read a story called *Mrs. Wishy-Washy*, by Joy Cowley. Let's look at the cover of our book and see if there are any clues that might tell us what this story is about. Can anyone tell me where to look for clues?"

The children responded:

> MICHAEL: You can look at the title of the book!
>
> JO: Hmm . . . well, we can look at the illustration of the woman on the cover!
>
> ALEXIS: We can take a picture walk!

Margo agreed with her young readers and continued with the opening of her lesson:

> "Yes, children, you are all right. Good readers always take a look at the illustrations and the title of the book to see if there are clues that will help us think about the story before we read it. So if we think about the title and the illustration on the cover, what can we predict the story may be about?"

The children responded:

Jo: Well, since the big woman on the cover is wearing an apron, I think the story is going to be about washing clothes! And the title of the book is *Mrs. Wishy-Washy*! I think she is going to wash something.

George: I think it's going to be about cleaning the house!

Margo intervened:

"So can we figure out anything else before we read? What do we think the problem in the story may be? Like most stories, this one has a problem. How can we predict the problem in the story?"

The children responded:

Michael: Let's take a picture walk!

Alexis: Yes, a picture walk may tell us what she is going to wash!

Other children agreed. Margo continued:

"Good idea! You are all thinking like good readers. Well, what do we see on the first page of the book? [The children responded accordingly.] And this page? [The children responded accordingly.] So, children, from the illustrations or the pictures in this text, we already know quite a few things about the story we are going to read, including the problem. I have written your thoughts on the easel to remind us while we read the story. Let's review them now."

<u>Mrs. Wishy-Washy</u> by Joy Cowley

We predict:
- The story takes place on a FARM.
- There are many ANIMALS in the story.
- ANIMALS like the PUDDLES of MUD.
- Mrs. Wishy-Washy is going to give the ANIMALS a BATH!
- The animals don't like the bath!!!

This vignette took place in a real classroom with emergent readers. Margo, the teacher, was reinforcing "good-reader" strategies she had previously taught. Children in kindergarten are not too young or inexperienced to begin learning what real readers do. In fact, our guess is that many of these children came to school already knowing that good readers make predictions *before* and *during* reading. We have learned that once children are introduced to good stories, their natural curiosities are engaged, and they begin to develop strategies for making meaning. Our job is to be sure that all readers develop strategies for understanding text.

Chapter 5 has been devoted to cognitive strategy instruction—that is, *how* to teach comprehension strategies. These next few chapters (Chapters 6–9) will clarify *what* to teach in the comprehension/reader response curriculum, and help build your knowledge about supporting the development of strategic readers.

> **BEST PRACTICES YOU WILL SEE IN THIS CHAPTER**
>
> ✓ Teaching "good-reader" strategies for *before*, *during*, and *after* reading engagement.

FACTORS THAT AFFECT A READER'S COMPREHENSION

In the last 25–30 years, research on the reading process has characterized reading as a socially constructive process with multiple interactive factors that affect a reader's comprehension of text. These factors include the learners' interests and motivations; the learners' background knowledge and ability to consistently activate schemas before and during reading; and the learners' strategy knowledge. In addition, researchers have concluded that the demands of the *reading task* and the *rigors of the text* affect readers' understanding (Brown et al., 1986; Flavell, 1985; Garner, 1987; Graves et al., 2001; Pressley, 2000). These factors that affect reading comprehension, when considered alongside the thinking of transactional theorists, help us to create a useful frame for our discussion of reading comprehension strategies. The work of Rosenblatt (1978) tells us that readers make a *transaction* with a text to create meaning. Her work helps us to think about comprehension instruction in terms of both the reader and the text.

To begin our examination of comprehension instruction, we present a concept map of a reader's comprehension process. We use Figure 6.1 to guide your acquisition of the factors that affect a reader's ability to make meaning.

The Reader + the Text

On the left side of Figure 6.1, under the heading "The Reader," you will see that many reader-based factors affect comprehension in a significant way. On the right side of this concept map, you will see many factors listed under the heading "The Text." These factors have to do with the readability and surface features of the text the reader is currently reading. Each of these text-based factors represents the changing natures of the many texts you are preparing readers to read. We discuss the text-based factors first.

Text-Based Factors

On the right side of Figure 6.1, examine the categories listed under "The Text." The first block points to *linguistic complexity* as a factor that affects readers' comprehension. Linguistic complexity usually refers to two features of a text: the *syntax* and the *semantics*.

Syntax

Syntax refers to the principles and rules regarding sentence structure in a given language. For example, in the English language, a typical simple sentence may have a structure like this:

The cat wandered down the street.

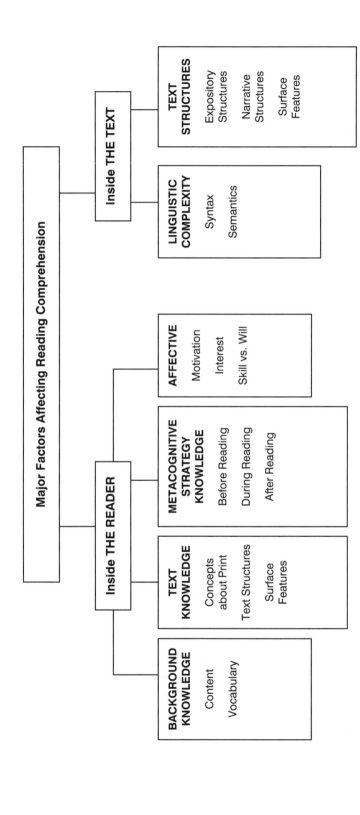

FIGURE 6.1. Major factors affecting reading comprehension: A concept map. Based on Samuels (1983), Flavell (1985), Garner (1987), Brown, Armbruster, and Baker (1986), and Alexander and Jetton (2000).

The syntactical structure of our sample sentence is typical because it begins with an article (*The*); the article is followed by a noun, which is the subject of the sentence (*cat*); the noun is followed by a verb (*wandered*); and the verb is followed by a prepositional phrase (*down the street*). This simple sentence is easy to understand. However, the syntactical structure could be made more complex, as in this example:

The cat that scratched me wandered down the street.

As the syntax increases in complexity, so do the rigors of the comprehension experience. Text representing an unfamiliar national or regional dialect can have the same effect. For example, *The Whipping Boy*, by Sid Fleischman (1986), is a Newbery Medal-winning book much loved by fifth and sixth graders. The characters in this book are from a fictional kingdom and the language of the text contains some tricky phrases that are syntactically different from what most American English speakers and readers have come to predict. Consider these lines from Chapter 5 of *The Whipping Boy*:

"The highwayman, are you?"
"Famous, he is," put in Cutwater. "Put to song, is Billy."

Notice the change in the syntax. Instead of "Are you the highwayman?" or "He is famous," Fleischman uses a dialect that is quite different from what an American reader expects. Therefore, the complexity of the syntax affects the reader's overall comprehension task.

Semantics

Whereas syntax has to do with form, semantics has to do with meaning. The term *semantics* refers to the vocabulary in the text and its applied meanings, both denotative and connotative. Consider these lines from Chapter 5 of *The Whipping Boy*, and spend a few seconds determining what the underlined words mean:

"Not much of a catch—two <u>sparrows</u>," said Billy. "But ain't they <u>trimmed up</u> in fancy <u>rags</u>, Cutwater?"

In this excerpt, Fleischman is using colloquial speech. From the story's context, you can figure out that Billy and Cutwater have captured two boys (sparrows) who are dressed (trimmed up) in fancy clothes (rags). Notice how your strategies had to change to meet the demands of the more rigorous text. Chances are you had to read the line a few times to construct meaning, or perhaps you had to ask someone what the word *sparrows* means in this context. The greater the linguistic complexity, the more complex the text (and therefore the comprehension task) becomes.

Text Structure

Another text-based factor that affects readers' comprehension is the structure of the text. *Text structures* are the ways in which whole texts, or chapters or chunks of connected text, are organized. For example, most stories have a beginning, in which the setting and characters are described; a middle, in which complications develop; and an end, in which the problems are resolved.

Expository texts also have text structures. Expository information is organized by classifying or sequencing the main ideas and details, or these ideas and details are organized by cause–effect, comparison–contrast, and problem–solution (Meyer, 1987). Researchers have found that the clearer the text structures, the easier the demands of the text (and therefore the comprehension experience) become.

For example, consider the complexity of a book that gives information about the sequence of how a seed becomes a tree, over six pages of text, with much descriptive information embedded, including the causes and effects of tree diseases. Now consider another text that neatly organizes the information of how a seed becomes a tree in a clear sequence labeled by subheadings. Which text presents the more rigorous reading experience? The former may present difficulty to young or inexperienced readers who do not have the strategy knowledge to isolate the information into identifiable categories. Therefore, the latter sequential text presents the less complex reading situation.

In Chapters 7 and 8, we provide more information on text structures and how to teach readers to use them to aid comprehension. For now, our aim is simply for you to understand that text and text difficulty play a significant role in readers' comprehension abilities. In fact, researchers have also suggested that the *surface features* of a given text all have an impact on comprehension. These surface features may include the table of contents, chapter headings and subheadings, a glossary, an index, and various typographical features, as we discuss in Chapter 7. They also include such basic text features as how well a text is written, whether or not it follows common rules for a specific genre, and its overall readability (Tracey & Morrow, 2002).

Reader-Based Factors

Researchers have identified four clear factors that affect readers' ability to construct meaning: background content knowledge, text knowledge, strategy knowledge, and readers' affect (Brown et al., 1986; Flavell, 1985; Garner, 1987).

Background Content Knowledge

Not surprisingly, the first factor is the extent of readers' *background content knowledge* about the text topic, including content-specific vocabulary. Recall our discussion in Chapter 5 regarding schema theory and the importance of readers' prior knowledge within a given learning event. As noted there, numerous studies have stressed the importance of readers' motivation to activate their prior knowledge before and during reading (Anderson & Pearson, 1984; Rumelhart, 1980). Brown et al. (1986) have further suggested that in order for readers to be metacognitive, they must not only have the background knowledge; they must consistently use it, regulate it, and monitor it in an interactive manner with the new print. Anderson (1985) has stated that "the click of comprehension occurs only when the reader evolves a schema that explains the whole message" (p. 375). Therefore, background knowledge plays a large part in a reader's ability to comprehend the text message.

Text Knowledge

A second factor that affects comprehension is readers' stored *text knowledge*. Text knowledge includes what readers already know about text features, linguistic quality, and text structures. It also includes what readers may expect when they read different types of texts (Garner, 1987).

For example, in kindergarten, we introduce children to simple print concepts. These include left-to-right and top-to-bottom progression, as well as the basic features of a book (author, illustrator, title, pictures, etc.). In first and second grades, we may progress to teaching children to use the surface features of simple chapter books, including the table of contents, glossary, chapter headings, and so on. By the intermediate grades, we expect that students will understand quite a bit about implicit text features, such as basic story structure and expository text structures. More about teaching these text features will be found in Chapters 7–8.

Strategy Knowledge

Another major factor listed on our concept web that affects comprehension is *strategy knowledge*. This factor includes the strategies readers use to make meaning from basic decoding strategies to advanced comprehension/response strategies. In this chapter, you will learn about general comprehension strategies that good readers use to make meaning from text.

Affective Characteristics

Finally, under "The Reader" heading in our concept map, you will see the *affective* characteristics that influence readers, such as their *motivations, interests,* and *attitudes* about the reading event. Alexander and Jetton (2000) synthesize these affective traits as follows:

> Learning from text is inevitably a synthesis of *skill, will,* and *thrill.* Few would argue with the premise that readers need to be skilled. Yet, learning from text cannot take place in any deep or meaningful fashion without the learner's commitment (i.e., will). Nor will the pursuit of knowledge continue unless the reader realizes some personal gratification or internal reward from this engagement (i.e., thrill). (p. 296)

In other words, skill is not quite enough. A reader's *will* (commitment to the reading event) and *thrill* (interest in and reward from the reading) are just as important for a successful comprehension experience.

In the balance of this chapter, we present the basic strategies that research suggests aid readers in the process of comprehension. What you have learned in Chapter 5 about cognitive strategy instruction will assist you in understanding how to teach comprehension strategies.

COMPREHENSION STRATEGIES TO TEACH

In the late 1970s, Durkin (1978–1979) studied reading instruction in several American classrooms. The results of her research suggested that teachers "tested" comprehension mainly by posing text questions after reading. Although she found some comprehension instruction, she concluded that not much was really known about how to teach reading comprehension. From the 1980s to the 1990s, researchers focused their attention on reading comprehension. This new research now informs our comprehension instruction practice and is summarized below.

From the abundance of research on comprehension strategies conducted over the last 25–30 years, Duke and Pearson (2002, pp. 205–206) have compiled what good readers do when they read. See Figure 6.2 for their summary of reading comprehension

---

WHAT DO GOOD READERS DO?

- Good readers are *active* readers.
- From the outset they have clear *goals* in mind for their reading. They constantly *evaluate* whether the text, and their reading of it, is meeting their goals.
- Good readers typically *look over* the text before they read, noting such things as the structure of the text and text sections that might be most relevant to their reading goals.
- As they read, good readers *make predictions* about what is to come.
- They read selectively, continually making decisions about their reading—what to read carefully, what to read quickly, what not to read, what to reread, and so on.
- Good readers *construct, revise*, and *question* the meanings they make as they read.
- Good readers try to determine the meaning of *unfamiliar words and concepts* in the text, and they deal with inconsistencies or gaps as needed.
- They draw from, compare, and *integrate their prior knowledge* with material in the text.
- They think about the authors of the text—their style, beliefs, intentions, historical milieu, and so on.
- They monitor their understanding of the text, making adjustments in their reading as necessary.
- They evaluate the text's quality and value, and react to the text in a range of ways, both intellectually and emotionally.
- Good readers read different kinds of text differently.
- When reading narrative, good readers attend closely to the setting and characters.
- When reading expository text, these readers frequently construct and revise summaries of what they have read.
- For good readers, text processing occurs not only during "reading" as we have traditionally defined it, but also during short breaks taken during reading, even after the "reading" itself has commenced, even after the "reading" has ceased.
- Comprehension is a consuming, continuous, and complex activity, but one that, for good readers, is both satisfying and productive.

FIGURE 6.2. What good readers do: A summary of reading comprehension strategies (Duke & Pearson, 2002, pp. 205–206).

strategies. In terms of the comprehension curriculum, we have found it helpful to group these strategies into what good readers do *before*, *during*, and *after* reading.

Before-Reading Strategies

In our visits to elementary classrooms, we often hear teachers introducing a new text by asking students, "What strategies should we apply before we begin reading?" or "What do good readers do before they read a new story?" Even the youngest children suggest that they should read the title and the author, look at the cover pictures, take a picture walk through the text, or predict what the story will be about. All of these are strategies that good readers use before they read. Strategies can be taught individually and then grouped together as a repertoire of strategies for greater effectiveness.

For our purposes, we have gathered a short list of strategies that are useful for younger readers to use *before reading*, and we present them in Figure 6.3 in a classroom-

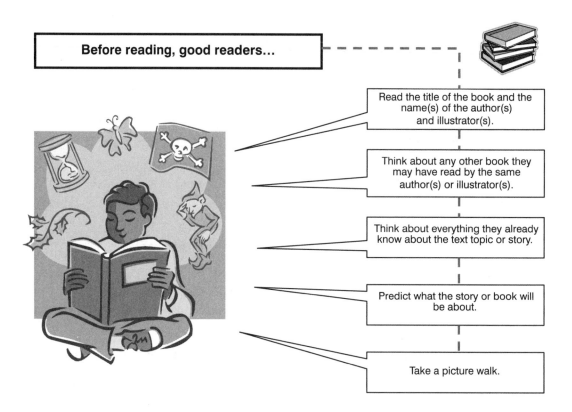

FIGURE 6.3. Before-reading strategies (grades K–3).

ready format. If you look at the strategies in the figure, you can conclude that these individual strategies are all ways to preview a text and set purposes for reading. We suggest that after you teach K–3 students the individual strategies, you then model how to cluster individual strategies, because good readers often apply a number of strategies simultaneously.

Figure 6.4 is an adaptation of the before-reading strategies for older students (grades 4–6). Notice that the strategies are basically the same as in Figure 6.3, but are more involved to match the rigors of an advanced text.

During-Reading Strategies

During-reading strategies are more complex and require readers to manipulate several strategies simultaneously. To remind yourself of the complexities of the strategies good readers use to comprehend text, read the excerpt on page 118 and jot down your reading strategies in the right-hand column. The first two are done for you.

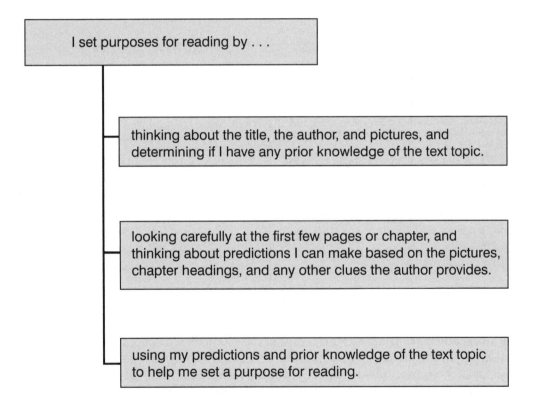

FIGURE 6.4. Before-reading strategies (grades 4–6).

Activity 1: The Text	Your Reading Strategies

Giant Pandas:
Meet Mei Xiang, Tian Tian, and Tai Shan
 	
   Mei Xiang and Tian Tian are the National Zoo's second pair of giant pandas. Both were born at the China Research and Conservation Center for the Giant Panda in Wolong, Sichuan Province. They are together for most of the day. It can be hard to tell the adult giant pandas apart, but Mei Xiang and Tian Tian do have a few differences.
   Tian Tian (t-YEN t-YEN), the male, was born on August 27, 1997. His name means "more and more." Tian Tian has black "knee socks." The black band across his shoulders narrows in the middle. His eye patches are shaped like kidney beans, and he has two black dots across the bridge of his nose. In spring 2007, he weighed about 275 pounds.
   Mei Xiang (may-SHONG), the female, was born on July 22, 1998. Her name means "beautiful fragrance." She has black hip-high "stockings" extending up her hind legs, and the black band across her shoulders is wider in the middle than Tian's. Her eye patches are oval, and a pale black band runs across the bridge of her nose. In summer 2008, she weighed about 250 pounds.
   Tai Shan (tie-SHON) was born early in the morning on July 9, 2005. He is Mei Xiang and Tian Tian's first offspring. At Tai Shan's first exam on August 2, we learned that the cub is a boy. He weighed 1.82 pounds and had a total body length of 12 inches. In March 2009, he weighed 187 pounds.
 	
(National Zoo, n.d.-c)
	• Read title and activated prior knowledge of giant pandas.
	• Read first line and predicted that the text was going to be about the differences between the two pandas.

What types of strategies did you record as your *during*-reading strategies? Since you are an expert reader, you may have recorded such strategies as *activating prior knowledge* about the various panda characteristics mentioned, *inferring* that giant pandas at the National Zoo probably need much care, and *evaluating* the differences among the three pandas mentioned. Finally, you may have *reread* a portion of the article for fact *clarification* and for answers to any other *questions* you may have had.

The purpose of this activity is to demonstrate how good readers have internalized reading comprehension strategies and how they apply them while reading. We call these particular reading strategies *in-the-head* strategies, because the reader engages in them mentally. There are other, more involved strategies, which we call "hands-on strategies."

To demonstrate what good readers do when presented with a rigorous, advanced text, we have designed another activity for you. This time, we are setting the purpose for reading for you. We want you to read the following short excerpt and think about what you would have to do to construct meaning from this text.

Before you read, consider this scenario: A close friend has been diagnosed with a MRSA (methicillin-resistant Staphylococcus aureus) infection while recuperating from surgery, and you are eager to help him with his understanding of this type of infection. So you go online to see what you can learn about MRSA infections. Read the following excerpt about MRSA, and record your reading strategies as you have just done in Activity 1. As you may recall, you have completed something similar in Chapter 1 of this text.

Activity 2: The Text	Your Reading Strategies
What is MRSA (methicillin-resistant Staphylococcus aureus)? MRSA is a type of staph that is resistant to antibiotics called beta-lactams. Beta-lactam antibiotics include methicillin and other more common antibiotics such as oxacillin, penicillin, and amoxicillin. While 25% to 30% of the population is colonized with staph, approximately 1% is colonized with MRSA. Staph infections, including MRSA, occur most frequently among persons in hospitals and healthcare facilities (such as nursing homes and dialysis centers) who have weakened immune systems. These healthcare-associated staph infections include surgical wound infections, urinary tract infections, bloodstream infections, and pneumonia. Staph and MRSA can also cause illness in persons outside of hospitals and healthcare facilities. MRSA infections that are acquired by persons who have not been recently (within the past year) hospitalized or had a medical procedure (such as dialysis, surgery, catheters) are known as CA-MRSA infections. Staph or MRSA infections in the community are usually manifested as skin infections and occur in otherwise healthy people. Most staph and MRSA infections are treatable with antibiotics. (Centers for Disease Control and Prevention, n.d.)	

You may have noticed that the demands of the text in Activity 2 are much more rigorous than those in Activity 1. We can presume that you must adjust your reading rate and strategies to meet the more difficult concepts and vocabulary included in the text.

In addition, you must consider your purposes for reading. In Activity 1, your purpose for reading may have simply been to appease your curiosity as you were drawn to the headline. Nonetheless, the task was easy due to the low readability level of the text. On the other hand, in Activity 2, since your purpose for reading has been to help a friend understand the MRSA infection, you may have used much more complex strategies to accomplish your goal.

When we had a group of graduate students participate in the reading of this text, we noticed that every one of them used what we call a *hands-on* strategy: They took out a pen and paper and recorded the text facts. Some used graphic organizers for their note taking; others used simple lists. Below is a graphic organizer one student drew and recorded to make sense of the MRSA infection information.

MRSA Definition: A type of staph infection				
Name of infection	Where do you contract the infection?	Type of infection	Treatment	Resistant to certain antibiotics
MRSA infection	Occurs *in* hospital or healthcare facilities Occurs more frequently in people with weakened immune systems	• Surgical wound infections • Urinary tract infections • Bloodstream infections • Pneumonia	Antibiotics	"beta-lactam" antibiotics, including oxacillin, penicillin, and amoxicillin
CA-MRSA Infection	Occurs *outside* of hospitals and healthcare facilities Can occur in healthy people	• Skin infections	Antibiotics	"beta-lactam" antibiotics, including oxacillin, penicillin, and amoxicillin

You can clearly see why we call note taking a hands-on strategy. We can assume that our student decided that the information in the text was far too much for her to process mentally. In order to make sense of the unfamiliar vocabulary and text concepts, she used what she *did* know from the text to make sense of what she didn't know. This is an example of a reader using background content knowledge and knowledge of text to construct meaning from text.

So what during-reading strategies do we teach in the elementary school? We find that it is easier to teach children individual during-reading strategies and to provide guided and independent practice in their application. Once they are proficient in applying these strategies consistently, we then group the strategies in a meaningful way and encourage our developing readers to select and employ those that are best for the given task. This stage of comprehension strategy instruction takes much coaching and lots of practice with applying strategies in a wide variety of texts. Individual during-reading strategies that are important to teach are presented in Figure 6.5 for grades K–3 and in Figure 6.6 for grades 4–6.

Finally, there are during-reading strategies called *comprehension-monitoring strategies*, which a reader employs to assure his or her comprehension success. *Comprehen-*

During reading, good readers . . .

Think about the topic or the story, and make pictures in their minds about the text information.

Predict what might happen next.

Write down ideas if there is too much information to remember.

Ask questions to help themselves understand the information.

Define unknown vocabulary.

FIGURE 6.5. During-reading strategies (grades K–3).

From *Teaching Reading: Strategies and Resources for Grades K–6* by Rachel L. McCormack and Susan Lee Pasquarelli. Copyright 2010 by The Guilford Press. Permission to photocopy this figure is granted to purchasers of this book for personal use only (see copyright page for details).

sion monitoring can be defined as a reader's active and deliberate awareness of comprehension success or comprehension failure, and of how to proceed in either case. For example, most readers can describe at least one incident in which their eyes continued to sweep the words on a page for some minutes before they realized they were thinking of something else instead of the text. What fix-up strategy should readers use in this case? Rereading! The most common of the fix-up strategies include rereading, self-questioning, summarizing, and adjusting speed for the purpose of text difficulty.

During reading, good readers . . .

Think about the topic or the story, and visualize the text information.

Predict what might happen next.

Think about what they know about the topic or story, and integrate their prior knowledge with what they are reading.

Read actively by posing questions to help themselves understand the information.

Use context to help themselves understand unknown vocabulary.

Make inferences while they read.

Take notes or draw graphic organizers to help themselves remember the text information.

FIGURE 6.6. During-reading strategies (grades 4–6).

From *Teaching Reading: Strategies and Resources for Grades K–6* by Rachel L. McCormack and Susan Lee Pasquarelli. Copyright 2010 by The Guilford Press. Permission to photocopy this figure is granted to purchasers of this book for personal use only (see copyright page for details).

> **During reading, good readers <u>know</u> if their comprehension is successful. If not, good readers . . .**
>
> Slow their reading rate to adjust to the text difficulty.
> Reread sections of the text for clarity.
> Look up unknown vocabulary.
> Use graphic organizers to outline difficult text information.
> Continue to pose questions for clarity.
> Stop reading and summarize periodically to check for understanding.

FIGURE 6.7. Comprehension-monitoring strategies.

From *Teaching Reading: Strategies and Resources for Grades K–6* by Rachel L. McCormack and Susan Lee Pasquarelli. Copyright 2010 by The Guilford Press. Permission to photocopy this figure is granted to purchasers of this book for personal use only (see copyright page for details).

We have placed the most common comprehension-monitoring strategies in Figure 6.7, ready for classroom use. As we do for all comprehension strategies, we use the cognitive strategy instruction model to teach comprehension monitoring.

After-Reading Strategies

After-reading strategies, such as self-questioning and summary writing, have been well researched. The most important of them have been included in Figures 6.8 and 6.9, again in classroom-ready formats for younger and older children, respectively. Summary writing is covered extensively in Chapter 7.

> **After reading . . .**
>
> After reading a story, good readers retell the story to themselves or a friend.
> After reading a fact book, good readers think about and retell the important information to a friend.

FIGURE 6.8. After-reading strategies (grades K–3).

From *Teaching Reading: Strategies and Resources for Grades K–6* by Rachel L. McCormack and Susan Lee Pasquarelli. Copyright 2010 by The Guilford Press. Permission to photocopy this figure is granted to purchasers of this book for personal use only (see copyright page for details).

After reading, good readers . . .

Think about what they read.

Summarize what they read.

Ask themselves questions for clarification and deeper understanding.

FIGURE 6.9. After-reading strategies (grades 4–6).

From *Teaching Reading: Strategies and Resources for Grades K–6* by Rachel L. McCormack and Susan Lee Pasquarelli. Copyright 2010 by The Guilford Press. Permission to photocopy this figure is granted to purchasers of this book for personal use only (see copyright page for details).

HOW TO TEACH COMPREHENSION STRATEGIES

As discussed in Chapter 5, we advocate using cognitive strategy instruction to teach reading comprehension. In our practice, we have discovered that teaching individual strategies within the context of before, during, and after reading, and then grouping the strategies for use before, during, or after reading, work well for K–6 populations.

In Chapter 5, we have presented a cognitive strategy lesson for teaching students how to activate prior knowledge. Using the same format, we now present a lesson plan that shows how to teach a "combined strategy" for the before-reading stage of the reading process.

Lesson: Combined strategy for previewing a text and setting purposes for reading

Text: *The Bus Ride That Changed History: The Story of Rosa Parks* (Edwards, 2005)

Lesson Grade Levels: 4–6

Lesson Objective: Students will demonstrate understanding of previewing a text and setting a purpose for reading an expository text (before reading).

Declarative Knowledge:

"Today I am going to model a strategy for you to use before we read one of our social studies or science books. The name of the strategy is *previewing and setting purposes for reading the text*. You will recognize some of the steps of the strategy, because I have been teaching you what good readers do before they read a textbook. Can you remember what good readers do before they read?" [Students respond.]

Ideally, your students will remember the individual strategies you have been teaching (activating prior knowledge, predicting what the text will be about, etc.). As they recall the individual strategies, write them on chart paper or a whiteboard and continue:

"The reason why we are learning this strategy today is because we know that good readers always combine a number of strategies to help them comprehend what they read. Previewing the text and setting purposes for reading help make our minds ready for the information we are going to learn. Watch me while I model for you how to preview a text and set purposes by combining all the strategies we have learned to use before we read."

Procedural Knowledge: The strategy steps we are modeling are given in **boldface**, so you can see how you will explicitly provide a strategy step and then apply it in the text.

"I am going to model our strategy with this book that we will be reading together as part of our social studies work. Listen to my thinking processes while I model for you how to apply our previewing and purpose-setting strategy.

"**I am going to start by reading and thinking about the title, in order to see if it helps me set a purpose for reading.** The title of the text is *The Bus Ride That Changed History: The Story of Rosa Parks*, by Pamela Duncan Edwards. Hmm. That is a long title and actually **reminds me of something I learned in school. I can recall my prior knowledge and realize that I already know a little bit** about Rosa Parks, an African American, and how she refused to give up her seat in the front of the bus. I also know that this famous incident took place before the civil rights movement, when African Americans did not have the same rights as other Americans. They had to sit in the back of the bus.

"**Thinking about this has led me to thinking** about Dr. Martin Luther King and the civil rights movement. **I know quite a bit about that**, but I really don't know much about the Rosa Parks incident, other than that she would not give up her seat on the bus.

"**So, next, I am going to think about what I might want to know about this incident. To help me determine this, I can look at the pictures and read all the information on the text cover.** Well, on the cover, there is a picture of a bus and people getting onto it. There are also children on the cover who are speaking. One girl on the cover says: 'This is a book about a bus, a law, and people who changed history.' And a little boy on the cover asks, 'How did they do that?' Then another boy on the cover says, 'Open the book, and let's find out!'

"So if I think about all of those things, I wonder if the book is going to tell us about Rosa Parks on the bus, the law that prevented her from taking a seat, and how she changed history. Since the little boy on the cover asks, "How did they do that?", I could probably assume that the book is going to tell us how Rosa Parks changed history. So maybe I can set one of my purposes for reading: to determine how Rosa Parks and the bus incident changed history.

"Wow, I didn't even need to go to the first page to set my purpose for reading, because the cover gave me so much information. [Think-aloud ends.]

"Now, children, let's review the steps of the strategy I just used to help me set a purpose for reading the text." [Write on chart paper the strategy heuristic as follows:]

My Purpose-Setting Strategy

First, I read the title and the author's name, and I think of all the things I know about the topic.

Next, I look very carefully at the cover pictures and read the text on the cover, and I ask myself:

- *Is there any prior knowledge I have about the text information?*
- *Is there any way I can predict what this text may be about?*
- *What do I want to know about this text topic?*
- *Does the author give any clues to what the text will be about?*

If a text cover does not have enough information, I open the book and preview the pictures, and the chapter headings to help me set a purpose for reading.

After you model the strategy steps and list them, it is important for students to practice the strategy immediately. For this guided practice, have the students practice with a new text.

Conditional Knowledge: Immediately following the guided practice, be sure to have your students evaluate the effectiveness of the strategy. Begin by debriefing the purposes they have formulated for reading the new text. This will help you assess how well they applied the new strategy. Next, debrief the strategy's effectiveness. You can do that by asking the children the following questions:

- "How effective was our strategy when you applied it in a different text?"
- "Did you have to go beyond the text cover to determine a purpose for reading?"
- "Did you think of other ways to help you set your purpose for reading? If so, let's add it to our strategy steps."

You want the children to understand that a strategy heuristic is just a guideline, and that it does not always work when you apply it to another text. The strategy may need adjustment to meet the demands of a different text.

Your final step in the strategy lesson sequence is to guide students to an understanding of when to use the strategy again. For example, you can tell them that they can use this strategy for any type of expository text or narrative text that has cover pictures and text. We do know that students will not automatically transfer the strategy to other texts unless we give them extensive guided and independent practice in a wide variety of texts.

CLASSROOM PRACTICES
TO PROMOTE READING COMPREHENSION

Researchers and practitioners agree that several activities promote reading comprehension development when they become aspects of regular classroom routine. The following, compiled by Duke and Pearson (2002), are those most widely practiced.

Time Spent Reading Texts

As with any new skill, time spent practicing is extremely important for proficiency development. Children should be given multiple opportunities to read for understanding while applying good-reader strategies, both in school and out of school. The most effective teachers are relentless—always talking about good-reader strategies, whether students are reading aloud, reading silently, or reading across the curriculum.

Reading Real Texts for Real Reasons

People read both for simple enjoyment and for learning new information. In your reading program, include books to read for enjoyment as well as books for reading instruction. Children need to have both in-school and out-of-school time when they are simply reading for the joy of reading. We have described this practice as *on-your-own reading* or *sustained silent reading* in Chapter 2 of this text.

Children also need practice in reading for information. Having students produce content-area projects in which they are independently learning about the world through books is an important aspect of a meaningful literacy curriculum. We are simply giving the children practice in doing what real readers do.

Reading a Wide Variety of Texts

A common problem with reading instruction in elementary schools is that students regularly read narrative text in the younger grades, and expository text is introduced much later. As we have stated in Chapter 2, even the youngest school-age children are fond of reading expository text and enjoy learning about their world through these experiences.

Classroom Discussion about Texts

Finally, one of the most important aspects of the comprehension curriculum, talk about text, has also been introduced in Chapter 2. Learners are supported through an environment that allows peer talk about books to take place on a daily basis. Talk about books deepens each reader's understanding of text and reinforces good strategy usage.

FINAL THOUGHTS

The general comprehension strategies good readers use to comprehend text must be explicitly taught and practiced in classrooms to assure student usage. See Figure 6.10 for a K–6 classroom-ready list of strategies good readers use throughout the reading process. Classrooms that emphasize these strategies help students to develop the habits of mind essential to becoming good readers.

Figure 6.11 is a photograph from one of our model second-grade classrooms. You can see that there are many ways to reinforce children's use of the good-reader strategies, including placing reminders around the room.

To complete our work on good-reader strategies, we have provided in Figure 6.12 (page 128) a list of trade books for each grade level that we have found useful for teaching comprehension strategies.

- Activating prior knowledge
- Formulating questions for setting the purpose
- Predicting
- Deciphering unknown vocabulary
- Taking notes for organizing and storing information
- Asking questions for clarification
- Summarizing for organizing, storing, and retrieval of information

FIX-UP STRATEGIES

- Rereading
- Adjusting speed
- Visualizing the characters
- Visualizing the events
- Self-questioning for clarification
- Summarizing

FIGURE 6.10. Strategies good readers use before, during, and after reading.

From *Teaching Reading: Strategies and Resources for Grades K–6* by Rachel L. McCormack and Susan Lee Pasquarelli. Copyright 2010 by The Guilford Press. Permission to photocopy this figure is granted to purchasers of this book for personal use only (see copyright page for details).

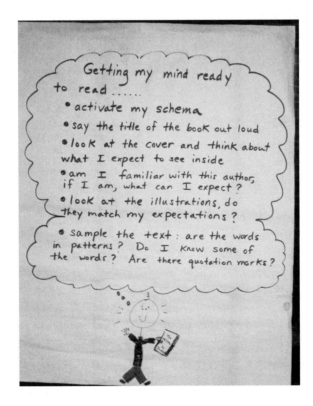

FIGURE 6.11. Classroom bulletin board for helping second graders prepare to read.

Book	Author
Grades K–1: NARRATIVE TEXT	
Sheep in a Jeep	Nancy Shaw
Henry and Mudge: The First Book (and all others)	Cynthia Rylant
The Last Puppy	Frank Asch
A Good Day	Kevin Henkes
Biscuit Finds a Friend	Alyssa Satin Capucilli and Pat Schories
Grades K–1: EXPOSITORY TEXT	
My Puppy Is Born	Joanna Cole
The Honey Makers	Gail Gibbons
Four Seasons Make a Year	Anne Rockwell
Sun Up, Sun Down	Gail Gibbons
Surprising Sharks: Read and Wonder	Nicola Davies
Grades 2–3: NARRATIVE TEXT	
Amazing Grace	Mary Hoffman
Stella Luna	Janell Canon
Tiki Tiki Tembo	Arlene Mosel and Blair Lent
The Snowy Day	Ezra Jack Keats
Miss Rumphius	Barbara Cooney
Grades 2–3: EXPOSITORY TEXT	
The Story of Ruby Bridges	Robert Coles
The Great Kapok Tree	Lynne Cherry
Mathematicians Are People, Too	Lucetta Reimer and Wilbert Reimer
Apples	Ken Robbins
Weather Forecasting	Gail Gibbons
Grades 4–6: NARRATIVE TEXT	
A Single Shard	Linda Sue Park
The Higher Power of Lucky	Susan Patron
Rules	Cynthia Lord
Sadako and the Thousand Paper Cranes	Eleanor Coerr
Michelangelo	Diane Stanley
Grades 4–6: EXPOSITORY TEXT	
Black Stars of the Civil Rights Movement	Jim Haskins
Pyramids and Mummies	Seymour Simon
Mosque	David Macaulay
Survivors: True Stories of Children in the Holocaust	Allan Zullo and Mara Bovsun
This Is My Planet: The Kids' Guide to Global Warming	Jan Thornhill

FIGURE 6.12. Books for teaching comprehension strategies.

Before you leave this chapter, be sure to assess what you have learned by thinking about the key terms presented in Figure 6.13 (page 130). Since you will be furthering your knowledge about comprehension strategies in the next two chapters, you want to be certain you understand the key terms for this chapter before moving on.

In the next chapter, we take a focused look at how to use expository text and teach specific expository text structures in the K–6 curriculum. These expository text strategies are important to your students' development as proficient readers of nonfiction or expository text.

REFLECTION ON ARTIFACTS FOR YOUR SELF-STUDY

For your self-study, record on Figure 6.14 (page 131) the artifacts you created while you read this chapter.

KEY TERMS FOR CHAPTER 6

In this chapter, the following key terms are essential to your understanding of reading instruction. Think about what they mean, and try to define them in your own words.

good-reader strategies

linguistic complexity of a text

syntax

semantics

text structure

prior knowledge

before-reading strategies

during-reading strategies

comprehension-monitoring strategies

after-reading strategies

FIGURE 6.13. Key Terms Chart for Chapter 6.

SELF-STUDY REVIEW CHART FOR CHAPTER 6

Name of Artifact	Teacher Instructional Actions and Language	Provisions for Individual Differences	Variety of Modes of Communication	Critical Thinking and Active Engagement	Opportunities for Assessment

FIGURE 6.14. Self-Study Review Chart for Chapter 6.

CHAPTER 7

Teaching Expository Text across the Curriculum

Rachael, a grade 6 literacy and social studies teacher, and Anita, a reading specialist, began planning a series of reading comprehension lessons for Rachael's class. Earlier in the school year, during social studies instruction, Rachael had discovered that many of her students could not identify main ideas and details in their social studies texts. In her consultation with Anita about the comprehension issues, she discovered that many of her struggling readers had already been referred to Anita for reading comprehension difficulties.

Instead of working with the children outside the classroom, Anita and Rachael decided to work together to meet each referred child's needs as well as the needs of the whole class. To determine the expository comprehension lessons they needed to prepare, Rachael and Anita assessed the children and then itemized the class needs.

As a result of their class assessment, they were able to determine that the class was distinctly divided into two groups: (1) readers with some basic knowledge of expository reading comprehension strategies and some awareness of how to apply these strategies, and (2) readers with little to no knowledge of expository comprehension strategies and no awareness of how to apply them.

To prepare for their instruction, the teachers consulted the research on the most essential expository comprehension strategies, and set out to provide their readers with the tools they needed to comprehend their social studies textbook. After an intensive 6-week intense training program in these strategies, the teachers reported that all readers had significantly improved their text comprehension abilities. Later in this chapter, you will see artifacts from their effective instruction on expository text features.

The research makes it clear that explicit teaching of expository comprehension strategies raises achievement in content-area reading and learning. However, as mentioned in Chapter 6, young children have little exposure to expository text until the later primary grades (Duke, 2000). Of more concern is the lack of explicit teaching of expository text structures, along with little knowledge about how explicit teaching works to increase comprehension of informational text (Pressley, 2002b; Pressley, Wharton-McDonald, Mistretta-Hampston, & Echevarria, 1998; Sweet & Snow, 2003).

Some researchers suggest that teachers are unaware of how to teach expository text comprehension and therefore avoid it; other studies have suggested that teachers think expository text is too difficult for children, and that this is why they emphasize story-books (Donovan & Smolkin, 2001; Duke, 2000; Kamil & Lane, 1997). However, Kamil (1994) found that children checked out many storybooks from school libraries, but a much larger number of informational books from their neighborhood libraries; this finding suggests that children have a genuine interest in expository text, but may not be getting sufficient access to it in many schools.

Children need to be exposed to expository text and expository reading strategies from the earliest grades. This chapter is designed to help you teach expository text comprehension for all elementary grades.

BEST PRACTICES YOU WILL SEE IN THIS CHAPTER

✓ Teaching expository text surface features.

✓ Teaching expository text structures/patterns.

✓ Using expository text to teach reading across the curriculum.

✓ Teaching children to use graphic organizers.

DEFINITION OF EXPOSITORY TEXT

In the previous chapters, we have used the term *expository text* to refer to all texts that contain information. Expository text is sometimes referred to as *nonfiction* and/or *informational text*. The mixing of these terms is evident in the literacy research as well as in practitioners' vocabularies. In an article on using informational books in the classroom, Saul and Dieckman (1995) discuss the terminology extensively. They suggest that many researchers use the terms *informational text* and *expository text* interchangeably (Kletzien & Dreher, 2004), while others use the terms *informational text* and *nonfiction* interchangeably (Alvermann, Swafford, & Montero, 2004; Freeman & Person, 1992). In this chapter and in all the chapters that follow, we continue to use the term *expository text* to define text that provides facts, gives "true" information, explains, informs, persuades, and/or describes various topics and phenomena.

Expository text is different in a number of ways from narrative text. These include differences in genres, surface features, and basic text structures. Figure 7.1 (page 134) lists the specific features of both expository and narrative text for comparison.

It is also worth noting that not all expository texts are written in the same way. First, two types of expository text—the autobiography and the biography—are written as stories. As readers approach reading these texts, they must use their narrative text strategies (described in Chapter 8 of this volume), as opposed to their expository text strategies (explained in this chapter). Second, many expository texts have a mixture of narrative and expository writing. For example, it is not uncommon to read an expository book on cloning that also includes stories about the first cloned sheep, Dolly. *The Quicksand Book* (dePaola, 1977) is also a book that interjects expository information into a narrative plot. Finally, there are also many children's books that present facts in a

Type of Text	Also Known as . .	Common Genres	Surface Features	Basic Text Structures
Expository	Nonfiction Informational These texts have true information about real things.	Trade books Reference books Textbooks Magazine articles Newspaper articles Almanac	Cover Author/illustrator Title page Table of contents Chapters Chapter headings Subheadings Multiple structures Illustrations Graphs/tables Photographs Maps Boldface or italics for vocabulary Glossary Index Appendix	Classification Sequence Comparison–contrast Cause–effect Problem–solution
Narrative	Fiction Story These texts have stories that are made up or imaginative.	Picture books Anthologies Short stories Novels Historical fiction Science fiction Realistic fiction Fables Fairy tales Tall tales Some forms of poetry	Cover Author/illustrator Title page Story text structure Photographs Illustrations	Setting (time/place) Problem(s) Solution(s) Resolution Consequence(s)

FIGURE 7.1. The differences between narrative and expository text.

story format such as texts that describe historical information by using real people as characters. Examples include *Can't You Make Them Behave, King George?* (Fritz, 1977) and *What's the Big Idea, Ben Franklin?* (Fritz, 1976).

The sections that follow begin with our work in the area of general surface features, and progress to expository text structures. By the end of this chapter, you will know what the most important elements of expository text are, and how to begin your teaching in this area of comprehension.

UNDERSTANDING SURFACE FEATURES OF EXPOSITORY TEXT

Think back to when you may have first learned about the surface features of expository text: a table of contents, a glossary, chapter headings and subheadings, and many others. You may have had a teacher who taught you how to use a glossary or an index,

Common Features	Chapter Features	Typographical Features
Cover Title page Dedication Table of contents Introduction Chapters Graphs and charts Illustrations Photographs Maps Appendix Glossary Index Bibliography	Titles Headings Subheadings Divisions Division headings Chapter summaries	Fonts Font size Boldface type Italicized type Bullets Numbering

FIGURE 7.2. Expository text surface features.

or maybe you learned on your own. Current researchers have also suggested that typographical features, such as special fonts, boldface type, italicized type, and bulleted information, signal the reader that important information is being communicated (Harvey, 1998). Figure 7.2 lists the important surface features of expository text that we teach in the elementary education curriculum.

HOW TO TEACH SURFACE FEATURES OF EXPOSITORY TEXT

The simplest way to teach expository text features is to model their functions. The most important information you need to communicate to your students is how each text feature aids comprehension.

As you are reading aloud or demonstrating how to find text information, you can point out the surface features. For example, you may want to draw attention to the chapter headings and show how these help you to set a purpose for reading. For the more complex surface features, such as an index or a glossary, your modeling must be more deliberate, with perhaps an entire lesson devoted to each feature's function and use. Ultimately, what is important is that you demonstrate how the features help readers focus on particular text information and aid their overall comprehension of the text topic.

We dedicate many of the following pages to the teaching of expository text structures, which further aid elementary students' comprehension.

UNDERSTANDING EXPOSITORY TEXT STRUCTURES

The term *text structure* can be defined as an author's overall plan of organization to convey main ideas and details (Meyer, 1987; Meyer & Rice, 1984). As mentioned in Chapter 6 most authors use five basic text structures or patterns to organize information:

1. *Classification structures.* These structures list, organize, or categorize information.
2. *Sequence structures.* These structures arrange text information in a chronological pattern or some other sequence. The information may be arranged by simple order, by historical dates, by sequential events, or by the order of steps in a process.
3. *Cause–effect structures.* As the name indicates, these structures arrange information to show causes and effects. Sometimes there are many causes and one or two effects, or vice versa. Sometimes there is a sequential cause-and-effect structure, in which one cause leads to an effect that causes another thing to happen.
4. *Comparison–contrast structures.* These structures arrange information to compare and contrast two or more objects, facts, events, or incidents.
5. *Problem–solution structures.* These structures arrange information to show problems, actions, and solutions within a certain event or an observable occurrence.

The five text structures are also detailed in Figure 7.3 (pages 138–139), along with sample text passages illustrating them, words that signal their presence to readers, and graphic organizers of their organizational logic. These five text structures can be used to organize information in simple or more complex ways. Generally speaking, the more advanced the text, the more complex the text patterns. For a complex example, in one social studies chapter describing the Boston Tea Party, the reader may encounter the causes of the Boston Tea Party interwoven with a description of the sequential events. We can assume that the author, who is a history expert, has written the text for content, not for readability. It is important to teach students how to identify the variety of text structures so that when they encounter complex patterns, they can identify main ideas and details.

We invite you now to participate in an activity to check your ability to *identify* the individual structural patterns of text. To prepare, refer again to Figure 7.3 (pages 138–139) and spend a few minutes reviewing the text structures. In particular, examine the last column of the figure, which shows a *graphic organizer* for each text structure. A graphic organizer can be used as a note-taking device and is a relatively simple method for helping students summarize text material and promoting understanding of content. Do you notice that the graphic layout indicates the relationship among ideas for that text structure? You have already seen a graphic organizer example in Chapter 6—the information matrix on MRSA infection. We invite you to engage in a similar activity here with new text.

TEXT STRUCTURE INQUIRY ACTIVITY

Directions: Read the following paragraph; determine the text structure; and, in the box provided, draw an appropriate graphic organizer containing the main ideas and details.

Text: "Mythological Roots of Mount Etna"

Sicily is the home of the largest active volcano in Europe, called Mount Etna. This volcano was once called Aetna, which was derived from the Greek word that means "to burn" (Lahanas, n.d.). The reason for Etna's winds and violent, fiery eruptions was often explained through classical Greek mythology (Best of Sicily, 2007). One prevalent myth suggested that Mount Etna housed the god of fire, Vulcan, who used the underbelly of the volcano as a forge, driving out other mythical creatures with his flaming explosions. It was also thought that the infamous one-eyed Cyclops used Mount Etna as a furnace to forge lightning bolts for Zeus to use as weapons against his enemies. Apparently, the work of the Cyclops caused great volcanic disturbances as they created and tested their weapons (Lahanas, n.d.). In one of the darker stories surrounding Etna's volcanic eruptions, classical Greek poets described the giant storm god, Typhoeus. In one version of this myth, Zeus imprisoned Typhoeus in the pit of Mount Etna where he tossed and turned, creating destructive winds and molten lava that flowed freely from the volcano (Atsma, 2000–2008). Whatever the reason, Mount Etna continues to erupt to this day, often creating havoc for one of Sicily's major airports and surrounding towns.

Draw your graphic organizer here:

The reasons for Mount Etna's volcanic eruptions, according to the ancient Greeks

If we asked all of our students to do this activity for homework, the chances are great that they would produce quite an array of different graphic organizers. They might share some characteristics, such as type of text structure graphic, but they would probably be quite different. This is the reason why we do not include a "correct" graphic organizer with this exercise. Since you are an expert reader, your graphic organizer probably portrays the information in a meaningful way.

How do you feel about this graphic organizer activity? Do you feel as if you were able to assimilate the material better after you organized the information in the organizer? If so, you understand the benefits of text structure instruction and of teaching children to draw their own graphic organizers. Next, we discuss how to teach expository text structures in the elementary school.

Text structure/pattern	Paragraph illustrating the text pattern	Words that signal the text pattern	Typical graphic organizer
CLASSIFICATION In the classification pattern, main ideas and details are classified in categories. For example, if the text topic is whales, the main ideas may be categorized into three types of whales: the orca, the narwhal, and the beluga. Details about each are included in the text.	Three *types* of whales that live in the Arctic include the orca, the beluga, and the narwhal. *Each* has its own characteristics. The orca, also called the killer whale, is a predator that feeds on other marine mammals. The orca has a sophisticated social structure and travels in family packs. The beluga	*many, several, one, each, another, still another; types, one type, another type; also, among, in addition to; characteristics, categories, classification*	Types of Whales
SEQUENCE In the sequence pattern, the main ideas are organized in sequential order, with details included within each step. For example, the text may describe in sequential order how a baleen whale filters its food.	The baleen whales feed by *first* opening their mouths very wide and swallowing ocean water. *Next*, they close their jaws a little while pushing out the water through their baleen plates. *After* the water is filtered through their baleen plates, krill and plankton are left behind for the whale to swallow.	*first, second, third; first, next, then; finally; yesterday, today, tomorrow; steps, sequence; later; before, after; to begin with; time, the history of; in 2004, 2005, 2006 . . . .*	FIRST: Open mouth and swallow water. SECOND: Close jaws and push out water. THIRD: Swallow krill and plankton.
CAUSE–EFFECT The cause–effect text pattern is either organized by causes that lead to certain effects or by effects that are caused by one or more phenomena. There are two kinds of cause–effect patterns. One type describes the causes and/or effects in no particular order. For example, causes of whale extinction may be listed in a text. Another type describes the sequential causes and effects of some occurrence. For example, the text may describe the sequential "domino" effects of the dangers of increased ultraviolet radiation in the earth's oceans.	In some areas of the world, ultraviolet radiation is increasing in ocean waters. *As a result*, tiny crustaceans called "krill" will be reduced. *Since* krill is a major food source for baleen whales, the whales' diet will be greatly *affected*. Starvation of these magnificent marine mammals may be a devastating *result*.	*cause(s), effect(s); as a result of, result(s); affected by, consequence of, consequently; therefore, if–then; for this reason, due to, since*	**Sequential Cause and Effect** | Cause	Effect	Cause
---	---	---
Ultraviolet radiation	Krill reduction	Baleen whales starve	 **Descriptive Cause and Effect** Causes — Effects

	Illustrative text	Signal words	Graphic organizer
COMPARISON–CONTRAST This text pattern compares and/or contrasts main ideas while providing specific details about the similarities and differences of two items. For example, the text may compare two types of whales and/or contrast them.	Baleen whales and toothed whales use distinctly *different* methods to obtain their food. Baleen whales filter krill through their upper jaw, which is *similar to* a strainer or a sieve. *On the other hand*, toothed whales are quite *different* because they have pointed teeth to help them prey on fish and squid.	*compare, comparison, contrast; same, different, like, as; similarities, differences; similarly, but, also; on the one hand; on the other hand*	<table><tr><td></td><td colspan="2">**Ways of Obtaining Food**</td></tr><tr><td></td><td>**Food**</td><td>**Food**</td></tr><tr><td>**Toothed Whales**</td><td>Teeth</td><td>Fish</td></tr><tr><td>**Baleen Whales**</td><td>Baleen</td><td>Krill</td></tr></table>
PROBLEM–SOLUTION This text pattern has main ideas and details organized by problems and corresponding solutions. Often the text lists actions that may or may not lead to the solution. For example, the text may describe the problems whale populations endure after an oil spill, provide actions scientists could take to repair the damage, and suggest final solutions that could eliminate the problem.	*Problems* with oil spills have forced many marine biologists *to act on* behalf of the many animals and birds who are affected by the spills. *Because of* the famous Exxon Valdez oil spill, stricter regulations of oil tankers now include more rigorous inspection techniques, more intensive training of oil company personnel, and field drills to check on preparedness in case of a spill. *As a result*, fewer oil spills have occurred.	*problem(s), issue(s); actions, to act; solution(s), resolution(s), to resolve; as a result, because of*	**PROBLEM** Ocean oil spills ↓ **ACTIONS** Stricter regulations: 1. Rigorous inspection 2. Intense training 3. Field drills **SOLUTION** Fewer oil spills

FIGURE 7.3. The five text structures/patterns, together with illustrative text, signal words, and graphic organizers for each.

HOW TO TEACH EXPOSITORY TEXT STRUCTURES

You can teach expository text structures in the same way as you teach all other comprehension strategies: by using the cognitive strategy instruction model discussed in Chapter 5 to design lessons for teaching children to identify all five text structures. To make it easier for you, we have included strategy steps (heuristics) for all five text structures in Figures 7.4, 7.5, 7.6 (page 142), 7.7 (page 143), and 7.8 (page 144). We have designed these strategies to be taught in grades 4–6.

---

1. Read the title, preview the text, identify the text structure, and read the text once through.
2. Ask yourself: What is the author's purpose for writing? What is the main topic?
3. Draw a classification graphic organizer to begin recording your ideas.

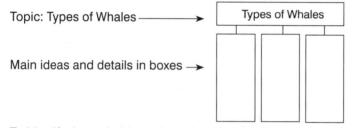

4. To identify the main ideas, do a close reading.
   - Ask yourself: What are the main parts of the topic? Can the topic be classified into smaller main ideas?
   - These signal words may help you identify the main ideas: *for example, characteristics are, such as, generally, types, kinds, categories, in addition to.*
   - Use all of your good-reader strategies to help you chunk the main ideas.
5. If you still cannot identify the main ideas, try the following steps:
   - Look at the boldface headings. Does that help you identify the main ideas?
   - Look at the illustrations. Does that help you identify the main ideas?
   - Look at the graphs and keys. Does that help you identify the main ideas?
6. Reread the text closely, line by line, to identify the supporting details:
   - Ask yourself: What are the characteristics, features, and details of the main ideas?
   - Use the question leads (*who, how, why, what, where, when*) to help you find the supporting details.
   - Look at the subheadings to help you identify the supporting details.
   - Use your good-reader strategies to help identify the details.

FIGURE 7.4. Strategy for the classification text pattern.

1. Read the title, preview the text, and read the text once through.

2. Identify the signal words, such as *first*, *second*, *third*, *then*, *next*, and *finally*. These signal words will help you identify the sequence pattern. However, some text may not contain these exact words.

3. Reread the text closely, and ask yourself how the events or steps or details are ordered.

4. Create your own sequence graphic organizer.

5. Record information in your graphic organizer as you ask yourself:

   a. What comes first? What comes next?
   b. Are they in order? Are you missing any steps?
   c. Have you included all the important steps and details?
   d. Have you tried using your good-reader strategies to help you find the sequence?

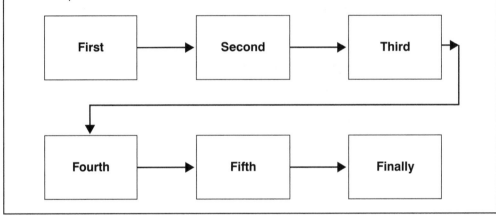

FIGURE 7.5. Strategy for the sequence pattern.

When teaching text patterns, you will always have to alter the strategy heuristic to match three variables: (1) the readers' vocabulary, (2) the text difficulty, and (3) the readers' prior knowledge of comprehension strategies. As an example, Figure 7.9 (page 145) presents explanations of the comparison–contrast pattern for younger or less experienced readers and for older, more experienced readers; notice the differences in language.

To understand the difference between teaching a general comprehension strategy that good readers use in most situations (Chapter 6) and teaching an expository text structure strategy, take a look at the lesson below. Of importance is the modeling/think-aloud portion of the lesson. You will see how all the good-reader strategies, such as activating prior knowledge and self-questioning, are embedded in the act of identifying main ideas and details in expository text. This lesson is based on the text shown in Figure 7.10 (page 146).

1. Read the title, preview the text, and read the text once through.

2. If the text appears to be listing causes and effects, draw an appropriate graphic organizer.

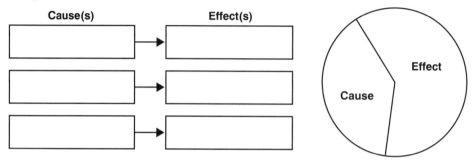

3. When you are looking for cause and effect, find something that happened as a result of another action.

4. Reread the text closely, line by line, and investigate:

   What is the cause? A cause is an action that triggers a reaction.

   To find the cause, use these signal words to help you: *when, because, since, if, due to, makes, produces*.

   What is the effect? The effect is the reaction.

   To find the effect, use these signal words to help you: *then, as a result, thus, therefore, consequently*.

   Use your good-reader strategies to help you find the main ideas.

FIGURE 7.6. Strategy for the cause–effect pattern.

1. Read the title, preview the text, and read the text once through.

2. Identify signal words, such as *compare*, *contrast*, *difference(s)*, *similarity*, *different*, *same*. These will help you identify the comparison–contrast pattern. However, some text may not contain these exact words.

3. Reread the text closely, and ask yourself: What is being compared?

4. Create your own comparison–contrast graphic organizer, and write in the two or three objects, events, or things that are being compared.

5. As you record information in your organizer, ask yourself:

   What are the differences? These signal words will help you find the differences: *different, differences, opposite, better than, on the other hand, rather.*

   What are the similarities? These signal words will help you find the similarities: *same, alike, similar, similarities, like, much as, on the one hand.*

   How are they being compared? Determine the category of comparison (for example, shape, length, width).

	Shape	Taste	Colors
Apple	Round, fat	Juicy, sweet	Red, green
Banana	Long, thin	Dry, sweet	Yellow, green

Remember that your good-reader strategies
will help you identify the main ideas and details.

FIGURE 7.7. Strategy for the comparison–contrast pattern.

1. Read the title, preview the text, and read the text once through.

2. If a problem is introduced, draw an appropriate graphic organizer to organize solutions. It is important to remember that there is not always a solution.

3. Reread the text closely, line by line, and ask yourself: What is the problem? Look for words like *problem, challenge, difficulty, trouble with, dilemma, puzzle,* or *question.*

4. Now ask yourself: What is a possible solution?

5. Sometimes the author gives information on ways a solution can come about. These are called *actions* that may lead to a solution.

6. To help find actions or solutions, look for words such as *since, therefore, if–then, as a result, nevertheless, consequently, will have to, this will mean, will be necessary,* or *must.*

7. It is important to remember that occasionally solutions come before problems.

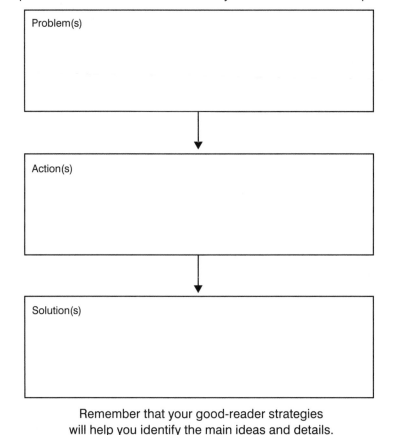

Problem(s)

Action(s)

Solution(s)

Remember that your good-reader strategies
will help you identify the main ideas and details.

FIGURE 7.8. Strategy for the problem–solution pattern.

COMPARISON–CONTRAST STRATEGY
FOR LESS EXPERIENCED READERS

1. Read the title of the book, take a picture walk, and read the text.
2. Think about what you are reading.
3. If the author is comparing two things, such as kinds of animals, people, countries, or other things, draw a graphic organizer to help you record what is the same and what is different about the two things.
4. Ask yourself: What is being compared?
5. Now ask yourself: What is the same or alike about the two things? The author may use words such as *same*, *alike*, *like*, *both*, *similar*, or *similarities*.

   Now ask yourself: What is different about the two things? The author may use words such as *different*, *differences*, *opposite*, *better than*, *different than*.
6. Write what is alike and what is different in your graphic organizer.

Apple	Round	Fat	Red
Banana	Long	Thin	Yellow

COMPARISON–CONTRAST STRATEGY
FOR MORE EXPERIENCED READERS

1. Read the title, preview the text, and read the text once through.
2. Signal words such as *compare*, *contrast*, *difference(s)*, *similarity*, *different*, and *same* will help you identify the comparison pattern. However, some text may not contain these exact words.
3. Reread the text closely, and ask yourself: What is being compared?
4. Create your own comparison–contrast graphic organizer, and write in the two or three objects, events, or things that are being compared.
5. As you record information in your organizer, ask yourself:

   What are the differences? These signal words will help you find the differences: *different*, *differences*, *opposite*, *better than*, *on the other hand*, *rather*, *but*.

   What are the similarities? These signal words will help you find the similarities: *same*, *alike*, *both*, *similar*, *similarities*, *like*, *much as*, *on the one hand*.

   How are they being compared? Determine the category of comparison (for example, shape, length, width).

	Height	Weight	Shape of Ear
African elephants	11 feet tall	14,000 pounds	Irregular—like the continent of Africa
Asian elephants	10 feet tall	11,000 pounds	Regular—rounded

FIGURE 7.9. Altering strategy heuristics to accommodate readers' skills.

WHAT IS THE DIFFERENCE BETWEEN PREDATOR AND PREY?

A *predator* is an animal that hunts another animal. The *prey* is the animal the predator eats. An example of a predator is a hawk. An example of a hawk's prey is a snake. Other predator–prey examples include cat–mouse and fox–rabbit.

Predators and prey are very different types of animals, but they share some of the same traits. Predators are usually very fast so they are able to catch their prey. Prey can run fast, too, because they need to run away from predators.

Both have a good sense of smell. The predator needs a good sense of smell to hunt and find the prey, but the prey also needs to be able to smell the predator who is hunting him or her.

Both predator and prey have good eyesight. Predators' eyes are close together so they can see long distances to find their prey, but most prey animals' eyes are on the sides of their heads so they can easily look out for predators.

Although predators and prey are very different, they share some common traits.

FIGURE 7.10. "What Is the Difference between Predator and Prey?"

Lesson: Strategy for comparing and contrasting text ideas

Text: "What Is the Difference between Predator and Prey?" (Figure 7.10)

Lesson Grade Levels: 2–3

Lesson Objective: Students will demonstrate understanding of comparing and contrasting expository text information.

Declarative Knowledge:

"Today I am going to model a strategy for you to use when we read fact or information books. The name of the strategy is *comparison and contrast*. The reason why we are learning this strategy is to help us become independent readers as we read fact and information books. Can someone tell me what it means to compare two things?" [Students' responses are written on the whiteboard as follows:]

To Compare:
Find what is <u>the same</u> about two or more things.
Find how two or more things are <u>alike</u>.

Example:
A cat and a dog have at least one thing in common: They are both pets.

"Yes, so we know that when we *compare* two or more things, we are looking for what is the same or what is alike about them. Now, does anyone know what it means to contrast two things?" [Students' responses are written on the whiteboard as follows:]

To Contrast:
Find what is <u>different</u> about two or more things.
Find how two or more things are <u>not alike</u>.

Example:

Dogs and cats are very different pets. One difference is that dogs like to go for walks and cats do not. Cats are much more independent than dogs and prefer to walk around outdoors by themselves.

Once you are sure that students have a conceptual understanding of what it means to compare and contrast, you can then model the strategy in a text. It is important for you to explain to students that comparing and contrasting two like or unlike things when you can *see* them is very different from extracting such information from a text. Following is the think-aloud/modeling portion of the lesson. While you read, look at the sentences in **boldface**. Notice how good-reader strategies are embedded in the instructional language, along with the steps of applying the text structure strategy.

Procedural Knowledge:

"Watch me while I model for you how to compare and contrast text information. I am going to model our strategy with this book that we have already read together on predators and prey. Remember? Listen to my thinking while I show you how to use our comparison–contrast strategy.

"**I am going to start by reading and thinking about the title, and see if it helps me understand what the text is about.** The title of the text is 'What Is the Difference between Predator and Prey?' [Figure 7.10]. Well, right away I know that the text is going to contrast or compare information about predators and prey, because the title tells me so. It even tells me what is going to be contrasted, because it says, 'the *Difference* between Predator and Prey,' and we have just reviewed that *differences* mean contrasts between two things.

"**So, next, I am going to think about everything I already know about predators and prey.** Hmmm. Well, since I have watched my cat chasing birds and mice in the garden, I know a little bit about how predators look for and catch their prey. **I am going to read the text again and see what important information the author is giving on predators and prey.** [Read portion of the text.] **Now I'm going to go back and ask myself, 'What is being compared?'** So **I am going to reread some of the text closely**.

"Well, this line of the text, 'Predators and prey are very different types of animals, but they share some of the same traits,' clearly tells me that the author is contrasting predators and prey. **I am going to draw a graphic organizer to help me record the main ideas and details**. [See graphic organizer below.] The two main sets of ideas the author is discussing are predator traits and prey traits, so I am going to write them in my organizer.

"Next, **I am going to read the text line by line to determine what is the same and what is different** about predators and prey. Well, the next line tells me that predators run really fast to catch their prey. So **I am now going to ask myself, 'What is the same as, or what is different from, how prey run?'** The author then tells me that prey are also fast runners so they can run away, so I am going to write that in my organizer. Now I have two similar traits.

"The next line says, 'Both predator and prey have good eyesight.' Hmm. The word *both* helps me, because it is saying that the predator and prey have something that is alike . . . eyesight! So I can write that in. That signal word, *both*, has really helped me to find a similar trait. So I am going to write that trait in my organizer for both predator and prey." [Write information on whiteboard as follows:]

	TRAIT 1	TRAIT 2	TRAIT 3
PREDATOR (HUNTER)	Runs fast to catch prey.	Great sense of smell to find prey.	Good eyesight. Eyes in front to spot prey.
PREY (HUNTED)	Runs away fast.	Great sense of smell to run away.	Good eyesight. Eyes on side of head to see predator.

As the think-aloud continues, be sure to say the name of each strategy step and then apply the step to the text. Do you see how this is done in the think-aloud above? You do this in order to be sure that the steps of the strategy are emphasized along with the text information. Once you identify the important main ideas and details, it is important to tell the children how you know that. This is the challenging part of conducting a think-aloud. It is important to say everything you are thinking.

After the think-aloud is completed, as you have seen before, it is essential to place the strategy heuristic on an easel pad or the whiteboard. Thus the lesson continues as follows:

"Now, children, let's review the steps of the strategy I just used to help me compare and contrast text information." [Write the strategy heuristic on chart paper as you verbally review the strategy as follows:]

Comparison—Contrast Strategy

1. Read the title of the book, take a picture walk, and read the text.
2. Think about what you are reading.
3. If the author is comparing two things, such as kinds of animals, people, countries, or other things, draw a graphic organizer to help you record what is the same and what is different about the two things.
4. Ask yourself: What is being compared?
5. Now ask yourself: What is the _same_ or _alike_ about the two things? The author may use such words as _same_, _alike_, _like_, _both_, _similar_, or _similarities_.
6. Now ask yourself: What is _different_ about the two things? The author may use such words as _different_, _differences_, _opposite_, _better than_, _different than_, or _but_.
7. Write what is alike and what is different in your graphic organizer.

After you provide the modeling and strategy steps, it is essential that students immediately practice the strategy. You can have them practice it in the same text if you still have information to add to your graphic organizer, or you can choose a new text for them to use as guided practice. Just remember that guided practice is *guided*. You can conduct a guided practice in a whole-group or small-group format, depending upon the amount of coaching you predict the students may need.

Conditional Knowledge: Immediately following the guided practice, you want to be sure to have the students evaluate the effectiveness of the strategy. You can do this by asking the children the following questions:

- "How effective was our strategy?"

- "Did you think of other ways of thinking to help you identify the similarities and differences? If so, let's add it to our strategy steps."

- "Did you find new signal words that help us to identify the main ideas being compared and contrasted?"

You want the children to understand that a strategy is just a guideline, and that it does not always work when you apply it to a variety of texts. In essence, the strategy may need adjustment to meet the demands of a different text or type of text.

Your final step in the strategy lesson sequence is to guide students to the understanding of when to use the strategy again. This is accomplished by telling them about all the types of texts to which they can apply the new strategy. For example, you can tell them that they can use this strategy for any type of expository text that has information being compared or contrasted. It is also important to give students multiple opportunities to transfer their strategy to other texts in the curriculum.

CHOOSING TEXTS FOR TEACHING EXPOSITORY TEXT STRUCTURES

When you are teaching expository text structures, it is important to consider which books to use for the initial modeling and which to use for further practice. For introducing and modeling each text pattern, you must use text that the children have already read and understood. This allows the children to focus on the strategy process instead of trying to learn new content at the same time. You will also want to look for books that have signal words for the patterns, as well as a relatively easy structure to determine. After students have had considerable practice with each pattern, then you can begin to choose books with more complex patterns and have them practice in these more difficult texts.

There is one more important point: Most textbooks do not present information in simple text structures. In such a case, readers may have to *impose* a text structure to extract the necessary information from the text. Imposing a text structure is more difficult for students, but you can coach them to success by having them practice on a wide range of text selections written in a wide range of text structures.

ENCOURAGING STUDENT USAGE OF TEXT STRUCTURES FOR COMPREHENSION

Do you remember our opening scenario in Rachael's sixth-grade classroom? To follow up with her text structure instruction, she had students construct simple flip books after she and Anita taught all five patterns of text organization. On each page of the flip book, the children included the strategy graphic organizer, the signal words, and a sample text written in the text pattern, to remind them how to identify the main ideas and details in expository text. Whenever children read expository text in Rachael's class

FIGURE 7.11. Expository text structure bulletin board.

now, they always have their flip books handy for easy reference. In addition, they can refer to Rachael's carefully designed bulletin board (Figure 7.11) to help with their strategy application.

    Crucial to the process of learning all comprehension strategies is repeated practice. In the following section, we present a very common model for a comprehension lesson to emphasize *reading across the curriculum*. This lesson model is one that you can use to introduce new books or portions of text and have your students practice the strategies they have learned. You will notice that the structure of the model itself emphasizes the good-reader strategies, but that its focus is on content. Figure 7.12 summarizes the model; below, we explain each part.

A LESSON MODEL FOR READING ACROSS THE CURRICULUM

The purpose of this before-, during-, and after-reading lesson model (Figure 7.12) is to have your students practice their good-reader strategies while they read expository content. You will notice that each step of the lesson plan consists of a good-reader strategy. After we explain each component of the model, we present a sample expository text lesson.

Before Reading: Activating Prior Knowledge

To introduce your book and topic, it is best practice to activate students' prior knowledge of the text topic and "connect" the readers to the text. As you have learned in Chapters 5 and 6, it is important for readers to access their prior knowledge and activate their schemas before and during reading. To do this efficiently and easily, we have discovered that the combination of *free recall* and *structured questions* works well.

BEFORE-READING LESSON ACTIVITIES: STUDENTS FOCUS THEIR ATTENTION

- Build, access, and activate students' prior knowledge of text concept.
- Review vocabulary words that might interfere with students' comprehension.
- Formulate questions to set a purpose for reading the text.

↓

DURING-READING LESSON ACTIVITIES: STUDENTS STORE INFORMATION

- Have students design a graphic organizer, or provide one for them to record text ideas.

↓

AFTER-READING LESSON ACTIVITIES: STUDENTS RETRIEVE INFORMATION

- Have students talk about the ideas they recorded on the graphic organizer.
- Ask questions to drive students to a deeper meaning of the text.
- *Optional:* Ask students to write a summary, using the graphic organizer as a template.
- *Optional*: Have the group engage in a cooperative, culminating content-area task.

FIGURE 7.12. A lesson model for reading across the curriculum. Use with a content-area book to emphasize content and reinforce known reading strategies.

Whenever you introduce a new text or a new text topic, you can begin with a simple open-ended question: "What do you know about predators and prey?" "What do you know about dinosaurs?" "What do we mean by the term *domestic animals*?" These free-recall questions are open-ended and serve well to stimulate a discussion about the text topic.

Once students provide prior knowledge of the text topic, you can ask specific structured questions to facilitate the discussion, or you can take the students to an area of the topic you would like to review before they read the text. For example, if you are accessing prior knowledge about dinosaurs, and students tell you the names of a few dinosaurs and some general facts, you can ask more structured questions to elicit more specific details. You may ask, "What do you know about the theories surrounding dinosaur extinction?" "What do you think dinosaurs ate?" "What specific traits made dinosaurs so different from animals that are free to roam the earth today?" The questions and subsequent discussion not only activate prior knowledge, but also help build prior knowledge for those students who may not know much about the topic.

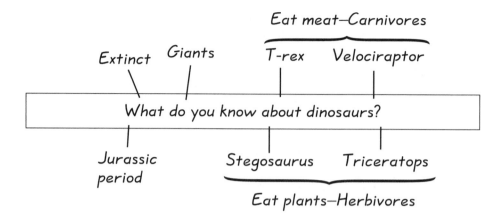

FIGURE 7.13. Activating prior knowledge about dinosaurs.

One word of caution about structured questions, however, is that the opening of this lesson should *not* cover all the points of the text. You want to leave the comprehension of the text topic to your able readers. Your lesson opening may look like Figure 7.13 when you are finished with it.

Before Reading: Vocabulary Instruction

As discussed in Chapter 4, vocabulary instruction is a crucial before-reading lesson component. Since your young readers' comprehension might be interrupted by encounters with unfamiliar vocabulary, it is best to choose approximately five words and teach them before reading.

Before Reading: Setting Purposes

Before you ask your students to read the text, it is important to set a purpose for reading. You can set a purpose or ask students to set their own purposes. For most content lessons, it is easy to impose a purpose that has to do with the main ideas in the text. For example, in regard to the predator–prey text (Figure 7.10), you may want to say to the children, "While you read, I want you to identify the differences and similarities of predators and prey."

During Reading: Encouraging Note Taking

For the during-reading section of the lesson plan, you can either provide a graphic organizer for your students or have them draw one once they become proficient at doing so. As you have learned earlier, a graphic organizer is a note-taking device that helps students summarize text material to promote understanding. Moreover, the graphic layout of the organizer indicates the types of relationships among ideas that the text presents or the reader imposes.

If you design a graphic organizer for your students to record information from the text during reading, it must match the purpose for reading. For example, if the students are reading the predator–prey text and have set the purpose for reading as identifying the similarities and differences, then the graphic organizer should be designed for students to record that information. Go back and look through the expository graphic organizers in Figure 7.3 to see the range of possibilities you can use for expository text.

After Reading: Free Recall

The next portion of the lesson takes place after students have read and recorded ideas in their graphic organizers. This is a perfect time to engage students in meaningful talk. Perhaps you have grouped students for the reading and note-taking portion of the lesson; if so, now is the time to bring them back to the whole group and debrief what they have learned. You can do this by asking students to present the information they learned by verbal recall, while you record the text information on a class-sized graphic organizer.

This portion of the lesson is designed to give students opportunities to share what they have learned. It also provides you with opportunities to examine their graphic organizers for accuracy and to assess their strategy usage. The after-reading discussion can continue with the aid of comprehension questions designed to help students think critically about the text information.

After Reading: Questioning

A common practice after students have shared the main ideas and details of the text is to invite them to have deeper discussions about the text material. We do this with questions designed to encourage readers to explore the deeper meaning of the text.

We can use the *question–answer relationships* (QAR) approach (Raphael, 1982, 1984, 1986) both to guide our understanding of what kind of questions to ask in an after-reading activity and to teach our readers how to find the sources of the questions to answer them correctly. The QAR strategy includes four types of questions divided into two categories of information—*in the text* and *in your head*—as shown in Figure 7.14.

In the Text		In Your Head	
Right There	Think and Search	Author and You	On My Own
Explicit questions	Implicit questions	Implicit questions	Implicit questions
The answer is right there on the page. Often the words used to form the question and the words that answer the question are the same.	The answer requires readers to search for an answer or put together an answer from different parts of the text.	The answer requires readers to fit together their understanding of the text and their background knowledge.	The answer relates to the text, but could be answered if the text has not even been read.

FIGURE 7.14. The question–answer relationships (QAR) strategy. Based on Raphael (1982, 1984, 1986).

The QAR approach to categorizing questions can be used to ask questions with answers that are explicit in the text, as well as those in which a reader must make an inference. For example, here are some categorized questions based on the predator–prey text in Figure 7.10.

Right There (reader uses explicit text information to answer)

1. What is a predator?
2. What is a prey?

Think and Search (reader searches for answer)

1. What defenses do prey use to get away from predators?
2. What traits do predators have to help them catch their prey?

Author and Me (reader uses the text plus prior knowledge to answer)

1. If predators and prey are both fast, how do you think a predator outruns a prey?
2. If prey have a good sense of smell, how can a predator catch them?

On My Own (reader uses prior knowledge to answer)

1. Would you rather be a predator or a prey? Why?
2. Have you ever seen a predator catch a prey? If so, what happened?

You can see that by using the simple guidelines in Figure 7.14, you can easily create questions that ask readers to think about text-explicit and text-implicit information. After you have mastered the QAR strategy yourself, you can then teach it to your students.

Vacca and Vacca (2005) describe a simple method for teaching young readers how to answer questions by discovering their sources. They suggest that first you introduce the four types of questions and the two categories of information sources: *in the text* and *in your head.* After you review the questions and the types of answers, give children several short text passages to read, followed by one type of question per passage. After answering each question, you and your young readers should only discuss what kind of question it is and why.

On a subsequent day, have the children practice again, except this time ask the children to identify the question type as well as to answer the question. As the children grow in proficiency of identifying both the answer to the question and the question type, you can raise the difficulty of the text passages as well as the length. You also want to be sure that each type of QAR is addressed. Finally, you can have the students apply the QAR strategy to actual content-area assignments.

What we have discovered is that you may need to repeat this routine several times before students are able to use it independently. When students are comfortable with identifying and answering the four types of questions, they can begin to generate their own questions and exchange with their peers for more practice.

Using the QAR strategy in the classroom can provide a useful framework for both students and teachers. It builds confidence among students in both question-asking and question-answering situations. As students become more aware of the different sources of information used to answer questions, they become more strategic in their reading and thinking, and their comprehension improves. Raphael and Au (2005) further researched the QAR approach and discovered that children who were taught how to answer text questions by understanding the sources of the questions were able to answer text questions with more clarity across grades and content areas, both in the classroom and on high-stakes tests.

AFTER READING: SUMMARY WRITING

Summary writing is an authentic task used in all disciplines across a wide variety of contexts. Although we continually ask students in the upper elementary grades to summarize text, there is little evidence that we are teaching them how to compose a summary.

Reading research has suggested that summary writing is an exemplary reading comprehension strategy for enhancing students' abilities to identify and recall specific text information (Brown, Campione, & Day, 1981; Brown & Day, 1983; Kintsch & van Dijk, 1978). Brown and Day (1983) developed the practice of using the following set of rules to guide the written summary:

1. Select a topic sentence from the text, or impose one.
2. Delete trivial information that is unnecessary for understanding.
3. Delete redundant information.
4. Replace subordinate terms with superordinate terms for a list of items. For example, use the word *animals* instead of *tigers*, *lions*, and *bears*.
5. Replace subordinate terms with superordinate terms for a list of actions. For example, use the word *exercising* instead of *lifting weights*, *running*, and *jumping rope*.

When you are teaching summary writing, it is important to communicate to students that the act of writing summaries actually consists of two separate literacy events: (1) reading for meaning and understanding, and (2) writing the summary itself. Over the years, we have taught students to write summaries as early as in first and second grades. First, we guide them in collecting the main ideas and details for their summaries by recording the salient information in graphic organizers. This assures that they are reading for meaning and understanding—the first step in writing a summary. Second, we model for them how to use the graphic as a "blueprint" for composing the summary. Finally, we model for them how to delete trivial and redundant information, and, depending upon the grade level, how to substitute superordinate terms for subordinate ones.

READING ACROSS THE CURRICULUM: A SAMPLE LESSON

Now that we have reviewed the components of a best-practice before-, during-, and after-reading lesson, it is time to take a look at what one looks like. Remember that the purpose of this lesson model is to focus on the *content* of the text topic, while simultaneously reinforcing good-reader strategies and providing practice in applying them. This lesson is based on the text shown in Figure 7.15.

Lesson: African and Asian elephants

Text: "What Do Asian and African Elephants Have in Common?" (Figure 7.15)

Lesson Grade Level: 3

Content Objective: Students will demonstrate understanding of the differences and similarities between African and Asian elephants.

Strategy Objective (reinforcement): Students will demonstrate understanding of the comparison–contrast text structure.

Before Reading: Activating Prior Knowledge:

"Today we are going to continue reading about indigenous animals in our science book and focus on elephants. Can you tell me what you know about African or Asian elephants?" [Write responses on chalkboard as shown on page 157.]

WHAT DO ASIAN AND AFRICAN ELEPHANTS HAVE IN COMMON?

Elephants are the largest land animals on earth. There are two kinds of elephants: African elephants and Asian elephants. Although they share similar traits, these elephants are actually quite different. African elephants are slightly larger than Asian elephants (National Geographic Society, 1996). They can grow to 25 feet long and 11 feet tall. A male African elephant can weigh up to 14,000 pounds (National Zoo, n.d.-a). Asian elephants, on the other hand, are smaller. They can be about 21 feet long and 10 feet tall, and can weigh up to 11,000 pounds (National Zoo, n.d.-b).

African elephants and Asian elephants have large but different-shaped ears. The African elephant has ears that look like the shape of the continent of Africa. Asian elephants have smaller, round ears (National Geographic Society, 1996).

Elephants use their trunks for breathing, eating, and just about everything else. Their trunks also work like our hands. African elephants have two finger-like features on the ends of their trunks that they can use to grasp small items, but Asian elephants only have one. Both African and Asian elephants like to play with water. They take water into their trunks and spray it all over themselves and others (National Geographic Society, 1996).

People use elephants for different things, like carrying water or lumber out of the forest. Asian elephants are better at this task, because African elephants are too difficult to train (National Zoo, n.d.-a, n.d.-b).

FIGURE 7.15. "What Do Asian and African Elephants Have in Common?"

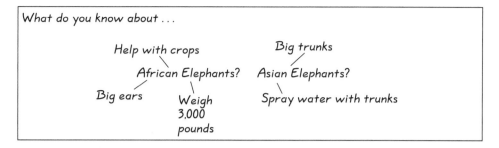

"Well, we do know quite a bit about elephants, but I can see that we don't know much about the difference between African and Asian elephants. Today we are going to read about both types of elephants, but first we need to review one vocabulary word that is important in the text."

Before Reading: Vocabulary Instruction:

"The text says, 'Although they share similar traits, these elephants are actually quite different.' What do you think the word *traits* means in this text? What kind of information about elephants do you think the author may talk about in describing how different types of elephants are alike and different?" [In order to integrate the word *trait* into students' prior knowledge, it is important to be sure students understand that *trait* means a physical feature of an elephant. Your finished vocabulary web may look like the one shown in Figure 7.16.]

Before Reading: Setting Purposes for Reading:

"Children, now you are going to work with your reading partner to read and understand the differences between African and Asian elephants. To help you do that, I want you to record the important main ideas and details in a graphic organizer. Remember how we learned the strategy to organize information that is being compared? Today you are going to practice that strategy while you learn about the differences between African and Asian elephants. First, I will pass out the texts and graphic organizers you will use for your note taking."

During Reading: Encouraging Note Taking:

"Now that you have your text and graphic organizer, let's review our comparison–contrast strategy and what information you should record in your graphic organizer." [Review the strategy and the use of the graphic organizer before students begin reading and working. A sample graphic organizer is shown on page 158.]

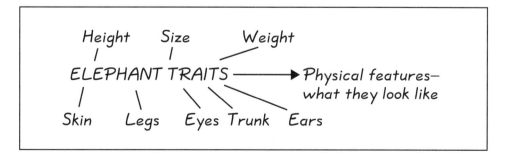

FIGURE 7.16. Before-reading vocabulary instruction on elephant traits.

Height		Weight	Length	Ears	Trunk
African Elephants					
Asian Elephants					

After Reading: Free Recall:

"Now, children, let's see what you learned about the differences between African and Asian elephants. I will ask each pair of students to supply information to fill in this enlarged graphic organizer I have placed on the overhead projector." [Allow students to have free recall of the text information and check their own graphic organizers as you write on the overhead transparency.]

After Reading: Questioning: To conclude the lesson, you can ask the following questions, to guide students to a deeper meaning of the text or identify further information that students may want to know.

- "If Asian elephants only have one finger-like structure and African elephants have two, do you think the African elephants can do more with their trunks?"

- "What other tasks do you suppose people have trained elephants to do?"

- "Why do you suppose African elephants are more difficult to train than Asian elephants?"

- "Which elephants, African or Asian, do you think are more commonly used to build houses?"

- "How long do elephants live? Does anyone know, or shall we look it up online?"

- "The text also did not give any information on what elephants eat. Can anyone guess what they eat? Then we can look that information up in our animal book as well."

This type of lesson focuses on the content of the text, but is structured to have students practice good-reader strategies. Following is another common lesson model designed to accomplish the same goal.

THE K-W-L INSTRUCTIONAL MODEL

The *know, what to know, learned* (K-W-L) instructional model, designed by Ogle (1986), has become common classroom practice. This instructional strategy prepares students for reading, guides their purpose for reading, and helps them comprehend text by clarifying details and extending their interest in the text topic. The K-W-L model is a three-step integrated instructional model that engages students in active reading. The title refers to three basic cognitive steps:

1. *Accessing what I KNOW about the topic before reading.* This step involves brainstorming what the group knows; it is similar to activating prior knowledge, as discussed in this and earlier chapters. The teacher's role is to record whatever students volunteer

about the topic *before* the students read. The critical component is to select a key concept for the brainstorming that is specific enough to generate the kinds of information that will be important to the reading.

A second type of brainstorming involves asking students to think of more general categories of information likely to be encountered when they read. This step requires much modeling and coaching if students are not used to thinking about the material they might learn in certain types of texts.

2. *Determining what I WANT TO KNOW and to learn during reading.* This brainstorming requires the teacher in a whole-group session to ask students *before reading* what they want to learn while reading about the text topic. This brainstorming encourages readers to set purposes for reading. As students read, they read purposefully, focusing on what they want to learn.

3. *Recalling what I have LEARNED as a result of the reading.* This step takes place *after reading.* Either individually or in the whole group, readers record what they have learned. They can talk about whether their questions were answered or whether they need to do further reading or research. This step helps readers to understand that they can actively pursue their own knowledge.

You can see that the K-W-L instructional model includes before-, during-, and after-reading instructional elements. Both of the lesson models presented in these last few pages are highly useful for helping students investigate expository text topics and learn from text while applying good-reader strategies.

FINAL THOUGHTS ON EXPOSITORY TEXT COMPREHENSION

We have started this chapter by defining *expository text* and briefly discussing surface text features, such as headings and boldface type. Surface features are basic elements that we take for granted, but they must be part of the comprehension curriculum in grades K–6. Most of this chapter has been devoted to text structure instruction. We hope we have impressed upon you the importance of *teaching* children to tap into an author's pattern of organization for comprehension success. Finally, we have presented two lesson models—the reading-across-the-curriculum model and the K-W-L model—that are useful in teaching science, social studies, health, music, or any other subject that uses expository text. These lesson models can be easily adapted for very young readers (grades K–1) in either a whole-group or small-group context.

In the next two chapters, we present ways of teaching children's literature or narrative text in K–6 classrooms.

To add to your self-study artifacts, try designing a text structure or a reading-across-the-curriculum lesson. Also, remember to check your knowledge of key terms in Figure 7.17 (page 160).

REFLECTION ON ARTIFACTS FOR YOUR SELF-STUDY

For your self-study, record on Figure 7.18 (page 161) the artifacts you created while you read this chapter.

KEY TERMS FOR CHAPTER 7

In this chapter, the following key terms are essential to your understanding of reading instruction. Think about what they mean, and try to define them in your own words.

expository text

surface features of expository text

expository text structures

classification text structure

sequence text structure

cause–effect text structure

comparison–contrast text structure

problem–solution text structure

graphic organizer

reading across the curriculum

free recall/structured questions

question–answer relationships (QAR) approach

summary writing

know, what to know, learned (K-W-L) model

FIGURE 7.17. Key Terms Chart for Chapter 7.

SELF-STUDY REVIEW CHART FOR CHAPTER 7

Name of Artifact	Teacher Instructional Actions and Language	Provisions for Individual Differences	Variety of Modes of Communication	Critical Thinking and Active Engagement	Opportunities for Assessment

FIGURE 7.18. Self-Study Review Chart for Chapter 7.

From *Teaching Reading: Strategies and Resources for Grades K–6* by Rachel L. McCormack and Susan Lee Pasquarelli. Copyright 2010 by The Guilford Press. Permission to photocopy this figure is granted to purchasers of this book for personal use only (see copyright page for details).

CHAPTER 8

Appreciating Children's Literature
Teaching the Language of Narrative Text

The following small-group discussion took place in a real second-grade classroom after students had finished reading a number of African trickster tales. While you read the transcript of the discussion, think about what these young children already knew about the elements of genre.

> KEVIN: Well, usually in African trickster tales, there are animals for characters.
>
> ANDREA: And it's usually a folk tale.
>
> PETER: They usually have yams, too.
>
> MICHELLE: Yup!
>
> MELISSA: There usually is a trick or outwitting.
>
> ANTHONY: You're right!
>
> RACHAEL: I love the tricking part.
>
> MELANIE: And there is always a lesson to be learned.
>
> ANDREA: And sometimes—and mostly every story is like someone is telling the story—you are not telling the story—someone else is telling the story . . .
>
> MELANIE: So you mean it is usually retold.
>
> ERIK: Usually there is a villain, too. But there is one thing I don't like about villains—is that—they always have to be women! I think they should be men a lot of times too.
>
> MICHELLE: Yeah, I agree!
>
> ANDREA: Yeah, both of them!
>
> PETER: We should check. Are we sure the villains are always women?

DEBRIEFING THE TRANSCRIPT

These second graders were talking about books. If you noticed, there was no teacher intervention. The children were charged with talking about a literature genre by themselves—and what a good job they did!

In the transcript, the children were talking about the genre of African trickster tales. In African trickster tales or similar folk tales from other cultures, the stories are about the specific country or region from which the tale originates, and all of the characters are animals. The animals always exhibit human traits, such as wisdom, foolishness, jealousy, and/or greed, and the stories teach valuable lessons through the animals' behaviors. The children in our transcript had just completed reading a series of African trickster tales, and their teacher had asked them to identify the most important elements of the genre. You can see that the children were quite adept at the task.

In this chapter, you will learn about teaching children's literature, including inviting children to read, think about, talk, and write about books in meaningful ways.

BEST PRACTICES YOU WILL SEE IN THIS CHAPTER

✓ Teaching literature genre by genre.
✓ Providing explicit instruction in story structure, oral retelling, and summary writing.
✓ Teaching narrative comprehension/response strategies.
✓ Guiding students in learning how to write book reviews.

USING CHILDREN'S LITERATURE IN THE READING PROGRAM

In their literature review, Galda, Ash, and Cullinan (2000) grouped the children's literature research into categories, including using (1) children's literature as text for the reading program, (2) children's own reading interests and preferences for book choices, (3) varying contexts to support children's engagement with literature, and (4) children's literature as read-aloud material in primary classrooms. Research has also examined best practices for teaching children the basic structures of narrative text, as well as reading strategies useful for navigating one's way to deep understanding of a story (Pressley, 2002a).

This substantial research base has helped us to understand the nature of children's engagement with good literature and has informed the ways in which we think about literature instruction. This chapter and the next are devoted to best practices in teaching narrative text or children's literature. We have divided the children's literature curriculum into two chapters, to scaffold your knowledge from the simple pedagogy to the more complex. Chapter 9 focuses on reader response, primarily through writing. This chapter presents practical suggestions to help children do the following:

1. Distinguish one genre of literature from another.
2. Identify basic story structure (setting, characters, and plot events).

3. Use cognitive strategies to understand elements of fiction/literature.
4. Write about favorite pieces of literature.

TEACHING GENRE BY GENRE

As our opening transcript of children's talk about African trickster tales suggests, our literature curriculum includes teaching children how to distinguish one genre from another. In the transcript, the children were quite aptly discussing the characteristics or elements of African trickster tales.

In the elementary school, we teach children about all literature genres, including picture books, short stories, novels, fables, biographies, all forms of poetry, and historical fiction. (See Figure 8.1 for a more inclusive list.) An essential part of our teaching includes teaching children to identify the elements of genre.

The *elements of genre* refer to the nature of the piece or the characteristics that make one genre different from another. For example, what makes a fable a fable? We can identify four elements of a fable:

1. It is a short, action-packed story.
2. It illustrates a moral or a lesson.
3. It features animals or forces of nature as characters.
4. It engages a universal (cross-cultural) audience.

Consider the famous fable "The Hare and the Tortoise." Hare challenges all the animals to a race. Tortoise accepts, and the race begins. Tortoise, having very short legs, heads for the finish line in his slow and steady way. Hare, on the other hand, runs very

---

- Autobiographies
- Biographies
- Drama (plays)
- Fables from around the world
- Fairy tales from around the world
- Fantasy
- Newspaper feature stories
- Folk tales from around the world
- Historical fiction
- Memoirs
- Myths and legends
- Picture books
- Poetry: Free verse, haiku, cinquain, sonnet, ballad, monologue, limerick, etc.
- Science fiction
- Short stories
- Realistic fiction
- Trickster tales from around the world

FIGURE 8.1. Common narrative genres for the elementary school reading curriculum.

fast almost all the way to the finish line, but gets so tired that he lies down to take a nap, knowing that he has plenty of time to be victorious. Meanwhile, Tortoise just plods along at his customary pace and passes the sleeping Hare. When Hare finally wakes up, he sees that Tortoise is just about to cross the finish line and win the race. The moral is "Slow and steady wins the race." As we introduce fables to children, we are careful to point out these elements for two purposes: (1) to boost their general comprehension of the genre, and (2) to help them understand what makes one genre different from another.

In Figure 8.2 (pages 166–167), we have highlighted the elements of the most common children's literature genres. The following section is devoted to the elements of basic story structure, as well as how to introduce these elements to your students.

DEFINING STORY STRUCTURE

In Chapter 7, you have learned about expository text structures. Similarly, narrative text (short stories or novels) has a basic structure. This text structure is sometimes referred to as *story grammar*, *story structure*, or *narrative text structure*. For our purposes, we refer to this text structure as *story structure*.

Stein and Glenn (1979) suggest that most conventional stories follow a typical story structure with the following elements: a setting, an initiating event, an internal response from a character, an attempt at resolution, consequences, and character reactions. This somewhat complex story structure can be taught in grades 4–6 and is described below. We have used the fairy tale "Cinderella" to illustrate each structural element.

Complex Story Structure (Grades 4–6)

• *Setting*. The setting introduces the time and place of the story, and usually introduces the main characters (*protagonists*). Sometimes the story begins with the supporting characters or with characters who are in conflict (*antagonists*) with the main characters. *Illustration*: Cinderella (protagonist) is a beautiful young woman forced to be a maid by her mean stepmother and her two ugly stepsisters (antagonists).

• *Initiating event*. Usually something happens that initiates trouble or a problem in the story. *Illustration*: One day the Prince announces that he is giving a ball. Cinderella cannot attend, because her stepmother and stepsisters will not allow her to go.

• *Internal response*. Usually the protagonist and other supporting characters have some sort of response or reaction to the event. *Illustration*: Cinderella is heartbroken that she cannot go to the ball. When her stepsisters leave in their handsome gowns, she cries.

• *Attempt at resolution*. The protagonist or other supporting characters make a plan or take actions to resolve the dilemma or problem. Usually there is a sequence of events that ends with a resolution. *Illustration*: A fairy godmother appears to Cinderella. The fairy uses her magic and creates a beautiful gown and tiny glass slippers for Cinderella. When Cinderella enters the ballroom looking so beautiful, the Prince falls in love with her. She falls in love with the Prince in return, but she has to leave the ball by midnight, or her magic dress and coach will disappear. As the clock strikes midnight, Cinderella

Genre	Plot Elements	Setting Elements	Character Elements
Autobiography	1. Story of the author's life. 2. Usually written in sequential order. 3. Is true to the life of the writer.	1. Vivid descriptions of settings with sensory details to create sense of place and time.	1. Strong physical and mental picture of main character. 2. Strong physical and mental picture of supporting characters.
Biography	1. Story of a person's life written by another person. 2. Usually written in sequential order. 3. Is true to the life of the subject of the text.	1. Real setting and time period of the person who is the subject of the text.	1. Strong physical and mental picture of main character. 2. Strong physical and mental picture of supporting characters.
Fable	1. Simple plot that reflects human weaknesses or strengths. 2. Story teaches a moral about life.	1. Place is anywhere. 2. Time is real time.	1. Very few characters. 2. Usually characters are animals with human traits.
Fairy tale	1. There is always a problem and a solution. 2. The "good" character usually "wins" or is triumphant in some way. 3. There is usually magic. 4. Things happen in threes or sevens.	1. Place usually has to do with castles and/or royalty. 2. Time is "Once upon a time . . . "	1. The main characters include a "good" and an "evil" character. 2. Both of these characters are well defined. 3. There are many supporting characters helping the main characters.
Fantasy	1. Plot involves elements that are not part of ordinary reality, with surprising turns and unusual developments. 2. Usually the plot has a theme of good versus evil. 3. Magic and imaginary inventions are often included.	1. Place is imaginary. 2. Time is any time.	1. Characters do not have to be realistic. They can have powers or special gifts. 2. Animals or inanimate objects can act like humans.
Memoir	1. Captures meaningful moments in life of writer. 2. Invokes emotion. 3. May just be one event or a series of events about one subject in the author's life. 4. Usually centers around a problem, its resolution, and the meaning derived from this experience.	1. Place is real. 2. Focus is on a specific period in time.	1. Character (the writer) has a strong voice. 2. Contains important supporting characters.

(cont.)

FIGURE 8.2. Elements of children's literature genres.

Genre	Plot Elements	Setting Elements	Character Elements
Historical Fiction	1. Plot is believable and shaped by the historical setting. 2. There is usually a problem for characters to resolve.	1. Place is a particular setting in history. 2. Time is specific to historical setting.	1. Characters are normal people who could have lived in the setting. 2. Characters usually experience some change.
Mystery	1. Suspenseful action. 2. Problem, usually involving a murder or other crime, with believable solution. 3. Possible "twist" to surprise reader.	1. Vivid descriptions of settings with sensory details to create sense of mystery.	1. Strong physical and mental picture of main character. 2. Victim described to gain sympathy from audience.
Realistic fiction	1. Plot has problem for character to resolve, with hopeful theme. 2. The plot must be believable and demonstrate real life. 3. Events can be imaginary, but have to be plausible.	1. Place can be real or imaginary. 2. Time is any time, but it is usually within 25 years of the present day.	1. Characters are realistic. 2. Characters change as a result of what occurs in plot.
Science fiction	1. Plot usually is woven around current or future science or technology. 2. Plot contains some feature that is totally different from the reality of the audience. 3. Plot is similar to that in the genre of fantasy.	1. Place can be anywhere—fictional or nonfictional. 2. Time is real time, past, or future.	1. Main characters can be real or imaginary (humans, animals, robots, aliens, etc.).

FIGURE 8.2. (*cont.*)

runs away from the Prince because she does not want to turn back into a maid in front of his eyes. As she is running away, she loses one of her glass slippers on the steps of the palace.

- *Consequence.* This is the effect of the protagonist's actions. *Illustration*: The Prince finds Cinderella's slipper and sends his men to every household in the land to find the beautiful girl to whom it belongs. He eventually finds Cinderella and asks her to marry him.
- *Reaction.* This is the protagonist's response to the consequence, and it ends the story. *Illustration*: Cinderella marries the Prince, and they live happily ever after.

After examining this complex story structure, you will notice that it is more complicated than that which is traditionally taught in the early primary grades. If you examine books written for young and inexperienced readers, the plot, characters, and themes presented are fairly simple. Therefore, the basic structural elements we teach in the K–3 classroom include the setting, problem, solution, and consequence. Below, we illustrate simple story structure with the fairy tale "Goldilocks."

Simple Story Grammar for Young Children (Grades K–3)

- *Setting*. Time, place, characters. *Illustration*: "Once upon a time," three bears live in the woods. They leave their lovely home one day and go out to forage for food.
- *Problem*. The major problem, trouble, or dilemma in the story. *Illustration*: While they are out, a young girl named Goldilocks enters the bears' home. Goldilocks is hungry, so she eats the bears' porridge. She is tired, so first she sits in Baby Bear's chair and breaks it. Then she tries out the beds and falls asleep in Baby Bear's bed.
- *Solution*. The solution to the trouble, problem, or dilemma. *Illustration:* The bears come home and are surprised to find that their food has been eaten and Baby Bear's chair is broken, so they look around. They find Goldilocks asleep in Baby Bear's bed and wake her up. Goldilocks runs away when she sees the family of bears.
- *Consequence*. What happens to the characters after the problems are solved. *Illustration:* The bears live happily ever after, and no one really knows what happens to Goldilocks.

TEACHING STORY STRUCTURE

How do we teach children to identify these parts of a story? Researchers suggest that more able readers will eventually develop this knowledge on their own, while less able readers benefit from direct instruction (Mandler, 1984; Short & Ryan, 1984). We suggest that children as young as kindergarten age be introduced to the basic elements of story structure.

Teaching Story Structure in the K–3 Classroom

In kindergarten through grade 3, story structure instruction can be accomplished through many contexts of storybook reading in your classroom. We have observed effective teachers of emergent readers pointing out the various story structure elements during read-alouds, shared reading, readers' theatre, small-group instruction, and the many other contexts you have read about in this book.

For example, while reading a story aloud to the class, you can read the opening of the story, which usually contains the setting and character introductions. Then pause and point out how you identify the aspects of the setting. On the whiteboard, you can write:

<u>Stories Have Settings and Characters</u>

Setting = Time + Place

Time = When does the story take place?

Place = Where does the story take place?

Characters = Who are the people in the story?

As demonstrated above, we suggest providing questions for young readers to ask themselves. This makes this simple teaching act a form of cognitive strategy instruction (see Chapter 5). Young children can come to "own" this strategy through constant teacher repetition during storybook reading. For example, in subsequent lessons you can read the opening, pause, and ask the children where and when the story takes place. You can also go on to model how to identify the characters, the problems, the solutions, and the consequences. With repetition and explicit teaching, you will be surprised at how quickly young children learn the language of stories.

Teaching Story Structure in the 4–6 Classroom

For children in grades 4–6, we suggest you use cognitive strategy instruction to model how to identify elements of the more complex story structure. When teaching older children, we build on what they know. For example, if your fourth graders already know how to identify the simple story structure, teach them the more complex structure to match the more sophisticated books they are reading in fourth grade.

You can also teach a more complex strategy for identifying each element of structure. For example, the following is a strategy for identifying the setting. Notice how much more detailed it is than the one presented above for younger children.

Identifying the Setting of a Story

Place

Read through the opening and see if the author tells you where the story takes place.

If the author does not tell you, look for clues as to where the story might take place. Ask yourself:

- Where are the main characters?
- Are they in a country? In a town? Is the place named?
- Is the place just a general environment, such as a school, a beach, or a city?
- Does the setting change often in each chapter? If so, note the setting each time it changes.

Time

Read through the opening of the story again, searching for clues about where the story takes place. Does the author tell you directly?

If the author does not tell you, look for clues as to when the story takes place. Ask yourself:

- Can I figure out what season it is by how the characters are dressed or the way the scenes are described?
- Can I find out what time of year it is by what the characters are doing? For example, are they in school?
- Is the time not listed because it is not important?

Characters

To find the main character, ask yourself who is described most often, or who is the narrator. The main character is called the protagonist.

Then find the character who opposes the main character. This character is called the antagonist.

Story Structure Identification Strategies

One of the most common ways to have students practice their story structure identification is to have them give an *oral retelling* of a story or write a *summary* of the main elements of the story. To prepare for an oral retelling or a summary, we teach children to record the main elements of a story in a *story map*.

The Story Map Graphic Organizer

A *story map* is a graphic organizer that allows a reader to record the basic elements of a story to aid comprehension. The story map was first introduced in the elementary reading curriculum in the early 1990s as a result of research conducted on using story maps with children who were both experienced and inexperienced readers, to determine whether identifying and recording elements of story aided comprehension (Idol, 1987; Idol & Croll, 1987). Figure 8.3 shows a story map that we have used in many K–3 classrooms or with inexperienced older readers. Figure 8.4 (page 172) is a story map for readers in grades 4–6 or for more experienced younger children. Once children record the elements of a story, either map can then be used as a source of information for discussing stories in book clubs, literature circles, and other literacy contexts. In addition, you can use either map as a blueprint for teaching children to retell a story orally or write a summary.

Oral Retelling

Morrow (1984, 1985, 1986) describes oral retelling as an ideal means of improving children's concept of story structure and overall story comprehension. We highly advocate the use of oral retelling as part of the K–3 reading program. Once you have taught children how to record the setting, characters, problems, solutions, and consequences in a story map, we find it is relatively simple to teach them to retell a story, using the story map as their guide. Here is our recommended procedure for teaching children to retell a story:

1. Place a completed story map on an easel, and tell children you are going to model retelling a story.
2. Model telling the story in your own words in proper sequence, while pointing to the various story elements on the story map. It is important to be very explicit. For example, when identifying the setting, you might say, "The setting of the story is at the lake at sunrise."
3. Debrief the retelling by asking children to tell you the steps you have used for retelling the story. Be sure they understand that the story needs to be told in sequential order.
4. Write the strategy steps for a retelling on a second easel chart, and review the steps with the children orally. Your strategy chart may look like Figure 8.5 (page 173) when you are finished writing.
5. Review the strategy steps, and then ask children to partner with another child to retell a story for which they have already made a story map (guided practice).

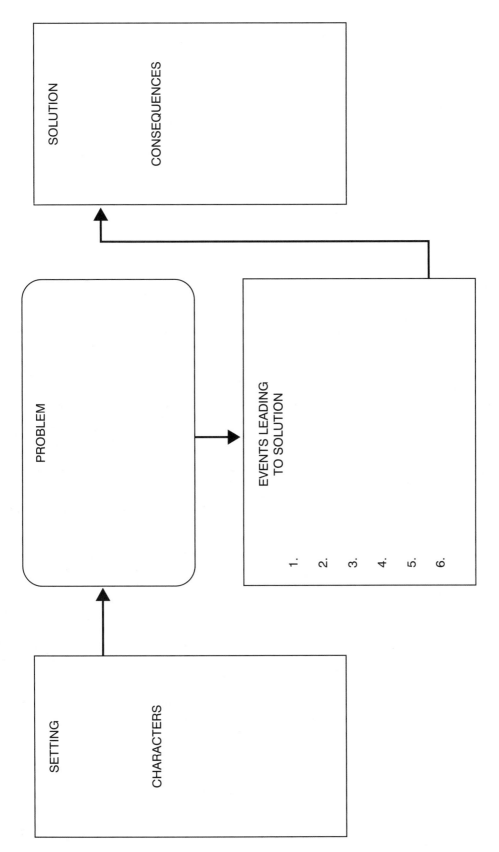

FIGURE 8.3. Simple story map.

From *Teaching Reading: Strategies and Resources for Grades K–6* by Rachel L. McCormack and Susan Lee Pasquarelli. Copyright 2010 by The Guilford Press. Permission to photocopy this figure is granted to purchasers of this book for personal use only (see copyright page for details).

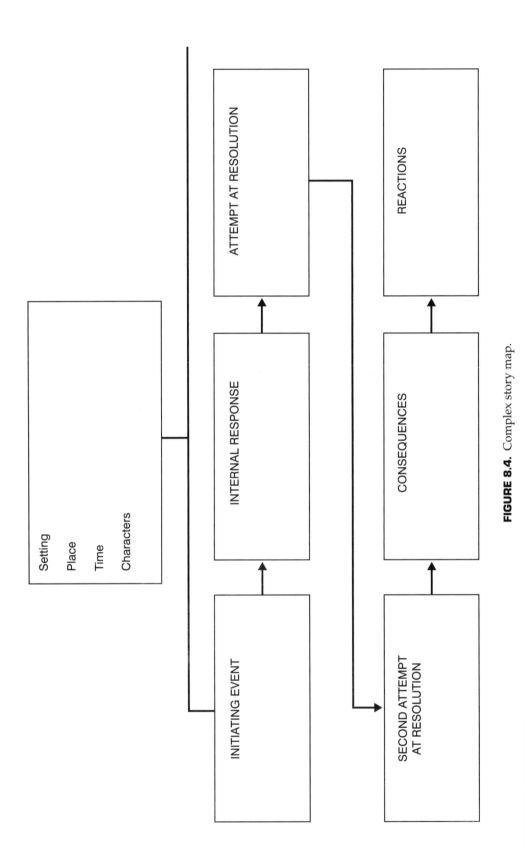

FIGURE 8.4. Complex story map.

From *Teaching Reading: Strategies and Resources for Grades K–6* by Rachel L. McCormack and Susan Lee Pasquarelli. Copyright 2010 by The Guilford Press. Permission to photocopy this figure is granted to purchasers of this book for personal use only (see copyright page for details).

1. *Hold your story map to guide your storytelling.*

2. *Start at the beginning of the story, and tell in your own words what happened at the beginning, the middle, and the end of the story.*

3. *Tell the story in sequence.*

4. *Don't forget to tell about:*
   - *The setting and each of the characters.*
   - *What the trouble or problem was in the story.*
   - *What happened to the characters at the end of the story.*

FIGURE 8.5. How to retell a story.

From *Teaching Reading: Strategies and Resources for Grades K–6* by Rachel L. McCormack and Susan Lee Pasquarelli. Copyright 2010 by The Guilford Press. Permission to photocopy this figure is granted to purchasers of this book for personal use only (see copyright page for details).

6. Walk around the room, coaching individual partners to success.
7. Debrief the students' experiences, and give them multiple opportunities for guided and independent practice.

We have had much success with oral retelling in grades K–2 with our emergent readers. Not only do children love retelling stories in their own words, but we find that it helps them focus on important story elements while reading, and subsequently raises their comprehension of the overall story. You will read about the use of oral retelling as a comprehension assessment strategy in Chapter 12.

Written Summaries

Writing summaries of narrative text is a good way for readers in grades 1–6 to record their understanding of major story elements. We teach children to write story summaries by using the same cognitive strategy instruction framework described in Chapter 5. For this task, they use a story map as a blueprint to write the summary. Summary writing is an advanced skill, and it requires much teaching and practice for children to produce a complete summary. Figure 8.6 is a second grader's summary of the story "The Ugly Duckling," by Hans Christian Andersen. You will see that even children as young as second grade or younger can be taught to write clear, concise summaries of stories. Again, you will see more examples of writing story summaries as a way of assessing comprehension in Chapter 12.

We have often found that in primary classrooms, the literature curriculum revolves solely around story structure and story maps. In the following section, we present ways to teach other story comprehension strategies that lead children to a deeper understanding of plot, characterization, and theme.

"The Ugly Duckling" by Hans Christian Andersen

A SUMMARY
By Matt, 2nd grade

"The Ugly Duckling" is a story about a mother duck and her six eggs. One morning she saw another egg. All the eggs hatched and most of the ducklings were yellow. The last egg hatched and the duck was UGLY. It was gray and large. All the animals on the farm made fun of it so the ugly duckling went away. He was so sad. One day he saw beautiful swans swimming. They all loved him and called him beautiful. So he wasn't a duck all along! He was a swan! Now he is one of the most beautifullest birds in the pond and he is happy.

FIGURE 8.6. Summary of "The Ugly Duckling."

TEACHING ELEMENTS OF PLOT, CHARACTERIZATION, AND THEME

Strategies leading to the deeper meaning of literature are often *implicitly* taught through literature discussions, small-group work, and written responses to literature. We advocate the *explicit teaching* of literature strategies that allow children to examine (1) characters' cultures, motivations, and subsequent behaviors; (2) more complex plots and story lines; and (3) complex themes. Figure 8.7 lists several strategies we have found useful to teach for these purposes; the list is by no means a complete list of the strategies good readers use while reading literature. We advocate the teaching of these strategies in K–6 classrooms as children encounter stories with more complex plots, characters, and themes.

Teaching students to interpret these more complex plots, characters, and themes is considered to be part of the reader response curriculum, which is described in detail in the next chapter. For now, we provide a lesson to illustrate how to teach a literature strategy, using the book *The Royal Bee* (Park & Park, 2000). It is meant to be a model to follow as you design lessons to teach other narrative text strategies, such as those listed in Figure 8.7. You will recognize how the cognitive strategy instructional model frames this lesson.

A Sample Lesson

Lesson: Strategy for identifying a character's personality traits

Lesson Grade Levels: 4–6

Lesson Objective: Students will demonstrate understanding of how to identify a character's personality traits.

Text: *The Royal Bee* (Park & Park, 2000)

Plot
- Identifying story structure
- Identifying sequence of events
- Identifying how events lead to characters' actions, behaviors, or attitudes

Characterization
- Identifying personality traits of characters
- Identifying physical descriptions of characters
- Identifying how main character's personality leads to outcome of story
- Identifying feelings and emotions of characters
- Identifying problems main character has throughout book
- Identifying how a character's motivations lead to actions

Setting
- Identifying setting
- Comparing settings of chapters
- Comparing book settings

Theme
- Identifying the theme of the story
- Identifying how characters' actions, behaviors, and/or attitudes lead to the theme of the story
- Identifying how characters' cultures affect the theme or the outcome of the story

---

FIGURE 8.7. Selected reading strategies for literature.

Declarative Knowledge:

"Today I am going to model a strategy for you to use while we are reading a story. The name of the strategy is *identifying a character's personality traits*. Can anyone tell me what a *personality trait* is?"

Keep in mind that during the declarative knowledge portion of the lesson, it is your responsibility as the teacher to conceptualize the strategy. Some children may know what a personality or character trait is; many will not. Therefore, the lesson starts with a vocabulary activity designed to prepare students for identifying character traits of storybook characters.

The question above invites children to brainstorm their understanding of *personality traits*. However, in the course of the discussion, it is essential to bring out and record two distinct sets of ideas: (1) a list of character traits, so children can have the list to use later when thinking about characters; and (2) a list of ways they know these things about people in their lives. You can use a visual structure like the one shown in Figure 8.8 to record the children's ideas.

Once you establish what a character trait is, and the children understand how "people" traits can be determined in real life, you can continue with the strategy teaching.

"The reason why we are learning this strategy on how to identify character traits is so it will help us gain a deeper understanding of characters in our books. Watch me while I model for you how to preview a text and identify a character's personality."

Procedural Knowledge: The strategy steps you will be modeling are given in **boldface**, so you can see how to provide each strategy step explicitly and then apply it to the book. As illustrated below and in Figure 8.9, a graphic organizer is used as part of this modeling process.

"I am going to model our strategy with the book *The Royal Bee*, by Frances Park and Ginger Park, since we have already read and enjoyed the book. I am going to begin by rereading parts of the book and thinking about the main character, Song-ho. It is his personality that we are going to try to identify. You remember that this book takes place a very long time ago in Korea, when only the privileged children were allowed to go to school. Now I am going to begin my think-aloud, so I want all of you to pay close attention to my thinking. Then I will let you try out our strategy.

[Think-aloud begins.] "In the opening of the book, the author tells us that Song-ho is a poor boy who is not allowed to go to school, but who very much wants to read books and write poetry. So right away, the narrator tells us that Song-ho is interested in reading and writing, so I am going to write that down in my graphic organizer under the heading '**What do others say about the character?**' In this case, the narrator has told us about Song-ho's hopes and dreams.

TRAITS	HOW DO YOU KNOW THIS ABOUT SOMEONE?
• Kind • Brave • Happy • Sad • Positive • Negative • Shy • Coward • Considerate • Thoughtful • Pleasant • Honest • Clever • Smart	• Things they do. • Things they say. • The way they talk to people. • Things other people tell you about them.

FIGURE 8.8. Personality traits.

Character: *Song-ho*

Event	What does the character say?	What does the character do?	What do others say about the character?	How does the character react to events or people?	Think about all this information and see if it helps you identify a character trait.
Page 1: Setting			*Interested in reading and writing.*		*Smart Motivated*
Pages 2–3: Morning	*Tells his mother he will do all his chores.* *Asks the teacher if he can stay outside the door and learn the lessons.*	*Sneaks to the school to listen to the lessons outside the door.*			*Respectful Crafty Brave*

FIGURE 8.9. Graphic organizer with Song-ho's personality traits.

"Then I will continue reading. [Read aloud the next event in the book.] Hmmm. The second event in the story takes us to Song-ho's home, where Song-ho tells his mother that he will do all his chores while she is in the fields working. I am going to write that down in my graphic organizer under the heading '**What does the character say?**'

"Also in this morning event, Song-ho hears the school bell and runs to stand outside the door and listen to the lessons, even though he is not allowed to go inside the school. Well, that tells us more about Song-ho, so I am going to write that information down under the heading '**What does the character do?**'

"As I continue to read, I learn that the teacher hears Song-ho outside the door. When the teacher comes out, Song-ho asks him if he can come to school, even though he is not one of the rich children. This is important too, so I am going to write that down in my graphic organizer under the heading '**What does the character say?**'

"Now, children, you can see that by just reading a few pages of text, I have found out quite a bit about Song-ho's character. Let's take a look at our graphic organizer and see what we've learned so far. Well, we've learned that Song-ho wants to learn to read and write. From that information, we can maybe infer that Song-ho is a *smart* boy, and that he is *motivated*, because he wishes to be educated. So I am going to write *smart* and *motivated* in my graphic organizer under the last heading.

"Then I am going to look at what I have listed under the second story event. First, I wrote that Song-ho tells his mother that he will do all his chores. So from that, I can determine that Song-ho is a *respectful* boy, because that is how he acts with his mother. I'll write *respectful* in my graphic organizer.

"Next, we see that Song-ho decides to sneak to the school to listen to lessons outside the door. Hmm. Well, we can infer that Song-ho is *crafty* to figure out a way to learn lessons, even though he is not allowed in the school. I am going to write *crafty* in my graphic organizer.

"Finally, when the teacher hears Song-ho outside the door and asks Song-ho what he is doing there, Song-ho asks the teacher if he can stay outside the door and learn lessons. I think he's very brave to do that, don't you? Considering that by the law of the land, only the privileged can go to school, Song-ho must have a lot of courage to address the teacher that way. I'll write *brave* in my graphic organizer. [Think-aloud ends.]

"Now, girls and boys, I am going to give you an opportunity to try out this strategy in this same book. Let's review our strategy before you work with your partner trying out the strategy." [Write on chart paper the following strategy steps.]

Strategy for Identifying a Character's Personality

1. Read the story once through to identify the setting, characters, events, and problems.

2. Skim the story again, paying attention to just one character.

3. While skimming, ask yourself these questions:
   What does the character think about?
   What does the character say?
   What does the character do?
   What do others say/think about the character?
   How does the character react to events or people?

4. As you answer these questions, record your answers on a graphic organizer. Once you have the character actions and thoughts recorded, think about words you can use to describe your character's traits.

   <u>Examples of character traits</u>:

<u>Positive</u>	<u>Negative</u>
Determined	Lazy
Thoughtful	Impulsive
Kind	Mean
Considerate	Inconsiderate
Outgoing	Shy
Honest	Devious
Pleasant	Unpleasant
Sweet	Hurtful
Brave	Coward

5. Once you come up with a list of character traits, try combining them to describe your character's personality.

After you provide the modeling and strategy steps, it is important that students immediately practice the strategy. While the students are engaged in guided practice, you can coach small groups or individuals to success in strategy application.

Conditional Knowledge: Immediately following the guided practice, you want to be sure to have students evaluate the effectiveness of the strategy.

First, it will be important to debrief the information they have included in their graphic organizers. The difficult part of this strategy is evaluating a character's words, actions, and motivations to determine his or her character traits. This requires interpretation and so will require much coaching. The children's responses at this point of the lesson will aid your assessment of how well they have applied the strategy.

Next, you must debrief the effectiveness of the strategy. You can do that by asking the children the following questions:

1. "How effective was our strategy?"
2. "Did you think of other ways of determining a character's personality traits? If so, we will add it to our strategy steps."

You want the children to understand that a strategy is just a guideline and that it does not always work when you apply it to every text. The strategy may need adjustment to meet the demands of a different story.

Your final step in the strategy lesson sequence is to guide students to the understanding of when to use the strategy again. You can accomplish this by having children practice the strategy in a wide variety of narrative text and debriefing how the strategy might change for each.

The lesson presented above is a reader response strategy lesson, because it requires interpretation by the reader. In the next chapter, we provide extensive information on reader response theories and practices as we continue our work in the area of literature strategy instruction.

CONTEXTS FOR LITERATURE DISCUSSIONS

Class discussions and peer talk are important contexts for the teaching of literature. Chapters 2 and 4 provide information on literature circles, book talks, and other contexts for talk about books. These contexts provide a framework for children's practice of reading strategies while providing opportunities to drive them to the deeper meanings of text. Refer back to these chapters to think about ways you can design your reading curriculum to include both comprehension strategy instruction and multiple opportunities for talk about good books.

TEACHING FIGURATIVE LANGUAGE
AND OTHER LITERARY DEVICES

Teaching children about *figurative language* and other literary devices is another important part of the literature curriculum. Figure 8.10 is a comprehensive list of such language and devices, as well as their definitions.

You can use the vocabulary-teaching strategies from Chapter 4 to teach figurative language terms. Choose one of the strategies that helps to illustrate a concept. For example, when teaching a simile, you can use a feature matrix to identify the parts of a simile, and then have children practice finding similes in text and add them to the matrix. Learning about figurative language gives children more of the tools they need to understand literature.

Type of figurative language/device	Definition	Example
Alliteration	The use of two or more sequential words with the same consonant sound.	Peter Piper picked a peck of pickled peppers.
Foreshadowing	The use of hints or clues to suggest what will happen later in a story.	The boy continued on his way, wary of strangers who might be lurking in the shadows.
Hyperbole	An exaggeration that helps to create an image for the reader.	Juan's eyesight was so good, he could see around corners.
Idiom	An expression or word usage that is common in one language but cannot be literally translated into another language.	I have a bee in my bonnet. A stitch in time saves nine.
Images	Words or phrases that appeal to the senses: smell, taste, touch, sight, or sound.	During the storm, thunder crashed, the surf pounded the beach, and lightning brightened the sky.
Metaphor	An *implied* comparison of two things that have at least one trait in common.	He is a lamb.
Onomatopoeia	Words that imitate a sound.	The bees were buzzing around the child's ears.
Personification	The assignment of human characteristics to nonhuman things.	The wind whispered its secrets to me.
Simile	An *explicit* comparison of two similar things, using the word *like* or *as*.	He is as gentle as a lamb.

FIGURE 8.10. Figurative language and other literary devices.

WRITING BOOK REVIEWS

Over the last several years, we have experimented with teaching children to write book reviews of good literature. We have discovered that book reviews are far more rigorous and certainly more academically challenging than the old-fashioned book report.

A comprehensive book review contains two clear components: a short summary of the book and an analysis of the book. If the review is to entice other readers to read the book, then the summary should not give away the end of the story.

Book review formats are not standardized. You can design one that is specific to the skills of your students or to your school's curriculum. We offer three book review formats below, to demonstrate the difference of what to expect across skill and grade levels.

Book Review Format (Emergent)

Tell *what* the story is about.

Tell *whom* the story was about.

Tell your friends why they should read this book.

Book Review Format (Primary)

- A short summary of the story.
- A short description of the main character and his or her goals and problems.
- Personal reflection—include:
  - How you liked the book, including your favorite parts.
  - What you did not like about the book.
  - Who should read this book?

Book Review Format (Intermediate)

Summary: Include a detailed setting, a description of the main characters, and enough plot details to entice readers to read the book.

Character Analysis: Choose one main character, identify his or her character traits, and include text evidence to support your points.

Theme: Describe the theme of the story, and include text evidence to support your thinking.

Reflection: Give your personal opinion of the book. Tell why you think it is a good piece of literature (or the opposite).

Recommendation: End with a strong recommendation that will either entice your classmates to read the book or dissuade them from doing so.

As you can see from the three formats above, the expectations for book reviews increase as we traverse grade levels. Employing a rigorous reading comprehension curriculum in each grade will ensure that our readers are progressing to meet the demands of more complex texts.

We have suggested to classroom teachers that children will be more likely to spend time on writing good book reviews if it is an *authentic* task—that is, if they know that their reviews will be enjoyed by many readers. Try placing the book reviews in your classroom library, your school library, or even your town library if the children's librarian agrees. In one district, we were able to talk a local independent bookseller into using the children's book reviews to "sell" her books. We helped her place the book reviews right on the bookshelf where the books were displayed. She was delighted, as were the townspeople who read the reviews and considered purchasing the reviewed books for friends or family members. In addition to libraries, classrooms, and bookstores, you always have the option of having students download their reviews onto Amazon.com or a similar website, to be considered for online publication.

The most prevalent types of writing about literature being taught in elementary school include reader response journals and written responses to literature. We devote the next chapter to these aspects of the literature curriculum. Also in Chapter 9, we describe *reader response theory* and present ways to help your students make personal connections to the literature they read.

Before you leave this chapter, think about the key terms we present in Figure 8.11, and jot down definitions in your own words. Also, you may want to design a literature lesson with your favorite children's book, using the information you have learned in this chapter while it is fresh in your mind.

REFLECTION ON ARTIFACTS FOR YOUR SELF-STUDY

For your self-study, record on Figure 8.12 (page 184) the artifacts you created while or after you read this chapter.

KEY TERMS FOR CHAPTER 8

In this chapter, the following key terms are essential to your understanding of reading instruction. Think about what they mean, and try to define them in your own words.

elements of genre

story structure

setting

characters: protagonist, antagonist

problem, solution, consequence

story map graphic organizer

oral retelling

figurative language

FIGURE 8.11. Key Terms Chart for Chapter 8.

SELF-STUDY REVIEW CHART FOR CHAPTER 8

Name of Artifact	Teacher Instructional Actions and Language	Provisions for Individual Differences	Variety of Modes of Communication	Critical Thinking and Active Engagement	Opportunities for Assessment

FIGURE 8.12. Self-Study Review Chart for Chapter 8.

CHAPTER 9

Supporting Children's Voices

Response to Literature through Writing

We, the authors of this text, are readers. Since we are literacy professors, there is no guilt associated with our leisure reading activities. We easily justify time spent reading as time spent working. We read everything—adult books or children's books, fiction or nonfiction, contemporary or classic—but our great love is modern fiction. We are always searching for new authors and savor new books by our old favorites. At the top of our list of contemporary American authors is John Irving. We wait for Irving to compose his next novel the minute we finish his last. As soon as the prepublication hype for a new Irving book hits the mass media, we arrange to pick it up from our favorite independent bookseller on the day of release. In short, we act like *Harry Potter* fans, and we cannot understand the lack of similar fanfare for Irving as for J. K. Rowling. The following is a true story about our reading of one of Irving's new books. This story will illustrate for you the importance of supporting readers' voices as they read and respond to literature.

Over a decade and several books ago, Irving (1998) wrote *A Widow for One Year*. I (SLP) remember waiting impatiently for the release date, and I cleared the following weekend to devour his latest work. As I began savoring the first few chapters, I was not disappointed. In fact, I was so enraptured with Irving's latest story and storytelling style, I uncharacteristically found myself placing sticky notes in the margins as I passionately responded to the work. I believe I was experiencing what Rosenblatt (1995), a legendary reader response theorist, has called "living through" a text (p. 33).

After I finished reading the last page, I experienced a feeling of deep loss, as all good readers who have greatly enjoyed a book do. I missed the characters! What were they doing today? How would they continue to transform their lives? How would the remainder of their lives unfold? Again, as any good reader does, I speculated on the answers to my questions and came to my own conclusions.

To assuage my feelings of loss, I went back to investigate what I had written on my sticky notes, and discovered that my notes were of two types. One type recorded my responses to the story, such as disenchantment with a character's action, elation over another's good fortune, or deep feelings of empathy with a scene or a character's dilemma. Another type of response was a reaction to Irving's writing style. For example, the last sticky note I placed in the book said, "Wow! 350 pages into the story, Irving changed his point of view and addressed the reader with a question I am more than willing to answer." As I reflected on my own responses that occurred *during* the text reading, I added more sticky notes. These responses recorded *after* reading were more reflective in nature, since I now knew the end of the story and the characters' resolutions to their troubles. These written responses were more critical and more thoughtfully composed, since I did not have a good story to hurry back to.

The next day, I gave my Irving book to a good friend, the coauthor of this book (RLM). She was about to take a vacation and I tucked the book into her carry-on luggage, with a written message: "It's one of his best!" Unbeknownst to her, I had left my sticky notes *in situ* for her to read as she enjoyed the novel. Three or four days later, I was not surprised to receive a phone call from a distant Caribbean island with her exclamations of pleasure at finding my responses in the book. She elaborated that my sticky notes were like having a friend reading side by side, sharing reactions and reflections. We talked a bit more about the novel, and closed the conversation by making a date to talk in depth about the novel's exceptional characters, events, and credible turn of events. She also added a caveat: Her text interpretations did not all agree with mine.

Such a satisfying conversation! We both delighted in sharing our thoughts and reflections with someone else who had read the novel. Not surprisingly, investigators of reader response classroom practice suggest that real readers gather to discuss and take pleasure in each other's personal responses. Sometimes disagreement ensues, which makes the interchange all the more enjoyable, as readers take opportunities to reinforce their own interpretations or even transform them as a result of talking about books (Beck, McKeown, Hamilton, & Kucan, 1997; Chinn, Anderson, & Waggoner, 2001; Evans, 2002; Maloch, 2002; Sipe, 2000).

In this chapter, we hope that our Irving tale will inspire you to learn about reader response theory and how to support children's voices, oral and written, while reading good literature. You may also refer back to Chapter 2 for more specific information on student talk about literature.

BEST PRACTICES YOU WILL SEE IN THIS CHAPTER

✓ Teaching reader response.

✓ Teaching children to write a "free" response to literature.

✓ Designing prompts for written responses to literature.

ROSENBLATT'S READER RESPONSE THEORY

Our current understanding of *reader response theory* is drawn from the work of Rosenblatt, as originally set forth in the first edition of her classic text, *Literature as Exploration* (Rosenblatt, 1938). More recently, Rosenblatt (2004) has suggested that "the reading of any work of literature is, of necessity, an individual and unique occurrence involving the mind and emotions of some particular reader and a particular text at a particular time under particular circumstances" (p. 1363). Rosenblatt (1995) has further posited that readers make a unique *transaction* with the text when they interpret the text through their own unique experiences and prior knowledge. In these words, Rosenblatt (2005) helps us conceptualize reader response theory:

> A story or poem or play is merely ink spots on paper until a reader transforms them into a set of meaningful symbols. When these symbols lead us to live through some moment of feeling, to enter into some human personality, or to participate imaginatively in some situation or event, we have evoked a work of literary art. Literature provides a *living through*, not simply knowledge *about*: not information that lovers have died young and fair, but a living-through of *Romeo and Juliet* . . . (pp. 62–63)

To further understand Rosenblatt's interpretation of readers' engagement with literature, let us consider a few tenets from her work:

1. "The reader brings to the work personality traits, memories of past events, present needs and preoccupations, a particular mood of the moment, and a particular physical condition" (Rosenblatt, 1995, p. 30). As Rosenblatt makes clear, readers bring to the text their own prior knowledge and experiences, and make a *transaction* with the text to create personal meaning and interpretations. Reader connections may be something as simple as sharing a feeling with a story character or reacting to an event experienced by the character. As readers respond to literature in a personal way, they are creating a private transaction with the text. Rosenblatt (1978, p. 24) further explains that readers can take either an *aesthetic stance* or an *efferent stance* while reading.

An aesthetic stance is reading for appreciation of the text and occurs *during* reading. Rosenblatt and other theorists suggest that in this type of stance, the primary focus is on private aspects of meaning. During aesthetic reading, "the reader's attention is centered directly on what he is living through during his relationship with that particular text" (Rosenblatt, 1978, p. 25).

An efferent stance is information-driven and also occurs *during* reading. In this case, the reader is reading for information, and the focus is on public aspects of meaning. In this type of stance, Rosenblatt (1978) suggests that the reader is not engaged with personal or qualitative responses, but is only focused on information gathering. This type of stance is often used with nonfiction or expository text, although Rosenblatt (1978) argues that it is possible for readers to take this type of stance while reading literature. She further argues that readers who take an efferent stance with poetry or other literature often miss the personal connections and enjoyment of the literary work. In her words, such readers will not be able to "savor the images, the sounds, the smells, the actions, the associations, and the feelings that the words point to" (Rosenblatt, 1991, p. 447).

2. "An intense response to a work will have its roots in capacities and experiences already present in the personality and mind of the reader. This principle is an important one to remember in the selection of literary materials to be presented to students" (Rosenblatt, 1995, p. 41). Over the last 30 years, a substantial amount of research has been conducted on reader response theory, children's literature, and classroom-based literature instruction (Beach, 2000; Enciso, 1997; Galda, 1982; Gee, 2000; Many & Wiseman, 1992; Martinez, Roser, Hoffman, & Battle, 1992; McGee, 1992; Pappas & Pettegrew, 1998). Some of this research suggests that readers will make personal connections to

literature because they see similarities between their own lives and plot events, characters' personalities, cultural backgrounds, and/or themes. These are all important points to consider when you are choosing literature for your elementary curriculum.

3. "The same text will have a very different meaning and value at different times or under different circumstances" (Rosenblatt, 1995, p. 35). As a reader's prior knowledge and experience changes, so too does the reader's interpretation of text. This tenet is best understood through your own personal experience with a piece of good literature. All of us have reread a favorite book and thought that someone had rewritten it between readings. Obviously, the text did not change; we changed! Rosenblatt suggests that readers' interpretations and appreciation of literature change as they change, therefore creating new meanings during different times in their lives.

4. "Awareness that others have had different experiences with it [the text] will lead the reader back to the text for a closer look. The young reader points to what in the text explains his response. He may discover, however, that he has overreacted to some elements and ignored others" (Rosenblatt, 1983, p. 286). Rosenblatt and other reader response theorists (Probst, 1981; Purves & Beach, 1972) have suggested that readers' sharing literary interpretations in a classroom or other social forum is just as important as readers' taking time for reflection on their own personal responses. As readers share their interpretations in a social context, they have opportunities to accept or reject the many different interpretations of text meaning.

The body of research and best practice on reader response in elementary classrooms is vast and is still growing. In this chapter, we suggest practical ways in which effective teachers can connect readers to the rich experiences the world of literature has to offer.

READER RESPONSE CLASSROOM ACTIVITIES

For the last 15–20 years, K–6 teachers have been implementing reader response theories and practice into their classrooms by having children respond to literature in many different ways. We have experimented with reader response instruction over the years and have found that the following activities are easily implemented in K–6 classrooms.

Time for Personal Reflection

Rosenblatt (1995) suggests that readers need time to think about their own responses and reflect on them before sharing. For example, following an initial reading of literature, you can ask children to think about the parts of the story that were meaningful to them—those with which they could make a personal connection. This can be accomplished by providing an open-ended prompt, such as "Think about the story we have just read before we have a class discussion," or a more structured prompt, such as "If you were the main character, would you have responded to the situation differently or in the same way?" We have found this opportunity for simple reflection to be invaluable. If children do not have the time or opportunity to form their own personal meanings before class discussions, some students, especially young children, will simply parrot what other children say. To that end, we always follow the initial text reading with time for personal reflection before we ask children to talk or write about literature.

Classroom Discussion

One of the most important reader response activities is classroom talk. In Chapters 2 and 4 of this book, we have described contexts for talking about literature, and have stressed the importance of such talk for vocabulary and language development. It is important for you to remember that book clubs, literature circles, whole-class exchanges, and small-group discussions are vital contributions to the literature curriculum. We have found that in discussion groups, children will ground their own personal interpretations in the text, as well as alter them as others enter the conversation. These discussion groups give the readers opportunities to arrive at deeper meanings of the literature. In many of her publications, Rosenblatt (1938, 1978) has suggested that readers confirm and/or deepen their responses by sharing and comparing their interpretations with others.

An essential guideline for leading literature discussion groups is that children must have a safe environment to talk about personal feelings, attitudes, and interpretations without fear of mockery from peers. You can support students' questioning and open reflection by offering a supportive environment within which to talk about books. Creating this respectful environment is vital to the success of your reader response instruction. Refer back to Chapter 2 for guidelines on how to create a supportive environment for student talk.

Finally, reader response practitioners make it clear that the teacher is not to be the "arbiter" of meaning while children are discussing works of literature. Children are to be encouraged to make personal responses, as long as they are able to provide text evidence to support their interpretations. Teaching children how to find text support is discussed later in this chapter, when we suggest pedagogy for teaching reader response principles.

Personal Response Journals

Perhaps the most prevalent reader response activity in the elementary classroom today is asking children to write in personal response journals after reading and discussing a story. There are two basic types of responses you can ask children to write in such journals.

The first type consists of "free" responses after discussions of stories. A free response means that a child is free to respond to any aspect of the text without constraints or a prompt from the teacher. Figure 9.1 provides examples of "free" journal responses from a third-grade classroom, and Figure 9.2 contains an older child's "free" journal entry in response to the book *Stone Fox* (Gardiner, 1980).

The second type of response is a more structured one. That is, children are asked to answer prompts, such as "What did the main character say or do in this story to make you like or dislike him or her?" This type of response to literature can be written in an ongoing journal or as a separate entity.

The remainder of this chapter is devoted to this second type of children's written responses to literature. Teaching children how to respond to a prompt is an important

---

Where the Wild Things Are by Maurice Sendak

The boy went on a big adventure. I like going on adventures.

Sometimes I get afraid of monsters like the boy in the story.

The Napping House by Audrey Woods

The boy left his bike out in the rain. I got into trouble
for doing that one time.

Charlotte's Web by E. B. White

I liked Wilbur because he is shy like me.

Charlotte is my favorite character because she is helpful.

I like Charlotte because she uses big words like my mom.

FIGURE 9.1. "Free" response journal entries by younger children.

Stone Fox
by John Reynolds Gardiner

I have just finished reading that Searchlight exerted himself so much during the
race that his heart burst. Searchlight knew how important it was that he and Little Willy
win the race so Searchlight sacrificed his own life. My heart hurt when I read the lines.
My own dog died last year of old age. It wasn't the same kind of death as Searchlight, but
I am sure that Little Willy felt the same way as I did. In the next chapter, I will see how
Little Willy is. I am sure I am going to understand his feelings because they are probably
very close to my own when I lost my dog.

Feelings when my dog died:

sad   Lonely

gloomy   Despair

Angry/Mad

FIGURE 9.2. "Free" response entry about *Stone Fox* (Gardiner, 1980) from an older child's journal.

skill to teach in the primary grades, for two reasons: (1) it provides an opportunity for children to lend their voices to literary interpretation, and (2) it allows opportunities to assess children's abilities to interpret and make personal connections to literature. You can read more about using journal writing to assess comprehension in Chapter 12.

We present a cognitive strategy and a model of a good written response on the following pages, to help guide your acquisition of the pedagogy associated with written responses to literature.

TEACHING CHILDREN TO CONSTRUCT WRITTEN RESPONSES TO LITERATURE: PROMPTS

In the last few years, many teachers have come to us for advice on how to teach children to construct a good written response to literature when presented with a specific prompt. State and national assessments now ask children to respond to a prompt in a written format. Here are some examples of common prompts:

As I read the story, I was reminded of . . . Because . . .
Compare the main character to yourself. How are you alike? Different?
What are the problems that the character _____ faced in the story, and how did he [or she] solve them?

We have experimented with teaching children to respond to prompts with a cognitive strategy that we have designed for this purpose. Although the strategy is helpful for children to remember the components of a good written response, it is not a substitute for teacher coaching and student practice. In our forays into written response composition, we have discovered that much can be accomplished through individual conferences with students. Following is a step-by-step outline for teaching children in grades 3–6 how to compose a written response. Later we demonstrate how to decrease the level of difficulty for younger or less experienced readers and writers.

Teaching the Elements of the Written Response Genre

We begin lessons in writing a specific genre by having children understand the nature of the piece they are about to write, or the *elements* that make up the genre. In this case, the genre we are teaching is the written response to literature. We always introduce the genre's elements and show children a model of the genre before we teach them how to write one.

The most important elements of a written response to literature include answering the prompt with details from the story; showing rather than telling; supporting the answer with evidence from the text; and using first- or third-person point of view. These elements are listed in Figure 9.3 in a classroom-ready format.

Perhaps you are puzzled as to why we suggest that young readers and writers must have *text evidence* to support their interpretations. Most response practitioners suggest that although readers should be allowed to freely express their reactions to text, we must also teach that subjective responses must be grounded in the text. As Rosenblatt (1995) has pointed out,

A good written response . . .

- Answers the prompt with details from the story.
- "Shows" the reader, instead of "telling."
- Provides clear evidence from the text that supports the answer. The evidence can be a quotation or a paraphrase of the text information.
- Uses first-person or third-person point of view consistently.

FIGURE 9.3. Elements of a good written response to literature.

From *Teaching Reading: Strategies and Resources for Grades K–6* by Rachel L. McCormack and Susan Lee Pasquarelli. Copyright 2010 by The Guilford Press. Permission to photocopy this figure is granted to purchasers of this book for personal use only (see copyright page for details).

When the focus of our teaching is the transaction between reader and book, such concerns do not lead away from the work into sheer emotionality and theorizing. The student scrutinizes the two-way circuit set up between himself and the literary work. He tests whether his particular personal response is justified, whether it has incorporated as adequately as possible what the printed page offers. (p. 70)

Asking children to tell how they arrived at an interpretation or a personal response is essential in teaching the act of responding. We can ask children, "How do you know that? Point to a line in the text that supports your idea." As Rosenblatt recommends in the passage quoted above, we must ask children to take a look at the "two-way circuit" between the text and their responses, and express that connection in their written compositions.

Our list of genre elements also includes writing a good response from either the first or the third person. Often children will start off writing in first person and switch to the second (e.g., "you understood"). This switching back and forth confuses the audience and children should be taught to fix this in the revision process. We believe children should be taught these writing techniques early in their development.

We also believe that elaboration in a written response helps students to deliver their message with detail and clarity. We teach elaboration as part of the process of *showing* the reader, as opposed to *telling* the reader. Often children will just put the main ideas down on paper. They need to be coached to elaborate with detail, as well as to provide evidence suggesting the connections between their interpretations and the text. Following is an example of a classroom chart we have used to illustrate the difference between showing and telling.

Show Your Reader, Don't Tell!

Telling: Tells the reader with no detail

> *Miyuki and Sophia planted a garden. Miyuki was a good gardener. Sophia was not. I am a good gardener, like Miyuki.*

Showing: <u>Shows</u> *the reader with much detail*

Miyuki and Sophia planted a beautiful garden in their backyard with many different flowers and plants. They planted lilies and roses, as well as lettuce and beans. Miyuki spent long hours caring for the plants by watering and weeding. Sophia was not such a good gardener and let the weeds grow around her plants. I am like Miyuki in the garden. I also plant string beans and lettuce. I water and weed the plants to help them grow.

Other elements of a good written response to literature may depend upon your school's literacy curriculum. We have not included such obvious elements as a strong organizational structure or grade-level application of the English language conventions, which we require for all written compositions.

Showing a Written Response Model

As suggested earlier, once children understand the elements of a response, we then show them a model. Figure 9.4 shows the composition of a third grader that contains all the elements of a good response to literature. The response is based on *The Last Puppy* (Asch, 1980), which is an enchanting tale about the runt of a large litter of puppies. The story is told from the point of view of this puppy, who ruins every opportunity to be adopted by being too eager with the families who come to the farm seeking a puppy. For example, when a beautiful woman comes to adopt one of the puppies, the runt gets so excited that when she picks him up, he bites her on the nose. After many trials, our puppy is the "last puppy" of the litter and is heartbroken. Finally, a family with a little boy comes to the farm and adopts the puppy. In the car on the way home, the little boy kisses the "last puppy" and says, "You know what? You are my first puppy!"

Now that you know the gist of the story, turn to Figure 9.4 and read the prompt and the sample response. While you read the response, keep an eye out for the elements of

---

The prompt:

The story *The Last Puppy*, by Frank Asch, is about a puppy who wants to be adopted. Can you think of an event in your life when you felt left out?

The response from a third grader:

<u>The Last Puppy</u>, by Frank Asch, was about a puppy who was so sad because no one wanted him. He tried and tried to be adopted. When someone came to adopt a puppy, he would act silly and the people picked a different puppy. I can think of one time when I felt like the last puppy. My friends and I were playing baseball. Sara and Billy took turns choosing teams. I was just like the puppy and acted silly. I jumped up and down and said, "Pick me! Pick me!" They did not pick me. I felt sad like the last puppy. They picked other kids to play first. I was just like the last puppy because they picked me last.

FIGURE 9.4. Prompt for, and model response to, *The Last Puppy* (Asch, 1980).

a good response that we have presented above. Notice that our third grader's composition has a personal connection backed up with text evidence; is written in consistent first person; and shows the reader (through elaboration of the event in the writer's life), as opposed to simply telling the reader that the event happened. These elements are essential to the success of a good response.

Components of a Written Response

Next, we need to take a look at the components of a response. Examine the response to *The Last Puppy* as we have annotated it for you in Figure 9.5, and notice that there are four clear parts:

1. Summary of the part of the story to which the personal connection is made.
2. The personal connection, or the answer to the prompt.
3. Direct evidence—tying the personal connection (answer) to the text by using a quote from the text.
4. More direct evidence—tying the personal connection (answer) to the text by paraphrasing the text.

The response format shown above and in Figure 9.5 is one that we prefer, but you can make up your own format, depending upon the age and skill of the readers and

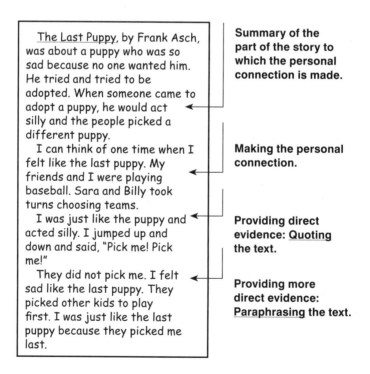

The Last Puppy, by Frank Asch, was about a puppy who was so sad because no one wanted him. He tried and tried to be adopted. When someone came to adopt a puppy, he would act silly and the people picked a different puppy.

I can think of one time when I felt like the last puppy. My friends and I were playing baseball. Sara and Billy took turns choosing teams.

I was just like the puppy and acted silly. I jumped up and down and said, "Pick me! Pick me!"

They did not pick me. I felt sad like the last puppy. They picked other kids to play first. I was just like the last puppy because they picked me last.

Summary of the part of the story to which the personal connection is made.

Making the personal connection.

Providing direct evidence: <u>Quoting</u> the text.

Providing more direct evidence: <u>Paraphrasing</u> the text.

FIGURE 9.5. Identification of elements of a good written response.

writers in your classroom. Your school or district officials may even suggest a format that they prefer. As we have mentioned in previous chapters, the way in which you teach any literacy lesson to your class will depend upon three variables: (1) the grade level of your class; (2) your class's current skill level; and (3) the text difficulty, including plot rigor and the characters' level of sophistication. To accommodate these variables, you will find it necessary to experiment with your teaching strategies.

Once children understand the genre's elements and the format of a good response, it is time to teach them how to gather information to compose their own responses.

Gathering Information for the Response

We teach the steps for gathering information for the response with tools you have become familiar with in previous chapters of this text: a graphic organizer and a cognitive strategy. Figure 9.6 (page 196) outlines a cognitive strategy that we have used successfully for older children in grades 5–6. While you investigate this overall strategy, direct your attention to two areas. First, note that we ask children to do a second close reading of the text, to help identify their answer to the prompt. Second, notice that we ask our writers to use a graphic organizer as a "planning step" in their writing. Once students have recorded the ideas in the graphic organizer, they have a blueprint for writing their responses. Our final teaching steps involve modeling how to compose a response, using the graphic organizer as a support.

Modeling How to Compose the Written Response

At the bottom of Figure 9.6, you will find the final three strategy steps for the act of composing the response. We ask children to summarize the part of the story that led to their answer to the prompt; next, we ask them to describe their answer or personal connection with elaboration and detail; finally, we ask them to provide text evidence to support their response. Remember that a strategy is a heuristic, or a guideline, to help readers or writers with their thinking processes as they engage in a new skill. The strategy steps we have provided for you may need to be adapted to fit the type of response you are asking children to write.

The lesson proceeds with modeling and providing a think-aloud of your strategy application. As in all strategies, the essential ingredient is the explicitness of your explanation during modeling, followed by multiple guided practices as children attempt to acquire the new skill. Be patient, provide solid feedback to each of your writers, and encourage revision. As your students' skill in writing responses grows, so too will their confidence in writing responses in the classroom and on state and national tests.

Teaching Written Responses to Younger Children

For emergent readers and writers, much of the reader response curriculum can be delivered orally. In particular, kindergartners may be inexperienced writers, so you can use a prompt to elicit oral responses after a read-aloud. For example, you can ask the following questions:

Steps for Gathering Information for a Written Response to Literature

1. **Read** the story for enjoyment and basic understanding.
2. **Read** the prompt, and think about what the prompt is asking you to do.
3. **Think about** your answer to the prompt. Can you think of an answer off the top of your head?
4. **Do a "close reading"** of the text, searching for your answer and/or evidence from the text that supports your answer.
   While rereading, remember to use your good-reader strategies.
   You can highlight the text, use sticky notes, or write in the margins of the text to mark the important information you need to answer the prompt.
5. During the close reading, **continue** to ask yourself the questions pertaining to the prompt, and record your direct answers to the prompt in a graphic organizer similar to the one below. You may have multiple answers to the prompt.

My answer(s)	Evidence from the text in my own words	Page number/line

6. **Choose** the answer that has the most—or the best—text evidence to support it.
7. **Compose** your written response from information you have included in the graphic organizer.

Steps for Composing a Written Response

1. **Summarize** the part of the story that leads to your answer to the prompt.
2. **Describe** your answer with elaboration and detail.
3. **Provide text evidence**, either by paraphrasing the part of the text that supports your answer or by quoting from the text.

FIGURE 9.6. Steps of the strategy for gathering information and composing a written response.

- "Has anyone ever felt left out of an event, the way the last puppy does?"
- "Has anyone had a dog that had a litter of puppies? If so, do you think one of the puppies may have felt like the last puppy?"

When you are determining prompts appropriate for your young readers and writers, try to create prompts that are easily tied back or connected to the text. It is never too early to teach children to think about responses that are grounded in the text. For example, if you ask children to tell you whether they have ever felt like the puppy in the book *The Last Puppy*, they may begin to relate many types of unhappy events, such as "I felt sad when my grandmother died," or "I felt sad when my friend went away." Such responses are not necessarily grounded in the text. A more appropriate response to the prompt might be "I felt like the last puppy when I was the last to be chosen to play baseball at recess." In order to help younger readers make the two-way transaction, you should always encourage them to connect their responses to the text events.

Designing Prompts and Guiding Responses

Using Graphic Organizers to Guide Responses

We have found that the ways in which we ask readers to connect to text can help keep their responses grounded in text or can have the opposite effect. For example, consider the graphic organizers we have designed for response activities in Figures 9.7 (page 198) and 9.8 (page 199). Notice that we have set up the graphic organizers to help readers stay within the text boundaries by guiding their responses. Instead of asking students simply to respond to an open prompt, we also provide them with practice in designing graphic organizers to respond to specific plot elements, maybe first as a book character and then as themselves. In other words, we ask them to make a response from the text and then to make a parallel response themselves. As you experiment with designing reader response activities, you will learn how best to lead your students to a good oral or written response to literature.

More Ideas for Prompts

We have used the following prompts in classroom settings with positive results, depending upon students' ability levels.

Personal Connections

- What feelings did you experience while reading what took place in the following event: _____?
- During the text reading, did you recall a memory? What was it? Why did the text help you to remember it?
- What confused you in the text?
- Is there an event in the text that you have experienced in your life?
- How are you like the character _____?
- How are you unlike the character _____?

Thinking about how I am similar to and different from the book characters

Characters in _____ Book name	How I am like this character	How I am different from this character
_____ Character name		
_____ Character name		

Thinking about how my school is the same as or different from the school in the story

	The school in the story	My school
My classroom		
Our special subjects		
Sports		

FIGURE 9.7. Reader response graphic organizers for young readers and writers.

Comparing Book Setting with Readers' Setting

	Place	Time
BOOK/CHAPTER:		
MY LIFE		

Comparing Characters' Problems with Readers' Problems

	Character	Problem(s) shared	Solution(s) shared
BOOK/CHAPTER:			
MY LIFE			

FIGURE 9.8. Reader response graphic organizers for older readers and writers.

Comparing Responses with Friends

- What meaning did your peers see in the story? Do you agree with them?
- Did the class discussion today cause you to change your understanding of the text? If so, how? And why?

Elements of Setting

- Why do you suppose the author created the setting for the book the way he or she did?
- What impact did the setting have on the story?
- What is the influence of the setting on the mood of the story?

Elements of Plot

- If you were a character in the book, what event would have been different?
- What events do you think were most important to the story?
- Did you ever see a movie version of this text? If so, how was it different? Which version did you like better, and why?

Elements of Character

- Were you especially interested in a specific character in the story? Why?
- Do you share a particular culture with a character? Describe the connection between you and the character.
- Is your culture very different from that of the main characters? If so, describe the differences.
- What is a specific character's motivation to do what he or she does in _____ scene? How would you have acted in his or her place?
- What is the conflict between two characters? Have you ever experienced the same conflict with a friend or family member?

Elements of Theme

- The character _____ made choices in this story that created problems for him or her. How would this story have been different if you were the main character?
- What message about life did the story suggest?

This chapter has provided only a glimpse of the possibilities for literature instruction in your elementary classroom. We hope you will investigate further such possibilities, as well as possibilities for your own growth as a reader and literacy instructor. It only takes one enthusiastic teacher to entice a whole host of children to become lifelong readers and writers.

FINAL THOUGHTS

Remember our Irving tale at the beginning of this chapter? It has an epilogue. Ten years after we read the Irving book, while we were sitting in a café in Siracusa, Sicily, on a January afternoon, I (SLP) narrated my Irving story to my coauthor (RLM), who was sitting by my side working on Chapter 2 of this book. We were once again reminded of the importance of providing opportunities for young readers to "live through" an engaging story, reflect and write personal responses, share those responses with others, and finally confirm or transform their own personal interpretations.

In the following chapter, we consider using multicultural literature to explore diverse themes and topics. The chapter also helps us to think about how to create a classroom context that supports a culturally responsive community of learners.

Now we invite you to assess your knowledge of key terms from this chapter, which we present in Figure 9.9 (page 202).

REFLECTION ON ARTIFACTS FOR YOUR SELF-STUDY

For your self-study, record on Figure 9.10 (page 203) the artifacts you created while you read this chapter.

KEY TERMS FOR CHAPTER 9

In this chapter, the following key terms are essential to your understanding of reading instruction. Think about what they mean, and try to define them in your own words.

reader response theory

aesthetic stance

efferent stance

personal connections

personal response journals

written responses to literature

text evidence

FIGURE 9.9. Key Terms Chart for Chapter 9.

SELF-STUDY REVIEW CHART FOR CHAPTER 9

Name of Artifact	Teacher Instructional Actions and Language	Provisions for Individual Differences	Variety of Modes of Communication	Critical Thinking and Active Engagement	Opportunities for Assessment

FIGURE 9.10. Self-Study Review Chart for Chapter 9

From *Teaching Reading: Strategies and Resources for Grades K–6* by Rachel L. McCormack and Susan Lee Pasquarelli. Copyright 2010 by The Guilford Press. Permission to photocopy this figure is granted to purchasers of this book for personal use only (see copyright page for details).

CHAPTER 10

Creating a Culturally Responsive Classroom Community

Aaron, a third-grade urban teacher, was preparing a reading lesson using the book *A Strong Right Arm: The Story of Mamie "Peanut" Johnson* (Green, 2002). Mamie was one of three African American women who played professional baseball for the so-called "Negro Leagues" in the 1950s. The book chronicles her life, from growing up with an absent mother to her experiences in attempting to gain access to male baseball leagues. As Aaron prepared his lesson, he considered how best to teach his reading lesson while considering the book's themes of racial segregation, gender inequality, and poverty.

The lesson he designed began with a shared reading of the first few chapters. As he read aloud to the whole class, Aaron taught his students how to identify a character's goal. He did this by asking them how they might set goals for themselves. He then asked students to work in small groups to identify Mamie's goal, which was to become a professional baseball player.

In a subsequent lesson, again in a shared reading format, Aaron asked his students to read with the purpose of identifying cultural obstacles that potentially prevented Mamie from accomplishing her goal. Together, students identified the following obstacles: poverty, gender, race, size, age, and a few other cultural elements. As students identified each obstacle, Aaron wrote each on a paper brick wall he had created on his whiteboard (see Figure 10.1). As they continued to read chapters, Aaron focused the reading purpose on identifying ways that Mamie was able to overcome her obstacles and "break down her wall." As the students pointed out each obstacle that Mamie managed to overcome, Aaron cut away the corresponding brick from the paper wall. Finally, he probed further by asking his students to identify how Mamie was able to overcome these obstacles.

Once the book was completed, as a culminating activity, Aaron asked the students to identify their own goals and build a "wall" of the obstacles (bricks) they would have to overcome to achieve their goals. As students completed their own "walls," he was not surprised to find that the conversations quickly turned toward whole-class problem solving for each other's cultural obstacles. Aaron was hopeful that the simple act of embedding cultural elements in his reading program would help the children in his classroom become sensitive to and respect each other's cultural diversity.

FIGURE 10.1. Mamie's "wall" of obstacles.

As Aaron experimented with building a culturally responsive classroom community, he understood that he could simultaneously maintain his rigorous academic reading program. This chapter describes a classroom context that is culturally responsive, works toward building a community of learners, and is suitable for the teaching of best-practice reading instruction.

BEST PRACTICES YOU WILL SEE IN THIS CHAPTER

Creating a culturally responsive classroom by:

✓ Building parent involvement in the reading program.

✓ Using multicultural books in the reading program.

✓ Creating lessons for teaching children about their own cultural identities and those of others.

WHAT IS CULTURALLY RESPONSIVE TEACHING?

Culturally responsive teaching has been defined and described by many multicultural educators and practitioners. We like the following definition: "Culturally Responsive Teaching is a pedagogy that recognizes the importance of including students' cultural references in all aspects of learning" (Ladson-Billings, 1994, p. 29). This broad, uncomplicated definition identifies the most important principle underlying culturally responsive pedagogy: It encompasses "*all* aspects of learning" (our emphasis).

So what do culturally responsive teaching and learning look like in a reading curriculum? Most researchers and practitioners agree that classrooms meeting the

Ladson-Billings definition share several characteristics. We have chosen to focus on a few of these characteristics that can be included in the reading curriculum. A culturally responsive reading curriculum does the following:

1. Builds positive home–school experiences (Gay, 2000; Nieto, 1996).
2. Incorporates multicultural text, information, and resources (Gay, 2000; Ladson-Billings, 1994; Nieto, 1996).
3. Teaches students about other students' cultural heritages, and shows them how to respect differences (Gay, 2000; Ladson-Billings, 1994; Nieto, 1996).

In the rest of this chapter, we define each of these characteristics, and we provide concrete ideas and activities to help you establish a culturally responsive reading curriculum.

BUILDING POSITIVE HOME–SCHOOL EXPERIENCES

Research suggests that families from all cultural backgrounds, education levels, and income levels encourage and talk to their children about school and keep them focused on learning and homework (Bowen & Bowen, 1998). Researchers have also investigated home–school partnership programs and similar interventions that engage families in supporting their children's learning at home (Melzi, Paratore, & Krol-Sinclair, 2000; Paratore, Melzi, & Krol-Sinclair, 2003). The overall results from these programs or interventions are clear. Home–school partnerships are linked to the following:

1. Higher student achievement (Dearing, McCartney, Weiss, Kreider, & Simpkins, 2004; Henderson, 1987).
2. Improved teacher, parent, and child attitudes (Ensle, 1996; Epstein, 1986).
3. Reduced dropout rates (Henderson & Berla, 1994).
4. Increased attendance (Henderson, 1987).
5. Improved student self-esteem, motivation, and behavior (Haynes, Comer, & Hamilton-Lee, 1989).

The Harvard Family Research Project has disseminated research on parent involvement programs (*www.gse.harvard.edu/hfrp*) and is a wealth of information for classroom teachers. Practitioners within the project suggest that *effective* parent involvement programs that engage diverse families must recognize, respect, and address cultural and class differences (Bouffard & Weiss, 2008). Following is a list of routines you can establish in your classroom to support home–school partnerships that promote reading engagement.

Conducting Parent Workshops

Effective practices for home–school partnerships include parent workshops in which teachers model for parents the type of talk used during reading instruction. For example, you can conduct an after-school or evening workshop for parents in which you model how to do a read-aloud. You can demonstrate how to read with expression, how to ask questions, and how to encourage children to predict what may come next. Parents can then have a "guided practice" by reading aloud to each other. You can conduct parent workshops on many other topics, including these:

- How to assist children with reading homework.
- How to help children with independent reading.
- How to help children choose appropriate books in the library.
- How to model fluency during parent–child storybook reading.

Sharing Assessment Tips

At open-house events, home visits, and parent information sessions during or outside of the school day, you can organize events to assist parents in learning how to use and interpret the results of the informal classroom assessment instruments. You can share key tools, rubrics, grading criteria, or strategies to help family members determine whether a child is successful in learning. You can also encourage parents to ask you how their children are doing and whether or not they need more help at home.

Engaging Family Members and Students in Reading Activities

You can invite parents and children for a special evening devoted to promoting reading. For this event, you can design new interactive activity centers or use those you have already created for daily instruction. Parents enjoy participating in phonics and comprehension activities, readers' theatre activities, and any other centers designed to reinforce the good-reader strategies. In turn, children are proud to show their parents what they can do, and enjoy working with them in the centers. Your goal for this type of home–school program is to thoughtfully connect the evening's activities to your daily classroom instruction, and ultimately to the home.

Creating Special Learning Kits to Lend to Students for Home Use

Family project kits can be made of inexpensive materials and organized for students to "check out." Following are some of the more successful kits we have designed:

- *Family storybook reading kit*—contains books to share with the whole family through readers' theatre activities.
- *Cultural history project kit*—contains instructions for writing a simple family cultural history, including a family tree.
- *Supermarket scavenger hunt kit*—contains instructions for parents to assist children in using reading skills in the supermarket.

Parents, family–school organizations, or community service organizations can help you assemble and maintain these kits. To be most useful, kits should include clear directions and should be tied to key learning events in the classroom.

Informing Parents of Activities in Your Classroom

Invite parents to attend oral presentations, class plays, author's chair, or any other "sharing" activities in your classroom. Parents enjoy seeing their children participate, and your whole class will love having a family audience. Invite parents to be volunteers in your classroom to help with book selection, a writing workshop publishing center, daily read-alouds, or just the management of school tasks.

Integrating Family Culture and Experiences into the Curriculum

Finally, you can expand your reading curriculum to include books by and about members of the many different cultures represented in your classroom. Parents can be involved by suggesting and sharing culturally specific books, presenting various aspects of their culture to your class, or just spending a half hour in your classroom reading aloud a book that represents their culture. This is an easy way to identify and share resources on students' family cultural identities.

INCORPORATING MULTICULTURAL LITERATURE INTO YOUR CLASSROOM

Defining Multicultural Literature

Multicultural literature refers to literature by and about members of groups considered to be outside the sociopolitical mainstream of the United States (Harris, 1992). This definition includes books written by and about members of ethnic minorities and/or non-mainstream ethnic groups, as well as by members of various other cultures—including persons with mental and physical challenges, gay/lesbian/bisexual/transgender populations, and alternative families. We take the position that every classroom in America should be well stocked with multicultural literature, so children have opportunities to read about themselves and the many cultures prevalent in our society. We do not advocate excluding books by and about mainstream Americans, including European Americans and other nonminorities; rather, we support a balance. It is our experience that American classrooms primarily use books featuring nonminorities throughout the reading program. Therefore, the following section of this chapter includes information on how to balance your classroom libraries and reading curriculum with multicultural literature.

Choosing Multicultural Literature

When you are choosing multicultural literature for your classroom, we advocate finding and choosing *culturally specific* literature and expository text (Harris, 1992). Culturally specific texts describe a particular culture with detail and elaboration. The details make the characters, events, or facts compelling and interesting. The specific details can include the names of characters; the forms of address for parents; the values and attitudes of the characters; and clear physical descriptions, either through the text or through the illustrations (Harris, 1992). According to Harris, culturally specific literature may include some or all of the following particulars:

1. Family relationships, interactions, and values.
2. Social interactions, customs, and interests.
3. Attitudes and behaviors.
4. Religious beliefs and practices.
5. Language dialects and participation structures.
6. Art and music preferences.
7. Geographic backgrounds and ways of life.

An example of a very popular culturally specific book is *Amazing Grace* (Hoffman, 1991). The story is about a young African American girl who loves to read, act, and make up stories. When her school plans to put on a production of *Peter Pan*, Grace wants to try out for the leading role. Trouble ensues once Grace makes her intentions known to her classmates. One of her friends says that she cannot be Peter Pan because she is a girl. Another classmate tells her that she cannot do this because she is Black.

When Grace goes home and tells her mother and grandmother what the other children have said, her family is displeased and tells Grace that she can be anything she wants to be. Then her grandmother proves her point by taking Grace to a production of *Romeo and Juliet* featuring a Trinidadian dancer. That gives Grace all the confidence she needs. She tries out for the part, and, of course, she becomes Peter Pan in the school's production.

We categorize this book as culturally specific because it gives readers an inside view of Grace's culture. The story contains details about Grace's family life, values, and attitudes, as well as a glimpse into how children are encouraged to pursue their dreams in her culture. Grace is a strong character with intelligence and drive, who is beginning to understand her own cultural identity.

Another point to consider when choosing multicultural literature is to read widely and investigate the authors' sources of information. Many multicultural educators suggest that books written by authors from the ethnicity or culture represented provide a helpful first-hand look at the cultural norms. Reading multicultural literature by "insiders" helps you and your students to recognize recurring themes that distinguish the body of literature from specific cultural groups. In addition, wide reading makes the differences between typical "insider" and "outsider" perspectives clear (Harris, 1992).

Remember that when you are choosing multicultural literature, a book of fiction should be well written, with strong characters and a compelling, meaningful theme. Good nonfiction should be up to date and accurate, with interesting illustrations, photographs, and other graphics. To help you choose multicultural literature for your classroom, refer to Figure 10.2 (page 210) for multicultural selection guidelines suggested by Harris (1992). In Figure 10.3 (page 211), we provide lists of our favorite culturally specific books for the K–6 reading program.

TEACHING STUDENTS ABOUT EACH OTHER'S CULTURAL HERITAGES AND WAYS TO RESPECT DIFFERENCES

Whether you teach in an urban, suburban, or rural environment, all students will benefit from reading and thinking about people from diverse cultures. In our work with (and as) teachers in schools, we have discovered that there are two clear components

Category	Information to evaluate
Author's attitude and language	• **The ways in which nonmainstream characters are depicted as part of a larger society.** Be sure that nonmainstream characters' contributions are as significant as those of the mainstream characters. • **The ways in which nonmainstream characters are depicted as part of their own group.** Be sure the author presents each character as a unique individual. • **Descriptions of characters' actions and behaviors.** Be sure the characters' actions and behaviors are not stereotypical in nature. • **Overall language.** Be sure that there are no historically racist terms that suggest a negative connotation, or terms that might offend a member of the culture.
Characters' language	• **Overall language.** Be sure the characters' language is appropriate to the historical time and place as well as the social situation in which the characters are placed. • **Characters' speech patterns.** If characters use the vernacular, check for accuracy and authenticity.
Illustrations	• **Accuracy.** Examine pictures for stereotypical images of characters. • **Authenticity.** Be sure the illustrations do not make every character look alike.

FIGURE 10.2. Multicultural literature selection guidelines. Based on Harris (1992).

to using multicultural literature. First, we must have students think about their own cultural identities. In order to understand differences and similarities, students must understand the elements that make up their own cultural backgrounds. Once students have a basic understanding of their own cultural identities, we can then have them read and engage with characters from different backgrounds. We examine each component below.

Exploring Students' Own Cultural Identities

With children in grades 3–6, we have been successful in using the frame for organizing cultural identity that was originally developed by Banks (2007). Banks is considered the "father" of multicultural education. Using this frame for what constitutes a culture, we engage the children in three separate inquiry lessons designed to help them examine culture and think about their own cultural identities. The following lessons set the stage for intriguing reading and conversations about diverse cultures.

LESSON 1: HELPING CHILDREN DEFINE CULTURE

Lesson: What is culture?

Lesson Text: None

Lesson Grade Levels: 3–6

Lesson Objective: Students will demonstrate an understanding of the definition of culture.

Books for Grades K–3	Books for Grades 3–4	Books for Grades 4–6
The Other Side Author: Woodson, Jacqueline	*Teammates* Author: Golenbock, Peter	*The Magic Paintbrush* Author: Yep, Lawrence
Show Way Author: Woodson, Jacqueline	*Baseball Saved Us* Author: Mochizuki, Ken	*Felita* Author: Mohr, Nicholasa
Amazing Grace Author: Hoffman, Mary	*A Strong Right Arm: The Story of Mamie "Peanut" Johnson* Author: Green, Michelle	*A Single Shard* Author: Park, Linda Sue
Starring Grace Author: Hoffman, Mary	*Coming to America* Author: Maestro, Betsy	*The Land I Lost* Author: Nhuong, Huynh Quang
Sam and the Lucky Money Author: Chinn, Karen	*Martin Luther King, Jr. and the March on Washington* Author: Ruffin, Frances E.	*Julie of the Wolves* Author: George, Jean Craighead
Abuela's Weave Author: Casteneda, Omar S.	*Julian, Dream Doctor* Author: Cameron, Ann	*Locomotion* Author: Woodson, Jacqueline
Butterflies for Kiri Author: Falwell, Cathryn	*The Ghost Dance* Author: McLerran, Alice	*Walk Two Moons* Author: Creech, Sharon
The Pot That Juan Built Author: Andrews-Goebel, Nancy	*Sadako and the Thousand Paper Cranes* Author: Coerr, Eleanor	*Mulberry Project* Author: Park, Linda Sue
Sweet Potato Pie Author: Lindsey, Kathleen D.	*Peace Begins with You* Author: Scholes, Katherine	*Esperanza Rising* Author: Ryan, Pam Munoz
Goldfish and Chrysanthemums Author: Cheng, Andrea	*The Royal Bee* Authors: Park, Frances, and Park, Ginger	*Bad Boy* Author: Myers, Walter Dean
Abuela Author: Dorros, Arthur	*Borreguita and the Coyote: A Tale from Ayutla, Mexico* Author: Retold by Aardema, Verna	*The Story of Muhammad Ali* Author: Garrett, Leslie
A Birthday Basket for Tia Author: Mora, Pat	*Fire Race: A Karuk Coyote Tale about How Fire Came to the People* Author: Retold by London, Jonathan	*Pablo Remembers* Author: Ancona, George
Too Many Tamales Author: Soto, Gary		*A Suitcase of Seaweed* Author: Wong, Janet
		Yolanda's Genius Author: Fenner, Carol
		Kira-Kira Author: Kadohata, Cynthia
		Yang the Eldest and His Odd Jobs Author: Namioka, Lensey
		Dia's Story Cloth Author: Cha, Dia
		The Devil's Arithmetic Author: Yolen, Jane
		Talking Walls Author: Knight, Margy Burns
		The Old African Author: Lester, Julius
		Going Home Author: Mohr, Nicholasa
		Roll of Thunder, Hear My Cry Author: Taylor, Mildred
		The Kite Fighter Author: Park, Linda Sue

FIGURE 10.3. Culturally specific books for your reading program.

Procedure: To begin the lesson, start drawing a web on the whiteboard and ask children to help you to complete the web. The center of the web should look like this:

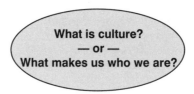

Then say:

"Today, children, we are going to think about what makes us who we are. Does anyone know what the word *culture* means?"

Older children may respond, but younger children may not have a response. With both older and younger children, continue with a general definition and more prompting questions:

"Culture has to do with our family background and traditions, such as where we come from and where we live. It describes the things that make us who we are. For example, I know that my family is from Italy. So that is my family's country of origin, or ethnic background, or *ethnicity*. I am going to add *ethnicity* to my web. Can you think of other things that make us who we are?"

Continue to fill in the web with students' responses until your web looks like that in Figure 10.4. The vocabulary in your web will obviously reflect your students' ages and ability levels. Once you have exhausted all possible responses, your goal is for the students to understand that people's cultures help to shape their beliefs, values, attitudes, and ways of life.

FIGURE 10.4. What is culture? Based on Banks (2007).

LESSONS 2 AND 3: HELPING CHILDREN THINK ABOUT THEIR CULTURAL IDENTITIES

Lesson: Making my own cultural pie

Lesson Text: None

Lesson Grade Levels: 3–6

Lesson Objective: Students will demonstrate understanding of their own cultural identities.

Procedure: This lesson is designed for students to explore their own cultural identities by making *cultural pies* (Barton, 2001). Figure 10.5 shows a completed cultural pie. We suggest that you model making your own cultural pie while you think aloud about what makes you who you are. Creating the pie is a two-step process. First, using the categories from the "What is culture?" web (Figure 10.4), identify the categories that define you best. Second, think about each category, and identify what percentage of "you" is invested in each category. Then guide students in creating their own pies. When they have made their pies, encourage them to share them with each other. We know that children love this activity—especially the final segment, the "share," as students get to know more about themselves and each other. An extension of this activity is to have students make cultural pies for book characters and compare the characters' cultures to their own. (For more information on using cultural pies with children's literature, see Barton, 2001.)

Lesson: Making my culture box

Lesson Text: None

Lesson Grade Levels: K–6

Lesson Objective: Students will demonstrate understanding of their own cultural identity.

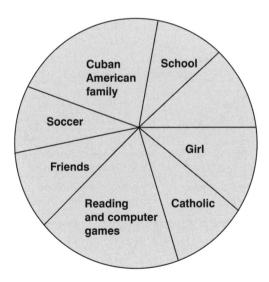

FIGURE 10.5. An example of a cultural pie.

Procedure: This lesson is an extension of the previous two lessons, but it can be used as a stand-alone cultural identity lesson for very young children. One of our graduate students extended the cultural pie activity to create this follow-up lesson. We have found that students reach a deeper understanding of their own cultural identities and appreciate them more after they create these culture boxes.

This three-step activity is simple to implement and to share. For the first step, ask your students to find five objects at home that best represent who they are, and to place them in a box that they decorate. Older children who have experienced Lessons 1 and 2 can be instructed to use their cultural pies as guidelines for what they should place in their culture boxes. You will have to give younger children (those in grades K–2) ideas about what to put in their culture boxes, since this is their first introduction to culture and cultural identity. For example, you can encourage them to choose a favorite book if they are avid readers, or a favorite pen if they love to write. You can suggest that to represent their families or their ethnicities, they can bring in photographs of their families or a symbol of traditions they share. Here are some of the items we have seen in culture boxes:

- Photographs of favorite activities, families, friends, and club activities
- Computer games
- Sports memorabilia (pennants, clothing, etc.)
- Wooden spoons or other kitchen tools to represent their cooking traditions
- Favorite games or toys
- An ethnic piece of clothing
- Religious objects

Encourage the children to decorate their culture boxes as symbols of their cultural identities. Figure 10.6 is a photograph of a few completed culture boxes.

The second step of the activity takes place once students have assembled their culture boxes. Ask them to fill out a matrix such as the one below to explain their objects. The last box, entitled "Classmates who shared a similar object," is left blank until the third step of this activity.

MY CULTURE BOX			
Object	Culture category	Why it is important to me	Classmates who shared a similar object
Computer game	Hobby and special interests	This is my favorite computer game. I play it with many friends after school.	| | | |
Yarmulke	Religion and gender	Symbol of my Jewish heritage and being a boy.	|

FIGURE 10.6. Examples of culture boxes.

The third step of the activity, "the sharing," begins by having each child share one object and tell why the object is a symbol of who he or she is. As children share, have them place a tally mark in the last box to identify classmates who have similar cultural objects. Since it takes a long time for children to share their five objects, you can follow up by placing the culture boxes in a learning center where students can share with smaller groups of children.

Through these activities, children investigate their own cultural identities and those of their classmates, and they will be in a better position to compare their identities to those of book characters. By exploring friends and book characters from diverse cultures, children will better understand the diverse world in which they live.

In the following section, we present suggestions for lessons based on multicultural literature. Each lesson is easily adapted to different grade levels and multicultural books.

Identifying and Comparing Book Characters' Cultural Characteristics

We have been experimenting very successfully with developing cultural lessons in K–6 classrooms. Through this work, we have come to know that once children start to understand culture, they engage in discussions about race, ethnicity, religion, and gender with remarkable maturity. We only need to give them the context and the vocabulary for doing so.

Following are some of the graphic organizers that we have used to initiate discussions about culture. From these cultural graphic organizers, you can see that we ask children to use their reading comprehension strategies to extract information about book events, characters, and themes, and then compare them to their own cultural information. These culturally responsive lessons are easily embedded in our reading programs and do not detract from our focus of teaching the reading curriculum.

For each of the following suggested lessons, we present only the graphic organizer that is the focus of the *during*-reading portion of a lesson. We leave it up to you to determine the *before*- and *after*-reading activities, because these will depend upon the multicultural book you are using and the grade level you are teaching.

The first lesson idea is a simple matrix (see Figure 10.7), similar to one we have presented in Chapter 4, asking students to gather information about a character's cul-

	Ethnicity	Gender	Hobbies	Family Traditions	Religious Beliefs
Book: Character:					
Me					

FIGURE 10.7. Matrix for a lesson on comparing a book character's cultural identity to your own. **Lesson Objective:** Students will demonstrate understanding of a character's cultural identity and how it is different from their own.

tural identity. You can see that students will have to use their good-reader strategies to extract the information needed. Students complete the activity by recording the same information for themselves. The fully recorded matrix provides high-quality information for cultural comparisons, which can be explored further in literature circles or whole-group discussions.

The second lesson (see Figure 10.8 on page 218) gives students opportunities to compare book characters' cultural identities. This lesson is best implemented after the students have read two to three multicultural books with very different characters.

The third lesson (see Figure 10.9 on page 219) is designed to encourage students to be thoughtful about a book character's cultural characteristics. We successfully used this lesson idea with students as young as second grade, working in a whole-class format. However, older children are more able to work individually or in small cooperative groups to complete the task.

FINAL THOUGHTS

This chapter is meant to be a short introduction to culturally responsive teaching and using multicultural literature to teach children about cultural diversity. We hope that it will be a catalyst for further exploration of how you can become a culturally responsive teacher. We end this chapter with questions to help you self-assess your introduction to creating a culturally responsive classroom community. Take a few minutes to jot down the answers to the questions. This too can be an artifact for your self-study. In addition, as always, we suggest that you assess your knowledge of key terms by using the chart designed for that purpose (Figure 10.10 on page 220).

Culturally Responsive Teaching Reflection Questions

- What are some effective ways for teachers to learn about their students' cultural backgrounds and experiences?
- How can teachers have students explore their own cultural identities?
- What are effective ways to explore diverse cultures, using multicultural children's books?

At this point, we have presented a great deal of research and practice on the elementary reading curriculum, including creating contexts and literate environments for your reading program. The next two chapters are about assessing your students' motivation and their reading abilities in all areas of the curriculum: phonological/phonemic awareness, phonics, fluency, vocabulary, comprehension, and reader response.

REFLECTION ON ARTIFACTS FOR YOUR SELF-STUDY

For your self-study, record on Figure 10.11 (page 221) the artifacts you created while you read this chapter.

Character/Book	Race/ethnicity	Traditions	Daily activities
Grace *Boundless Grace* by Mary Hoffman			
Tree-Ear *A Single Shard* by Linda Sue Park			
Esperanza *Esperanza Rising* by Pam Munoz Ryan			
Character from Independent Reading Book:			

FIGURE 10.8. Matrix for a lesson on comparing cultural backgrounds of book characters. **Lesson Objective:** Students will compare the cultural backgrounds of characters from diverse cultures.

Book Event:	Character's Problem:	Character's Solution:	Given your culture, how would your solution have been different?	Why?
Book Event:				
Book Event:				

FIGURE 10.9. Matrix for a lesson on the influence of culture on a character's problem solving. **Lesson Objective**: Students will demonstrate understanding of how a character's problem solving is influenced by culture.

KEY TERMS FOR CHAPTER 10

In this chapter, the following key terms are essential to your understanding of reading instruction. Think about what they mean, and try to define them in your own words.

culturally responsive classroom

home–school experiences

multicultural literature

culturally specific literature

cultural identity

cultural pie

culture box

FIGURE 10.10. Key Terms Chart for Chapter 10.

SELF-STUDY REVIEW CHART FOR CHAPTER 10

Name of Artifact	Teacher Instructional Actions and Language	Provisions for Individual Differences	Variety of Modes of Communication	Critical Thinking and Active Engagement	Opportunities for Assessment

FIGURE 10.11. Self-Study Review Chart for Chapter 10.

From *Teaching Reading: Strategies and Resources for Grades K–6* by Rachel L. McCormack and Susan Lee Pasquarelli. Copyright 2010 by The Guilford Press. Permission to photocopy this figure is granted to purchasers of this book for personal use only (see copyright page for details).

CHAPTER 11

Assessing Children's Reading Development

Part 1. Motivation, Phonological/Phonemic Awareness, Word Identification, and Fluency

I have noodles in my nostrils.
I have noodles on my nose.
There are noodles on my cheeks and chin
and dripping down my clothes.

I've got more upon my forehead.
Some are sticking to my neck.
It's completely disconcerting.
I'm a noodle-covered wreck.

These playful, silly, engaging verses are the first two stanzas of the poem "I Have Noodles in My Nostrils" (Nesbitt, 2007, p. 12).[*] When students read poems such as this one, skillful teachers gain lots of information about how their students read and feel about reading. If you listen (and watch) *very, very carefully* as a student reads this, you can learn about the student's attitudes, phonological/phonemic awareness, accuracy, and fluency. In this chapter, we describe ways to look very carefully at your students to learn as much as you can about their reading development. (And you will see this poem again.)

WHAT IS ASSESSMENT?

Caldwell (2002, p. 213) defines *assessment* as a four-step process:

1. Identifying what to assess.
2. Collecting evidence.

[*]Copyright 2007 by Kenn Nesbitt. Reprinted from *Revenge of the Lunch Ladies* with the permission of Meadowbrook Press.

3. Analyzing the evidence.
4. Making decisions based on the analysis.

Let us apply this process to a common situation. Suppose you want to try out a new diet in order to lose a few pounds. Using the four steps of assessment suggested by Caldwell, you might approach it like this:

1. *Identifying what to assess*: Ability to lose weight on new diet.

2. *Collecting evidence*: Before: A friend has asked if you are putting on weight.

The number on the scale is increasing.

Your jeans are tight.

You avoid mirrors.

During: You are losing weight each week.

People ask you if you are losing weight.

Your clothes fit better.

You are always hungry.

You start looking in the mirror periodically.

After: You have lost 15 pounds.

Your "skinny jeans" fit.

You are getting compliments about looking great.

You cannot wait to start eating normally again.

3. *Analyzing the evidence*: The diet seemed to do what it said it would do.

You were too hungry all the time.

4. *Making decisions based on the analysis*: Eat sensibly, monitor your weight, and follow the diet again if necessary.

In real life, we are continually going through the process of assessment. We collect data, analyze them, and make decisions based on what we have found. In classrooms, teachers follow the same process. We are keen observers of our students' reading behaviors; we collect evidence of what they know and can do; we analyze this evidence; and then we adjust our instruction to match the needs of the learners.

In this chapter, we use the same framework for thinking about what, how, and why to assess our students as we learn about them as *developing readers*. We think that Caldwell's four-step process helps demystify assessment by organizing it into a sensible structure. More importantly, it reminds us that classroom-based assessment has a purpose: to inform us about the kinds of instruction we need to use to meet the needs of all our students. Assessing students without using the information as a driving force for teaching minimizes the efficacy of the task. If we do not act on the information, then all we are doing is collecting information and not using it.

We offer an overview of several types of assessments that are easily implemented in a classroom setting. However, the ones we suggest *by no means* exhaust the range of assessments available to teachers; rather, they represent and highlight some types of assessments we see in many excellent classrooms.

Before we can begin to describe good assessment practices, we need to remind you about a few key terms: *reliability, validity, summative assessment,* and *formative assessment.*

What Do We Mean by Reliability?

Reliability is the degree to which a test's results yield consistent scores from time to time and from one set of conditions to another. Standardized tests are considered to have a high degree of reliability.

What Is Validity?

Validity is the degree to which an assessment measures or evaluates what it says it measures. Classroom-based literacy assessments, such as the ones we describe in this chapter, have a high degree of validity.

What Is Summative Assessment?

Summative assessment is a final assessment. The purpose of a summative assessment is to assign a grade or score at the end of a unit or marking period.

What Do We Mean by Formative Assessment?

Formative assessment, or *ongoing assessment*, is assessment we use to make instructional or curricular decisions. The main goal of formative assessment is "to inform teachers of the active knowledge, skills, and strategies that their students have under their control" (Blachowicz, Buhle, Frost, & Bates, 2007, p. 246). Most of our suggestions in this chapter focus on formative assessments.

Principles of Good Formative Assessment Practice

We follow Winograd, Flores-Duenas, and Arrington (2003) in presenting a summary of five of the best practices in literacy assessment. We agree that reading assessments should do the following:

1. Draw from the classroom experiences and the expertise of excellent teachers.
2. Begin with what the students currently know, with a clear eye on the endpoint.
3. Promote trust and cooperation between teachers and students.
4. Make seamless connections to instruction.
5. Include multiple measures over time and in a variety of meaningful contexts.

In the remainder of this chapter, we focus our attention on those assessments that give us the best information about our developing readers' attitudes about reading, phonological and phonemic awareness, ability to decode words, and fluency.

BEST PRACTICES YOU WILL SEE IN THIS CHAPTER

✓ Assessing motivation.

✓ Assessing phonological and phonemic awareness.

✓ Assessing word identification.

✓ Assessing reading fluency.

ASSESSING MOTIVATION

Identifying What to Assess

In Chapters 2 and 3, we have discussed the importance of establishing a motivating environment. We have suggested that a print-rich classroom with consistent and well-designed routines will promote literacy learning. We have also noted that there is no guarantee that our students will be as engaged as we would like them to be. We can never really know whether all our hard work has paid off unless we assess how our students feel about reading and how our efforts contribute to their willingness to read. When we assess our students' motivation, in other words, we are really assessing two things: (1) their attitudes about learning *while they are in our classrooms*, and (2) how well *we* provide and sustain a motivating environment for our students.

Collecting Evidence

You can collect the evidence, or data, for assessing motivation through observation, surveys, and book logs.

Observation

You can collect evidence of your students' attitudes about reading in many ways. One way is informally through observation. If your students are speaking or acting enthusiastically about your independent reading program, you can get a general sense that they like the time of day when they are allowed to choose their own texts and read on their own. You can have class discussions about the kinds of books they like to read and the titles they would like to see in the classroom library. Unsolicited comments, such as "I love when you do a read-aloud right before we go home! It gives me good ideas about the kinds of books I want to read," provide important and genuine information. You can jot down notes and collect the observations you make about what motivates your students about reading and learning in a daily log or notebook. These are called *anecdotal records*.

Interest and Attitude Surveys

Surveys given at the beginning of the school year—and at other times—can help you learn about your students' reading habits and interests. We present two examples of such surveys here. The one in Figure 11.1 can be adapted for any grade; it questions students about their interests in a multiple-choice format. The one in Figure 11.2 (page 228) asks students many of the same questions, but the format encourages elaboration. (A slightly different version of this second survey is included as part of our second-grade sample reading performance assessment in Appendix B.)

When you are designing and using surveys such as these, remember that you are assessing students' interests and attitudes, not the processes they use to read. We discuss assessing those processes in Chapter 12. Keep the survey simple, and focus on the things you want to learn about your students. You might want to know, for example, how much they read at home, or whether they like reading at all. If so, what kinds of things do they like to read about? Each class of students you teach is different, and surveys yield very different information from year to year. You may want to repeat the same survey at the end of the year. That way, you and your students can compare the ways their attitudes and interests have changed.

We offer the following suggestions for designing and scoring reading surveys.

STEP 1: WHAT KIND OF A SURVEY WOULD YOU LIKE TO MAKE?

The first step in making a survey is to decide whether you would like a survey that invites students to answer open-ended questions, such as "Do you like to go to the library to take out books?", or rate statements on a scale of 1–4, such as "I like to go to the library to check out books." We know from experience that the type of survey depends on the age and literacy abilities of the children in your classroom. For example, open-ended questions are best for older students who have the stamina to elaborate, as well as the writing skill to respond.

STEP 2: WHAT DO YOU WANT TO KNOW ABOUT YOUR STUDENTS?

Second, make a list of questions or statements about your students' reading habits. Your questions/statements can range from school to home and ask students to think about their attitudes toward reading, their motivations for succeeding in reading endeavors, and maybe even their likes and dislikes in regard to reading multicultural books. Do you want to know their independent reading habits at home? Do you want to know if they go to the library to take out books? Do you want to know how they feel in your classroom during reading groups or whole-group instruction? Every survey is different and should reflect what you *need* to know to carry out your reading curriculum.

STEP 3: HOW DO YOU DESIGN THE SURVEY INSTRUMENT?

The answer to the third question depends upon the answer to the first question above. If you have written a list of questions to which students must respond, the questions should just be typed on a page, with lots of room for students to respond with elaboration.

1. I like to read in class . . .
   ☐ Yes
   ☐ No
   ☐ Sometimes
2. I read at home . . .
   ☐ Every day.
   ☐ About three times a week.
   ☐ Less than once a week.
   ☐ Never.
3. The books I like to read the most are . . .
   ☐ Fantasy stories.
   ☐ Adventure stories.
   ☐ Mysteries.
   ☐ Stories about real people.
   ☐ Stories about history.
   ☐ Other: _____
4. Every week I try to read ____ books.
   ☐ One
   ☐ Two
   ☐ Five
   ☐ More than five
5. I think reading is . . .
   ☐ Fun.
   ☐ Hard.
   ☐ Easy.
   ☐ Boring.
6. I have . . .
   ☐ Many books at home.
   ☐ Some books at home.
   ☐ No books at home.
7. Most of the books I read come from . . .
   ☐ Home.
   ☐ Library.
   ☐ School/classroom.
   ☐ Friends or relatives.
   ☐ Other: _____
8. I would read more if our class had . . .
   ☐ More interesting books.
   ☐ More time for reading in class.
   ☐ Easier books.
   ☐ Other: _____

FIGURE 11.1. Reading survey.

Write the answers to the following questions in the space provided. You can use the back.

1. How would you describe yourself as a reader?

2. What would you like to be able to read?

3. What makes reading hard?

4. What makes reading easy?

5. How often do you read?

6. What kinds of things do you like to read or read about?

7. How can you improve as a reader?

8. What is the title of one of your favorite books?

9. What is the title of the last book you read on your own?

10. What do you think teachers can do to motivate their students to read?

FIGURE 11.2. Open-ended survey.

If you have chosen to make a survey with a rating scale, it is best to design your survey so that the rating system is next to each statement. Be sure the students can easily recognize what the numbers on the scale mean—for example, 1 = "not at all," 2 = "sometimes," 3 = "often," and 4 = "always." If you use a rating scale, it is important to note that you always want the #4 option to be the most positive answer, and the #1 option to be the least positive answer. For example, the following statements ask the same thing, but the #4 option gives very different results:

"I don't like going to the library." In this case, 4 = "always" is a negative answer.
"I love going to the library." In this case, 4 = "always" is a positive answer.

You can see that if your statements are skewed incorrectly, you will not be able to use a quantitative scoring system to evaluate your students' responses.

You also want to include directions for your students on the survey. Perhaps you may explain your purpose in administering the survey, as well as either an explanation of the rating system or directions for elaborating responses to open-ended questions. When you are administering the survey, be sure to tell students that there is no grade attached to the survey, and encourage them to answer truthfully.

STEP 4: HOW DO YOU EVALUATE THE SURVEYS?

If you are using statements with a numbering system, add up the students' responses. For example, if a student circles 4, 4, and 3 for the first three statements, you can add up those numbers to 11 (out of a possible 12) and know that the child feels positive about those items. If the child scores 7 on those three items, then you know that the child feels negative about those items. Of course, you also want to do a qualitative analysis of the results, being sure to record when individual students are extremely negative. For example, if a student is negative about reading at home, you might follow up to find out why and see what you can do to intervene.

Book Logs

Another way to assess your students' motivation and interests is through having them keep a *book log*. Figure 11.3 is a very simple sample form for a book log. For each book, the students log the book title, author, date finished, and genre, and give a few comments. This log helps students keep track of the books they read on their own and can give you the information they need to monitor the kinds of books their students read. You should *model* the process of filling out a book log, so that the students write more thoughtful comments than just "Good," "Bad," or "I liked it."

This type of book log does not interfere with the amount of reading we want our students to do and the amount of reading they must do to be competent and skillful readers. Following up each self-selected text with a traditional book report does *not* motivate children to read more. A student once said to us, "The whole time I was writing this book report, I could have been reading another book!"

Book title	Author	Date finished	Genre	Comments

FIGURE 11.3. Sample book log.

Analyzing the Evidence

The next step is to ask yourself, "What have I learned about my students' reading interests and motivation to read?" You may want to aggregate the results by making a chart of their responses, or follow up with a class discussion. If you have used an open-ended survey, you can read the students' responses and look for themes among their answers. For example, if some students respond that they do not like to read in school during sustained silent reading, do not like to go to the library, and do not read at home, you can safely deduce that these children do not read unless reading is assigned. You can also make notes about the reading habits and attitudes specific to each student as well as the overall class, and make appropriate interventions for your classroom.

Making Decisions Based on the Analysis

After collecting data on their students' attitudes and interests, many teachers learn that they do not have nearly the number of books or the types of titles they need to keep their students happy. Fifth- and sixth-grade teachers also often report that their students say that they hardly ever read at home. If that is the case in your class, you will need to make the most of the classroom time by providing rich reading experiences for your reluctant readers.

If many of your students indicate that they want to read books that are not currently part of your classroom library, you may want to follow up with the survey in Chapter 2, Figure 2.6 (page 17), called "How Does Your Classroom Library Rate?" This will give you more information about the kinds of books needed in the classroom and whether there are basic gaps you need to fill. Even so, the data you have collected are the main indicators of what is needed to satisfy the needs of your classroom. Based on the responses you get from your students, you may have to do the following:

- Add more books to your classroom library.
- Schedule additional time to visit the school library.
- Showcase more books that match the interests of the students.
- Allow more time for independent reading in school.
- Read aloud more books in the genres they like, to keep them interested in reading.

The most important point is to use the results to make your classroom fit your students' interests and help make your students a classroom of motivated readers.

TRY THIS

Design a survey you can use with your students to assess reading attitudes and interests. First, choose a grade level. Then use the tips described previously for designing surveys. You may combine the types of questions and examples shown in Figures 11.1 and 11.2 (pages 227 and 228). After you design your survey, try it on a child to see what kind of information the survey gives you. Write your survey in the space on the following page:

ASSESSING PHONOLOGICAL AND PHONEMIC AWARENESS

Identifying What to Assess

In Chapter 3, we have discussed the importance of phonological and phonemic aware-ness—that is, awareness that spoken words are divided into parts: syllables, onsets–rimes, and phonemes. It makes sense to assess this awareness orally. The oral assess-ment can determine the students' performance at rhyming, counting words in sentences, counting syllables, segmenting and blending syllables, segmenting and blending onsets and rimes, segmenting and blending phonemes, and substituting one phoneme with another. In our oral speech, these features are not always apparent to younger children. Giving them deliberate attention helps children develop it; the assessment determines whether they have gained this awareness.

Collecting Evidence

To assess how well your students can orally segment words into individual phonemes, you can use the Yopp–Singer Test of Phoneme Segmentation (Yopp, 1995). The assess-ment is available online and can be downloaded from many websites. This oral assess-ment takes only a few minutes, and is administered on a one-on-one basis.

You can also design an assessment yourself. Take a look back at Figure 3.1 (page 39) in Chapter 3, which lists the phonological and phonemic awareness tasks suggested by Yopp (1993). As you can see, the order in which the tasks are listed there reflects their increasing difficulty. You can use Figure 3.1 as the basis for a checklist for recording the performance of each student. Figure 11.4 is an example of such a checklist.

Name of student	Rhymes	Counts words in sentence	Counts syllables in words	Segments and blends syllables	Segments and blends onsets and rimes	Segments and blends phonemes	Substitutes phonemes

FIGURE 11.4. A checklist for assessing phonological and phonemic awareness.

Analyzing the Evidence

Once you have assessed your students' performance, you can then target skills in need of instruction and make a plan for teaching them. Remember that distinguishing individual sounds within words or syllables is much harder than being aware that words and syllables are separate units, so it is best to start with the easier tasks.

Making Decisions Based on the Analysis

In Chapter 3, we have also presented Yopp's (1993) recommendations for the instruction of phonological and phonemic awareness. We have stated there that although the instruction should be deliberate and planned, it should also be playful, be developmentally appropriate, and take place within real literacy-learning tasks (Yopp, 1993). Teaching and assessing phonological and phonemic awareness should not be stressful for you or your students. Oral word play can easily be integrated into your literacy curriculum. All developing readers can benefit from oral word play and reading poems. Students who already have a strong foundation in phonological awareness will still benefit from the songs, stories, and poems that you recite together.

ASSESSING WORD IDENTIFICATION

Identifying What to Assess

Once students begin reading in kindergarten (or before), we need to assess many aspects about the way they read words. What, for example, do they do when they encounter unknown words? How do they use meaning to give them clues as they read? What instruction do we need to provide to help them feel competent in decoding words?

Collecting Evidence

Listening to your students read orally, one on one, is an authentic way to assess how your students are reading. If your students are accustomed to sitting with you to read, it is also a low-risk and low-stress experience for them. You can learn a great deal about what your students do when they read *silently* by listening to them read with you orally, and you can begin this assessment practice in kindergarten.

Running Records

Most teachers use some type of coding system to record how their students are reading. The most common way we have seen classroom teachers collect information about their students' oral reading is the use of *running records* (Clay, 1979). A running record is a record of a student's oral reading that can be analyzed and used for instruction. To take a running record, you need only a blank sheet of paper, a pencil, and a student with a real text. You then record what you see and hear, using a series of symbols. Clay's running records measure accuracy, not grade level. In other words, a running record will help a teacher determine how difficult a *particular text* is for a *particular child* under a *particular condition*. For instance, a student reading a text that is familiar or has been read many times will perform very differently than when the student reads a new text for the first time. Taking into account all the conditions of the reading makes it a more valid assessment.

Taking a running record is a way to collect data—both qualitative and quantitative—about a student's oral reading. In addition to calculating a score of the words read accurately (quantitative information), it also allows you to take notes on the ways in which the student makes attempts at unknown words, fixes his or her own errors while reading, and thinks out loud (qualitative information). That is why Clay strongly recommends using a blank sheet of paper and not using a prepared text to record your observations. She also discourages working from a tape. You can learn more from recording the information when you are watching students as well as listening to them.

Assessing a student's reading performance by taking a running record requires good instruction and sufficient time and practice. Watching knowledgeable and experienced teachers perform the assessment is a must. Sitting with the teachers afterward to analyze the records is also essential. Then you should go through a period of guided practice as you perform the assessment on several students and analyze the results with another teacher.

We also suggest using Johnston's (2000) self-tutorial on running records. This valuable resource walks you through the process gradually and gives you ample practice in taking running records. It also gives detailed descriptions of the coding system and other procedures related to the assessment.

Informal Reading Inventories

Some teachers and many reading specialists use an *informal reading inventory* (IRI) instead of, or in addition to, running records. IRIs are published assessment instruments that contain many narrative and expository passages in a variety of reading levels, typically from preprimer to 12th grade. They are organized according to reading levels, and they include the coding systems and all the directions for administrating and analyzing the assessments.

Many teachers like IRIs because the information they collect is recorded directly on the prepared passages, and the instrument determines the approximate grade level of an individual student's reading ability. They are convenient and require little preparation. However, as it does for running records, learning to administer and analyze IRIs well takes practice and patience. To learn more about using IRIs, see Caldwell (2002, 2008).

Analyzing the Evidence

The assessment methods just described provide an abundance of information to be analyzed. You can start by asking a few questions to guide your analysis. For example, as you look at the record of the student's reading, what have you learned about the way the student approached the task? Do you see a pattern of behaviors or errors? Did the student read for meaning? Did the substitutions make sense? Was the student just reading words? What strategies did the student use to decode unfamiliar words? Did the passage seem easy, hard, or appropriate?

McKenna and Stahl (2003, pp. 59–60) suggest the following series of questions to guide teachers as they review and analyze the word identification errors or miscues their students make:

- *Meaning*: Did the reader choose a substitution or phrasing that made sense in the passage, sentence, or part of the sentence?
- *Structure*: Did the reading sound like language that follows a grammatical form? Did the reader follow the structure of the text?
- *Visual*: Did the child read a word that had graphic similarity to the word in the text? Was the graphophonic system being used?
- *Self-correction*: What cueing system did the reader use to fix incorrectly read words?

By answering these questions about a student's reading, you can then make decisions about types of interventions and subsequent instruction. In most cases, the errors students make fall into two categories: Either the students did not read for meaning, or the students were not decoding the unfamiliar words correctly. Often you will see a combination of both. By looking for a pattern of errors, you can plan instruction based on your analysis.

Let us use a real text to take a look at examples of different types of errors. In a version of the Aesop's fable "The Fox and the Stork" that we use for second-grade assessment (see Appendix B), the first sentence reads, "On a summer day, Fox went for a walk in the forest and met Stork." If a student reads the sentence like this: "On a summer day, Fox went for a walk in the woods and met Stork," substituting the word *woods* for *forest*, the meaning of the sentence does not really change; nor does the substitution affect the overall understanding of the fable. There is a chance that the student, if asked to reread the sentence slowly, will self-correct and say "forest."

Now imagine that a different student reads the same sentence this way: "On a summer day, Fox went for a walk in the first and met Stork." In this case, the word *first* looks very similar to the word *forest*, but it does not make any sense syntactically or semantically. If the student is asked to reread the sentence slowly, and self-corrects and says "forest," you may say that the student used his or her knowledge of letter–sound relationships to a certain degree at first. If, when asked to reread the sentence slowly, the student does not self-correct, you have received very different information about the student. This student is not attending to the meaning of the sentence in the same way that the first student did.

Making Decisions Based on the Analysis

Making decisions about what to teach after taking oral reading records also requires experience and a good deal of knowledge about teaching phonics and comprehension. If you find students making a pattern of errors that does not interfere with the meaning of the text, you can share the oral reading records with the students—showing them substitutions they made that did not interrupt the meaning, and leading them to look more closely at the words.

If you find that your students are making patterns of errors that interfere with the meaning of the text, teaching (and reteaching) comprehension-monitoring strategies will be beneficial. All students will continue to encounter unknown words as they become more experienced and expert readers.

If the record shows a student's pattern of unsuccessful attempts at decoding unfamiliar words, then the instructional decisions should lead to improving the student's ability to decode words through explicit phonics instruction. In previous chapters, we have provided examples of instruction in both decoding and comprehension. You can refer to these when making decisions on how to improve your students' oral reading performance.

ASSESSING FLUENCY

Identifying What to Assess

A fluent reader is a joy to listen to. When fluency is accompanied by excellent comprehension, the reader exemplifies the kind of strategic reader that we all aspire to develop. As we have cautioned in Chapter 3, fluency does not guarantee comprehension; however, it does free a reader's cognitive resources enough so he or she can focus on the real task of reading—constructing meaning from text.

When we assess fluency, we take a look at the three important characteristics identified by Rasinski (2003) and discussed in Chapter 3: *accuracy*, *automaticity*, and *prosody*. We explain how to assess these aspects of fluency next.

Collecting Evidence

According to Kuhn (2007), determining the number of *correct words per minute* (cwpm) is the easiest and most commonly used method to assess your students' reading accuracy and automaticity. She suggests three variations, which are described below. (In Appendix B, we use the first one for our second-grade sample assessment.)

Procedure 1

- Choose a 100- to 200-word passage from a text in the literacy curriculum. Ask the student to read aloud for 1 minute from the beginning of the text.
- As the student is reading, count the number of correct words. Stop after 1 minute.
- Calculate the score as cwpm.

Procedure 2

- Choose a selection from a text in the literacy curriculum. Ask the student to read aloud for several minutes.
- After the student is comfortable with the text, begin timing for 1 minute. Count the number of correct words.
- Calculate the score as cwpm.

Procedure 3

- Choose three passages of approximately 100–200 words each from the same text from the literacy curriculum.
- Ask the student to read each one aloud for 1 minute.
- As the student is reading, count the number of correct words.
- Calculate the score as cwpm for each passage.
- Average the three scores to determine the student's cwpm.

After we assess a reader's accuracy and automaticity, we must also collect information about the student's prosody. This simple assessment includes listening to a student read a piece of short connected text (approximately 200 words) while collecting information on the student's ability to use natural speech and expression, proper phrasing, smoothness, and appropriate volume.

Kuhn (2007) suggests using texts from the literacy curriculum when you are assessing fluency, so that you can determine how the students are performing when using the day-to-day instructional materials. Knowing how easy or difficult the classroom texts are is important; it helps you to determine how much support to give students who are reading them. If you decide to use a text for fluency assessment that is also being used for teaching reading in small ability groups, the results can help you determine whether that text is appropriate for the students. If not, you can adjust the level of the texts accordingly.

Rasinski (2003) suggests administering fluency assessments several times a year as needed, to keep track of your students' growth over time. Because these assessments are easy to administer, they can be conveniently worked into your repertoire of assessment strategies.

Analyzing the Evidence

Many grade-level norms and guidelines are available in texts about fluency (see, e.g., Moskal & Blachowicz, 2006). Many are derived from a common chart used to analyze the results of oral reading fluency assessment (Figure 11.5; this chart is also included in the second-grade sample assessment in Appendix B). This chart represents the average and should be used carefully when you are making decisions about your students' ability to read fluently. The norms chart shows fluency target rate norms that correlate with fall, winter, and spring in grades 1–8. You can easily determine whether a student falls within the norms indicated on the chart.

To analyze a student's prosody, you can use a Likert scale, such as the one we have likewise included in Appendix B. This scale covers the following criteria:

- Student uses consistent and appropriate volume.
- Student uses punctuation for effective phrasing.
- Student reads easily and efficiently, making more self-corrections than errors.
- Student reads at a steady conversational pace.
- Student uses expression while reading aloud. For example, student changes tone for dialogue or to differentiate among characters.
- Student reads with the appropriate tone for the mood of the story or to exemplify the emotions of the character.

Grade	Fall (WCPM)	Winter (WCPM)	Spring (WCPM)
1		10–30	30–60
2	30–60	50–80	70–100
3	50–90	70–100	80–110
4	70–110	80–120	100–140
5	80–120	100–140	110–150
6	100–140	110–150	120–160
7	110–150	120–160	130–170
8	120–160	130–170	140–180

FIGURE 11.5. Oral reading fluency target rate norms. WCPM (words correct per minute) is the same as cwpm (correct words per minute) as described in the text. Retrieved February 20, 2008, from *www.prel.org/products/ re_/assessingfluency.htm*. Reprinted by courtesy of Pacific Resources for Education and Learning.

Making Decisions Based on the Analysis

Once you have determined where a student falls within the accuracy/automaticity norms, the next step is to make decisions on the appropriate support and interventions. As mentioned above, the cwpm fluency assessment is a good general method for determining the difficulty of a text you use for your instructional materials.

If the text you used is the grade-level core text—such as a literary anthology, science text, or social studies text—and the student has performed within or above the norms, you can reasonably expect that the student can read this text independently without too much support (after the selection has been introduced by you). However, taking a reading from a science text will only inform you of what to expect when the student is reading from that science text. The same is true for any other text you use in the classroom. You should continue to monitor these students as texts change and the level of difficulty increases.

Students who can read the grade-level text with relative ease should read the text independently. If the text appears to be too difficult, as determined by the fluency scale and your informal assessments of the students' performance, you will need to put some interventions in place. For example, when you are using the instructional materials that are too difficult for some students, you may want to use Paratore's (2000) flexible multiple-grouping model (described in Chapter 2). The community reading component of this model provides for varying levels of support when your students are reading grade-level text. You may designate reading buddies to give support to the students who cannot contend with the text independently. Chapter 3 describes additional ways to support students who are not yet fluent readers.

To design appropriate interventions for prosody, you can refer back to Chapter 3 to refresh your memory of fluency instructional methods. Children who do not use natural expression or proper phrasing will benefit greatly from your modeling of the various aspects of prosodic reading. After modeling the various aspects of prosody, you can decide whether individuals or groups of students would benefit from partner reading, echo reading, choral reading, or readers' theatre to practice being fluent readers.

STUDENT LITERACY PORTFOLIOS

A *literacy portfolio* is an assessment system that enables you to systematically collect and analyze performance-based evidence over time. However, *literacy portfolios* are also containers used to collect artifacts that demonstrate students' growth over time. Literacy portfolios provide one way for us as teachers to work together with our students to make sense of the information we collect during classroom-based assessments (Paratore & McCormack, 2005), and they help us to manage all the assessment information.

Portfolios can include work samples and other evidence that are both formative and summative. You can include anything that demonstrates what students know and are able to do. If you decide to use literacy portfolios, you can assess your students' development as readers in several ways. Some of these types of assessments are described in this chapter:

- Attitude and interest surveys
- Book logs
- Writing samples that show development of word knowledge
- Scoring rubrics and checklists
- Running records that have been shared with the students
- Results from IRIs
- Fluency assessments

Glazer (2007) offers suggestions for a portfolio system, based on over 25 years of development.

- The data in the portfolios should demonstrate each child's learning needs and strengths, as well as the kind of instruction that is most beneficial to the learner.
- Students should be involved in using the portfolios to monitor their own progress.
- The routines you establish should be consistent with other literacy routines that promote independence.
- The portfolios should be easy to handle, retrieve, store, and refer to.

Literacy portfolios provide excellent evidence when you are reporting progress to parents or participating in meetings about students with whom you have concerns.

FINAL WORDS

Making thoughtful choices about the classroom-based assessments you use and the instruction you give takes a great deal of experience. Whenever you can, consult with other teachers who have more experience and training in administering and analyzing reading assessments. Likewise, share your knowledge with others.

We have started this chapter with two stanzas from the poem "I Have Noodles in My Nostrils." Here now is the last stanza. There are a few more stanzas, but you will have to read Nesbitt's (2007) hilarious book of poems to read the whole thing.

> So try not to do what I did:
> I'm a total nincompoop,
> and I fell asleep at lunch
> while eating chicken noodle soup.

With what you now know about assessment, what could you learn by listening very carefully to a child read the poem?

Record your ideas here.

Before you read the next chapter, please review the Key Terms Chart in Figure 11.6 (page 242) and write definitions in your own words. In Chapter 12, we continue with assessment of vocabulary, comprehension, and response.

REFLECTION ON ARTIFACTS FOR YOUR SELF-STUDY

For your self-study, record on Figure 11.7 (page 243) the artifacts you created while or after you read this chapter.

KEY TERMS FOR CHAPTER 11

In this chapter, the following key terms are essential to your understanding of reading instruction. Think about what they mean, and try to define them in your own words.

validity

reliability

summative assessment

formative assessment

book logs

running records

informal reading inventories (IRIs)

correct words per minute (cwpm)

literacy portfolios

FIGURE 11.6. Key Terms Chart for Chapter 11.

SELF-STUDY REVIEW CHART FOR CHAPTER 11

Name of Artifact	Teacher Instructional Actions and Language	Provisions for Individual Differences	Variety of Modes of Communication	Critical Thinking and Active Engagement	Opportunities for Assessment

FIGURE 11.7. Self-Study Review Chart for Chapter 11.

Assessing Children's Reading Development

Part 2. Vocabulary, Comprehension, and Reader Response

A student wrote the following piece after reading the text *Coming to America* (Maestro, 1996).

> Hi! I am Stephanie your tour guide. Today we are going to Ellis Iland. But first let me tell you about It. Ellis Iland is a place were people from different contry's came to Ellis Iland for hope for a better life in America. They get blood test's and they get there eyes checked, ears, and there walkin checked. People who are blind or deph, and criminal's (which i'll explain later). can not come to America. Ellis Iland is in New York city. And it take's about three week to get there. They don't want criminal's to get away with MUR DER so they don't let them come into America!!

Johnston (1997) often asks his readers to look carefully at a student's writing while asking the following questions: What does the student know? What does the student almost know? What does the student still need to learn? He guides his readers to consider the writing from more than one perspective, but *always* asks his readers to focus on what their students know and are learning. We have learned a great deal from Johnston's work about looking at how well children perform in reading tasks. We have learned to focus on what students *know*, instead of what they do *not* know.

Using Johnston's framework, take a careful look at the student's writing above. Imagine that Stephanie, the author of this sample, is a fifth grader. How would you assess her performance? Would you say that she has good ideas, but her writing is unsophisticated? Would you focus on the spelling and mechanics, and overlook her demonstration of text comprehension? Jot your ideas below.

What does she know?

What does she almost know?

What does she still need to learn?

What if we told you that Stephanie is not a fifth grader, but is actually a second grader? Now how would you assess her performance? Would your assessment of her performance change, or would it stay the same? Jot down your ideas below.

What does she know?

What does she almost know?

What does she still need to learn?

In fact, Stephanie is a second grader. We hope that you noticed, as we did, how sophisticated her writing is, how she has woven her own background knowledge into the piece, and how she strongly demonstrates her reactions to the information in the text. You were probably not as distracted by the mechanics, because she is a second grader who is, undoubtedly, still learning the standard conventions for writing.

In this chapter, we investigate ways to assess your students' understanding of texts by collecting evidence of comprehension and reader response strategy knowledge. In Chapters 5–9, we have discussed how to teach these strategies in terms of when they are best used: before, during, and after reading. As we have explained in Chapter 11, assessment has a very important purpose: to guide us as we make decisions about what our students need to learn as they become competent readers. After we collect evidence, we need to make very *deliberate* plans about what to *teach*, and then reassess the effectiveness of our instruction.

The assessment tools we describe in this chapter are grouped in a similar before, during, and after sequence. They cover the wide range of assessment strategies.

BEST PRACTICES YOU WILL SEE IN THIS CHAPTER

✓ Assessing metacognition: Strategy knowledge.
✓ Assessing vocabulary knowledge.
✓ Assessing reading comprehension.

ASSESSING METACOGNITION: STRATEGY KNOWLEDGE

Why Assess Metacognition?

In Chapter 5, we have discussed metacognition and cognitive strategy instruction. Cognitive strategy instruction involves explicitly teaching our students expert reading behaviors that will be performed mostly in their heads. Expert readers are aware of the strategies they use to construct meaning, and they know why, how, and when to use them. This can make for *very* difficult reading assessment in a traditional sense. How do we know, for example, what our students think about before they read? What processes do they use to construct meaning while reading? What strategies do they employ after reading to help them clarify or extend their understanding?

Some strategies are obvious and visible. We may observe our students talking to each other while reading as a way to get a definition for an unknown word. We may see them consult a dictionary. Some students may highlight text or consult a website on a computer. Some students may rely on us for answers to their questions while reading.

Other processes are far less simple to observe. For example, we cannot see what is going on in our students' heads as they encounter unknown words or come across a passage that is syntactically complex and difficult to understand. Of course, if we ask our students to read a text, and then we ask them to tell us about what they read—*and they can*—we can suspect that they are using strategies, even though we cannot see them or hear them. However, the extent to which they use strategies and the ease in which they perform them is unknown to us. Moreover, we know that all students sometimes run into some trouble with understanding text. What about those times when the text becomes very difficult? We know that the more difficult the text is, the more purposeful the strategies need to be. But what if students do not have a good grasp on the strategies they need? How would we know?

As is true of many informal assessments administered in the classroom, assessing metacognition is more of an *art* than a *science*. It lacks a bit of the reliability that we would like to see when considering the kinds of informal assessments to use in our classrooms, because it leaves a great deal of the interpretation up to us as we are doing the assessment. The act of "getting inside the heads" of our students is complex, and we can never be quite sure whether we are really finding what we are looking for. This is especially the case with younger children, whose oral language skills may not be adequate to explain what is going on inside their heads. Nonetheless, these drawbacks do not diminish the importance of assessing metacognition. Done well, assessing our students' metacognition—their knowledge about what they do, how they do it, and why they do it—gives us an abundance of information about their thought processes, their reading processes, and ultimately our own instruction.

How to Assess Metacognition

Metacognition is typically assessed in the form of an interview and/or an observation. An interview is better for encouraging a student to elaborate; an observation allows us to take notes about what we see and hear. We recommend a combination of both. Why? We cannot rely on students to report accurately what they do to make sense of text. We may ask, "What do you do before you read?", and they may report that they look at the front and back of the book, do a picture walk, and write predictions in their reading journals. Then, as we observe them before reading, we may see them pick up a book and begin reading. A combination of an interview and an observation thus gives us more information.

We have designed and used many instruments to informally assess strategy knowledge. Figure 12.1 (page 248) and Figure 12.2 (page 249) are examples of interviews you can use to assess before-, during-, and after- reading strategy knowledge. (The Metacognitive Process Interview, Figure 12.2, also appears as part of our second-grade sample reading performance assessment in Appendix B.) Figures 12.3 (page 250) and 12.4 (page 251) provide observation assessments for before- and during-reading strategies, respectively.

BEFORE READING: ASSESSING VOCABULARY, COMPREHENSION, AND RESPONSE

Why Assess before Reading?

If we ask our students to tell us what they know about the Cold War before reading about it, they can reasonably expect that the social studies lesson that day will have something to do with the Cold War. If we ask them what they know about biofuels, they may recall hearing about them on the news or reading about them on the Internet. Assessing our students before asking them to read has many benefits both for them and for us. For students, it gives them a preview of what they will learn that day; it helps them get their minds ready to read. For us as teachers, it can help drive the type

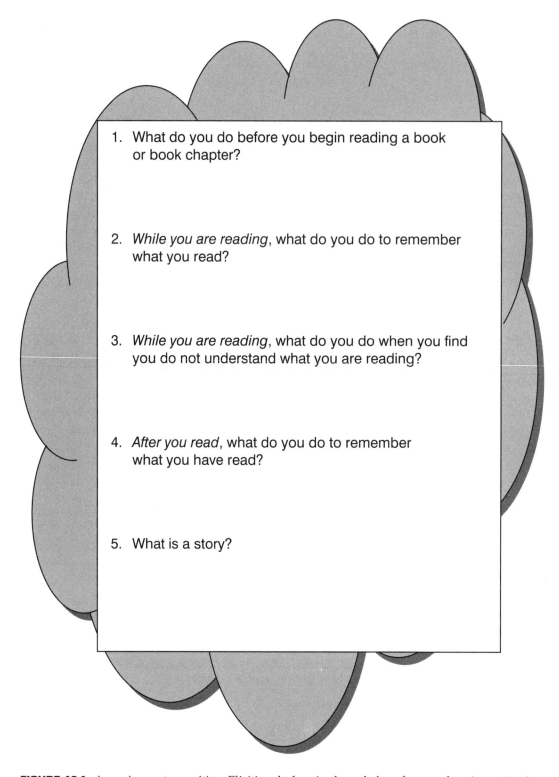

1. What do you do before you begin reading a book or book chapter?

2. *While you are reading*, what do you do to remember what you read?

3. *While you are reading*, what do you do when you find you do not understand what you are reading?

4. *After you read*, what do you do to remember what you have read?

5. What is a story?

FIGURE 12.1. Assessing metacognition: Eliciting declarative knowledge of comprehension strategies.

1. What is reading?

2. If someone asked you how to read, what would you say?

3. What's hard about reading?

4. What's easy about reading?

5. What do you do before you start reading? (You want students to explain the process.)

6. What do you do when you come to a word you don't know? (You want students to explain the process.)

7. What do you do to help you remember what you have read? (You want students to explain the process.)

8. What do you do when you finish reading? (You want students to explain the process.)

9. What is a story? (You want students to tell you specific information, such as "It has characters and a plot.")

FIGURE 12.2. Metacognitive Process Interview.

Ask the child, "Show me what you do before you read a story." As the child demonstrates, check off responses. Remember that the child must show how to *apply* these strategies.

Before-Reading Strategies	✓	Notes
Look/read the title		
Take a picture walk		
Acknowledge author		
Examine front cover/illustration		
Activate prior knowledge		
Read back cover/inside flap summary		
Make predictions		
Make connections		
Other:		

FIGURE 12.3. A metacognitive observation checklist to elicit procedural knowledge of before-reading comprehension strategies.

Ask the child, "Show me what you do while you read a story." As the child demonstrates, check off responses. Remember that the child must show how to *apply* these strategies.

During-Reading Strategies	✓	Notes
Make connections		
Take notes/use graphic organizer		
Look at pictures		
Make predictions		
Visualize		
Reread		
Draw a picture		
Talk to someone/ discuss		
Ask questions		
Use key words		
Think about story elements		
Other:		

FIGURE 12.4. A metacognitive observation checklist to elicit procedural knowledge of during-reading comprehension strategies.

and depth of the instruction that day, especially if it is a new topic. The wide range of background knowledge and experiences that our students bring to lessons greatly affects what and how we teach them. By assessing students before reading, we gain insight about their background knowledge, vocabulary, and attitudes about the topic and the texts. Below, we describe several examples of informal techniques to use as before-reading assessments.

Brainstorming through Webbing

We have described brainstorming through webbing in Chapter 4 as a vocabulary-learning event. But you can also use this technique as an informal assessment of your students' prior knowledge about a topic. Figure 12.5 shows a brainstormed web on mammals. Its creation gave the teacher insight into how much the students already knew about mammals. This type of informal "checking in" helped her make decisions about how to adjust instruction based on what the students already knew.

Self-Assessing Vocabulary Knowledge

Many content-area texts are so heavily laden with new terms and concepts that it is difficult to decide which words and concepts are the most important ones to teach. Figure 12.6 is a chart you can use to assess your students' prior knowledge about words by engaging them in a self-assessment of the words they already know or think they know.

For this assessment, you need to select the words your students will encounter during a unit of study. Then list the words on a chart and distribute a copy of the chart to each student. As the students read the words, they ask themselves, "Do I know this word?" If they do (or think they do), they check it off and define it. Then they ask them-

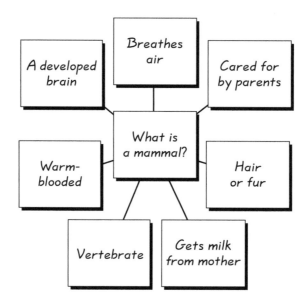

FIGURE 12.5. "What Is a Mammal?": Before-reading assessment web.

Directions: Check each word you know. Define it. Then use it in a sentence.

Word	I Know it	Definition	I can use it in a sentence	Sentence

FIGURE 12.6. A chart for assessing students' prior word knowledge.

selves, "Can I use the word in a sentence?" If they indicate that they can, they provide a sentence for the word.

This type of assessment can give you multiple layers of information. For example, it can give you a general sense, as you look over all the students' charts, of which words and terms need the most attention during whole-class instruction. It can also inform you of the degree to which each student knows the words. Knowing the definition of a word is not the same as knowing how to use the word meaningfully. Although this method of assessing vocabulary before teaching is not perfect, it does have the potential for narrowing down the sets of words and terms you teach in the content areas.

Assessing Strategies: "My Best Guess"

In Chapter 4, we have described the importance of developing vocabulary by teaching *strategies* to decipher the meanings of unknown words. A way to assess this ability could be through an activity similar to the one provided in Figure 12.7: "My Best Guess." Students are given this recording sheet with new, unknown words or terms listed (Figure 12.7 provides one example). The form asks them not only to guess the word meanings, but also to describe the strategy behind each guess. Because the form provides no context for the words, this activity is useful for assessing whether or not students are using word parts to figure out new words.

This assessment can also be used during reading or after reading to assess different knowledge. Used while reading, it can help you determine whether or not the students are gathering the clues given by the author. In the case of a content-area text, it lets you know whether or not the students are using the text features—words in boldface or italics; deliberate definitions within the sentence or sentences; graphic clues, such as illustrations or charts; or glossaries.

We caution you not to overuse this and similar assessment tools, or to use them as worksheets. We urge you to use them judiciously. These are meant to be assessment tools that ultimately provide information about your performance as a teacher and things you may need to teach or reteach later.

Journal Writing

Journal writing before reading—that is, doing a "quick write" before starting a selection—is a good way to get your students thinking about a text before they read it, and it is an efficient way for you to assess their background knowledge and prior experiences. Asking students to respond before reading results in writing that is more reader-based than text-based, because there is no threat that the text will influence their responses.

For example, before reading *Hatchet* (Paulsen, 1987), a fifth-grade teacher might want to get his or her students thinking about what it might feel like if they were lost for a certain amount of time. Many children may have experienced becoming lost or separated from their parents—even for just a few minutes. It is not an experience they easily forget. Writing about it can bring their feelings to the surface and help them show empathy for the character.

Figures 12.8 and 12.9 (page 256) show a first grader's journal entry (drawing and text) before reading the book *Grandpa and Me* (Gauch, 1972). The students were asked to write about the things they do with their grandparents. This student chose to write

Word or Term	My Best Guess	Strategy	Meaning
Water cycle	Water is used over and over.	I related it to the word recycle. I know recycle means to use again.	

FIGURE 12.7. An activity for assessing vocabulary strategy: "My Best Guess."

From *Teaching Reading: Strategies and Resources for Grades K–6* by Rachel L. McCormack and Susan Lee Pasquarelli. Copyright 2010 by The Guilford Press. Permission to photocopy this figure is granted to purchasers of this book for personal use only (see copyright page for details).

FIGURE 12.8. First grader's journal entry.

about the times his grandmother and grandfather babysat him and the fun they had. After reading the text, the students were able to make connections between their own experiences with their grandparents and the experiences the character in the text had with his grandfather.

We have used journal writing as a before-reading assessment many times. We give a very short time limit (5 minutes) for writing, and then ask the students to pair up and share their journal entries. We have found that this short journal activity gives them just the right amount of experience of getting ready to read. You can follow up by asking two or three students to share their entries with the whole class. That way you can get a

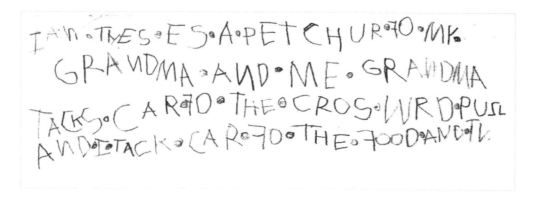

FIGURE 12.9. First grader's journal entry. "Ian. This is a picture of my grandma and me. Grandma takes care of the crossword puzzle and I take care of the food and TV."

general sense of how the students are responding, and, by doing so, you may generate more discussion.

Anticipation Guides

An *anticipation guide* is a before-reading self-assessment activity that contains a list of true or false statements related to the topic or the text your students will be reading (Duffelmeyer, 1994; Wood, Taylor, Drye, & Brigman, 2007). Anticipation guides can include statements that trigger disagreement among students and challenge their own beliefs about something they will be reading. Using an anticipation guide is an effective way to determine the level of background knowledge your students have.

Anticipation guides foster collaborative thinking and learning, so this activity should not be done by students individually. As in many of the activities involving peer-led grouping that we have described, the talk around the task should be highly encouraged and highly valued. During the interaction, small groups of students are expected to read the statements and discuss their opinions, merging their ideas, beliefs, and understanding about the topic.

Anticipation guides are typically used in older grades; however, we advocate using versions of them in any grade, beginning in kindergarten. Figure 12.10 (page 258) shows an anticipation guide designed for kindergartners and used before reading the text *Animals Born Alive and Well* (Heller, 1982). The students worked at their tables in groups of four, while the teacher moved around the classroom. Figure 12.11 (page 258) shows an anticipation guide designed for sixth graders who were about to read the book *Out of the Dust* (Hesse, 1997), a fictional account in free verse of a family's experiences during the Dust Bowl era.

Here are some suggestions for using anticipation guides:

- Group your students in pairs or in small heterogeneous groups of four or five.
- Choose—or let them choose—roles for each person (e.g., group leader, reader, scribe, and reporter).
- Give each student a copy of the anticipation guide.
- Ask the reader to read each statement; the leader should lead the discussion.
- Ask the scribe to record what the group says. The group does not need to reach consensus.
- At the end of the session, read each statement aloud. After each one, elicit a report from the reporter in each group.
- Revisit the anticipation guide after the reading of the text, and compare the students' thoughts and ideas before and after the reading.

Now try designing an anticipation guide on your own:

1. Choose a grade level.
2. Select an expository text or a trade book that you might use to teach a concept in social studies or science.
3. Think of broad concepts that the students may learn as they read this text.
4. Write statements that either support or oppose each concept.

Do you agree? Put an X next to the one you think is true.

	Before Reading	After Reading
All mammals live on land.		
A whale is a mammal.		
All mammals have fur.		
All mammals have four legs.		
A dog is a mammal.		
All mammals have live birth.		
Mammals cannot fly.		

FIGURE 12.10. Anticipation guide before reading the text *Animals Born Alive and Well* (Heller, 1982).

In your groups, read each statement about the Dust Bowl, and decide whether you think each statement is true or false. Feel free to talk about anything else you know about the conditions during the time of the Dust Bowl.

Statement	Agree	Disagree
1. The Dust Bowl was a series of dust storms.		
2. The Dust Bowl spanned the period from 1930 to 1940.		
3. The Dust Bowl took place in Central Florida.		
4. The dust blew eastward in large black clouds.		
5. Much of the soil was deposited in the Atlantic Ocean.		
6. About 500,000 Americans were left homeless.		
7. The Dust Bowl was caused by severe drought.		
8. The Dust Bowl was caused by lack of crop rotation.		
9. Skies were blackened all the way to Chicago.		
10. People died from dust pneumonia.		
11. The Dust Bowl could happen again.		

FIGURE 12.11. Anticipation guide before reading *Out of the Dust* (Hesse, 1997).

When you have completed your guide, you can use it as an artifact for your self-study (see Figure 12.28 at the end of this chapter).

DURING READING: ASSESSING VOCABULARY, COMPREHENSION, AND RESPONSE

During the reading process, you can assess your students with some of the same tools and strategies as you would use before reading and after reading. We have already mentioned some such tools and strategies in the preceding section. In addition, some of the teaching activities described in Chapters 6–9 can also function as assessments, as described below.

Asking Questions

Using the question–answer relationships (QAR) protocol described in Chapter 7, you can help guide your students through the text by giving them questions to think about or write about while they are reading.

Keeping Journals

Journal writing while reading helps keep some students on track. Prompts to respond to while reading can help students interact with text. An assessment of those interactions can provide valuable information about the kinds of connections students are making.

Organizing Text

You can ask students to design a story map while they read narrative text, or to design another kind of graphic organizer while they read either narrative or expository text. This learning activity requires repeated reading of the text. Then the students can use their graphic organizers to write a summary or practice an oral retelling—two ways students can demonstrate their comprehension after reading.

A Practice Activity: Assessing Strategy Knowledge through Think-Alouds

In Chapters 5–9, we have walked you through explicit instruction of comprehension and reader response strategies that all readers must have to understand the many kinds of texts they will be reading. Included in the scripted lessons are transcripts demonstrating the ways in which expert readers think while interacting with different texts. These teacher think-alouds enable students to "hear" a teacher's thought processes. You can use this same process to "hear" what your students are thinking about while they are negotiating a difficult text. Reflecting on what you know about assessment so far, and using what you know about cognitive strategy instruction, how would you assess a student's think-aloud? What would you have to listen for? How would you record your observations? How would it inform your instruction? (See the box on the following page.)

Record a procedure for eliciting a think-aloud here.

AFTER READING: ASSESSING VOCABULARY, COMPREHENSION, AND RESPONSE

Assessing Story Structure

Oral Retelling

As Johnston (1997) reminds us, oral story retelling, although it is a "straightforward" assessment of comprehension, is not entirely authentic. In other words, retelling the stories we read with the amount of detail and elaboration that we want our students to do is not something that we ordinarily do in real life. For example, if a friend asked you, "What did you do last Saturday?", you would not begin with the moment you woke up and relate every detail of the day. The question implies, "What did you do last Saturday *that is interesting or important or worth mentioning*?" A reply such as "I went to the Red Sox double-header," would be an appropriate—and very coveted—response. Similarly, if you are reading a book and a person sitting next to you on the bus says, "Tell me about that book you're reading," you would not begin by saying, "Well, it starts off by . . . " and then continue to retell every detail.

However, this *is* precisely what we expect from our students when we ask them to retell. We expect them to skip the implied version and go right to the detailed, sequential version. We have tried using a prompt such as "Tell me what you remember about the story you just read," and we do not get the same results as when we use a prompt such as "Tell me everything you remember about the story you just read, from the beginning, in order, in your own words." This is a valid difference. The same student retelling the same story using the two different prompts performs much better with the second prompt than with the first prompt. The only difference is that the second question asks them for the elaborated, inauthentic version. For example, we have asked students after reading *Martha Speaks* (Meddaugh, 1992) to tell us about the story, and we have received this for a retelling: "Oh, the dog wouldn't stop talking because she ate the alphabet soup and the family got mad." Although this is the gist of the story, it is not even close to resembling a complete story retelling. After using the second prompt, we have heard the same child say, "Oh, you want the whole thing!" and retell it in detail.

Although we agree with Johnston that story retelling is not very authentic, we find it an effective way to assess comprehension. To elicit a retelling from your students as a means of assessing comprehension, we make the following suggestions, based on a procedure described by Rhodes and Shanklin (1993):

1. Select a story that has a clear story structure. The student should be able to easily identify the story parts.
2. Ask the student to read it silently. Tell the student that you will be asking him or her to retell the story from beginning to end after the reading. This gives the student a purpose for reading, as well as opportunities to reread sections of the story to prepare for the oral assessment.
3. After the student reads silently, say, "Now tell me everything you remember about the story you just read, from the beginning, in order, in your own words."
4. When the student is finished, ask if there is anything else he or she would like to add to the retelling.
5. Analyze the retelling.

Analyzing the Retelling

To analyze the retelling, you can use a retelling checklist similar to the one in Figure 12.12 (page 262). This checklist (which also forms part of our sample second-grade assessment in Appendix B) is a version of an *intervention assessment* (Paratore & McCormack, 2005). It gives specific criteria to be met for a successful retelling. When a student is not completely successful, the assessment is then used to determine under which conditions the student can become successful at retelling. The assessment calls for you to administer interventions until the student is successful. Interventions range from giving prompts to calling for a complete rereading. The "Narrative" column in Figure 12.12 is used for jotting down the story parts before the assessment (it is filled out for "The Fox and the Stork" in Appendix B). To guide your assessment, use the following steps:

1. Follow the procedure for eliciting a story retelling.
2. As the student retells, check the details the student gives in the "NI" (no intervention) column.
3. If the retelling is complete and you are satisfied with the student's performance, you can stop. The student was successful without any interventions. If not, begin administering the following interventions, in this order (check off the ones you use in the corresponding columns of Figure 12.12):
   a. "P" = Prompt. Give a prompt, such as "Every story has a problem."
   b. "Q" = Questioning. Ask, "What else can you tell me about the way the problem was solved?"

Narrative		NI	P	Q	V	R
Setting						
Names main character(s)						
Names other characters						
Time and place						
Problem/Goal						
Refers to problem and/or primary goal						
Major Events						
Relates event(s) leading to solution						
Resolution						
States how problem is solved or goal is attained						
Consequence						
Ends retelling with a concluding statement						
Sequence						
Retells the story in structural order						

Key

NI =	No intervention	V =	Visual cues
P =	Prompt	R =	Reread
Q =	Questioning		

FIGURE 12.12. Story-retelling assessment and analysis: Oral response. Adapted from Paratore and McCormack (2005). Copyright 2005 by The Guilford Press. Adapted by permission.

c. "V" = Visual cues. Say, "Take a look at the picture. Does that give you a clue about why the character was unhappy?"

d. "R" = Reread. Say, "Let's reread this section of the story to see if we can figure out what happened at the end."

4. Write a summary of what you have learned about the student. How well did the student perform? What were the conditions of success? What further instruction is needed?

We like using this intervention assessment procedure for assessing story retelling, because we think it gives us far more information about what students know and under which conditions they are successful.

Story Maps and Story Frames

In Chapter 8, we have described *story maps*, which provide effective frameworks for practicing retelling stories and writing summaries. Another strategy for writing story summaries is a *story frame*. An example of a simple story frame is provided in Figure 12.13 (page 264).

As with all graphic organizers, it is what the students *do* with the story maps or frames that is important; in other words, the graphic organizers are means to an end. Their purpose is to help students organize their thinking before writing or speaking. If a student writes a good summary from a simply drawn story map or graphic organizer, it is the summary that should be assessed, not the graphic organizer. This way, we value the way our students think—as each child thinks differently—and intervene only if the thinking does not produce the outcomes we expect.

Assessing Vocabulary Knowledge through Word Banks

Whenever we ask teachers how they assess the vocabulary their students learn while reading new texts, we invariably get the same answers: (1) matching, (2) filling in the blanks, and (3) writing each definition and using each word in a sentence. Instead of employing these decontextualized assessment formats, we have had success in asking students to demonstrate their understanding of new words by using vocabulary from a *word bank* to answer a question or prompt about a text. In this type of assessment, the word bank is derived from the vocabulary words and terms the students have previously encountered in the text. Look at Figure 12.14 (page 265), which illustrates an assessment used by a second-grade teacher after using the book *Ruby the Copycat* (Rathmann, 1991) to teach a reading lesson. In order to assess her students' knowledge of the vocabulary words they encountered in the text, she provided a bank of the words they had discussed before, during, and after reading, and asked them to answer the following question: "How do you know Ruby and Angela are friends?" This assessment was challenging, but it gave the second-grade teacher important information about how well the students knew the meanings of the words they encountered in the story. This is an effective way to give your students practice using the words meaningfully, while assessing their understanding of the vocabulary in context.

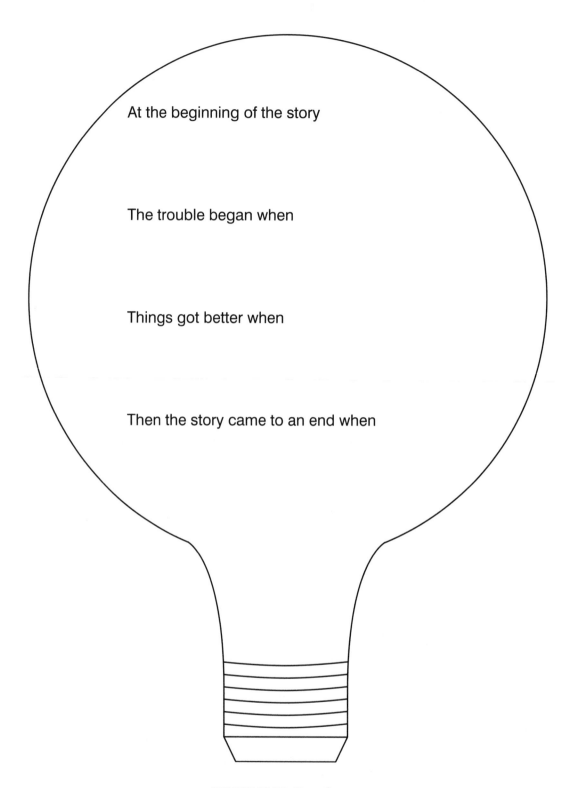

At the beginning of the story

The trouble began when

Things got better when

Then the story came to an end when

FIGURE 12.13. Story frame.

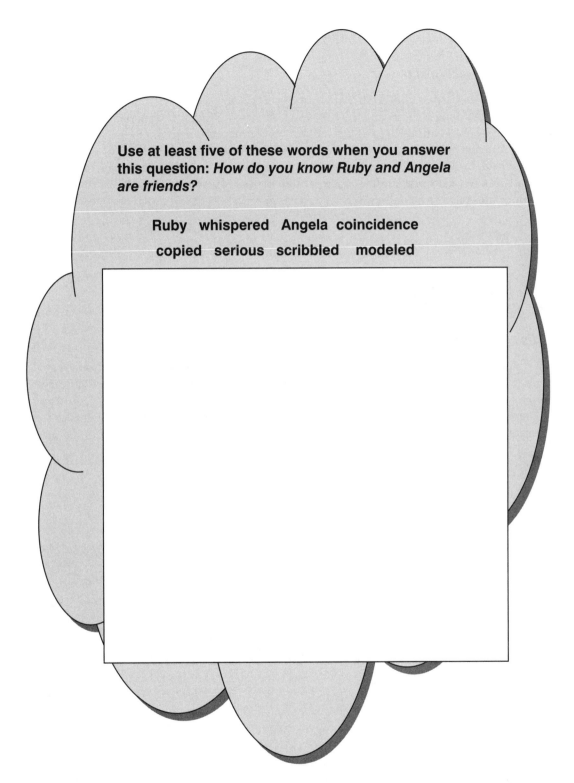

FIGURE 12.14. Using a word bank to assess vocabulary: *Ruby the Copycat* (Rathmann, 1991).

Using Journal Writing

We have already mentioned journal writing as a valuable form of before-reading assessment. When done well, it can also help you assess your students' understanding of text and provide a meaningful (and private) way for students to respond to text.

You can use journals to ask students to record written summaries of what they have read. In Chapter 7, we have described the rules for summary writing and indicated that we have seen first graders successfully write story summaries. Recall that story summaries need to contain the main parts of a story:

- Setting
- Characters
- Problem or goal
- Events leading to solving the problem or attaining the goal
- Consequence or conclusion

Using Summary Writing: Trying It Out

In Figures 12.15 and 12.16, you will find two story summaries. In the first one (Figure 12.15), the student was asked to write a summary for the story *The Doorbell Rang* (Hutchins, 1986). The second one (Figure 12.16) is a summary of the story *The Teeny-Tiny Woman* (Galdone, 1984). How do you think these first graders performed on this assessment? Did they follow the rules for writing story summaries? Can you recognize the story parts? If you wish, you can follow up your assessments of these summaries by using the grade K–1 story summary rubric in Figure 12.17.

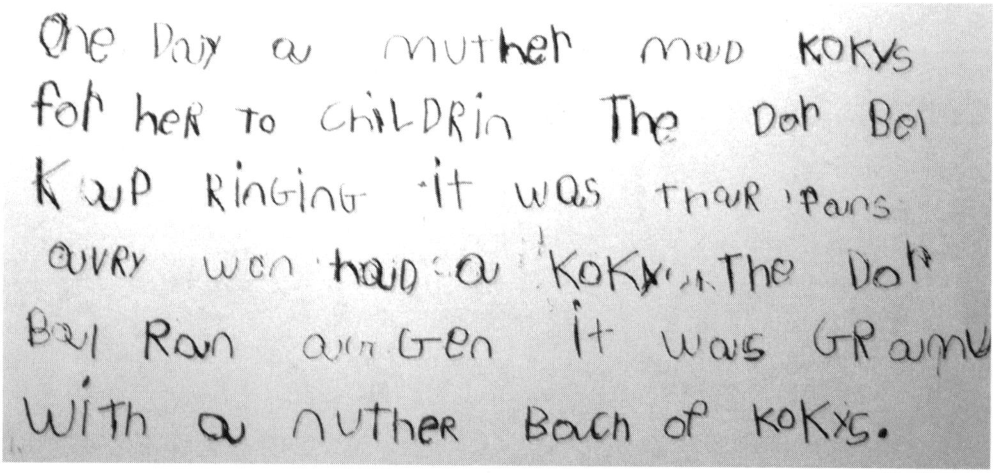

FIGURE 12.15. First grader's summary of *The Doorbell Rang* (Hutchins, 1986). "One day a mother made cookies for her two children. The doorbell kept ringing. It was their friends. Everyone had a cookie. The doorbell rang again. It was Grandma with another batch of cookies."

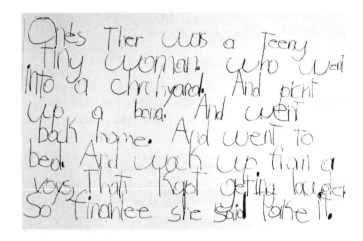

FIGURE 12.16. First grader's summary of *The Teeny Tiny Woman* (Galdone, 1984). "Once there was a teeny tiny woman. who went into a churchyard. And picked up a bone. And went back home. And went to bed. And woke up from a voice, that kept getting louder. So finally she said, 'Take it.'"

Score each bulleted item separately.

Score	Organization/story structure	Mechanics
4	• Accurately writes events in sequence. • Frequently incorporates detailed drawings or other graphics. • Throughout the piece, the child includes sophisticated storybook/literary language, such as "The message in the story . . . ," "The main character is . . ," "The plot is . . . ," "Once upon a time . . . ," etc.	• Includes a majority of sight words and some invented spelling.
3	• Most of the events are in sequence. • Frequently incorporates drawings or other graphics. • Frequently includes important storybook/literary language (see examples above).	• Includes some sight words but is mostly invented spelling.
2	• Some events are in sequence. • Incorporates some drawings or other graphics. • Some storybook/literary language is used (see examples above).	• Mostly invented spelling and random letters.
1–0	• No sequence is evident. • Incorporates few or no drawings or other graphics. • Does not use storybook/literary language at this time.	• Includes little or no use of invented spelling and sight words (scribbles).

FIGURE 12.17. Grade K–1 story summary rubric.

Other Written Responses to Writing

As described in Chapters 8 and 9, we have seen highly effective teachers teach writing genre by genre (Pasquarelli, 2006a), and then ask their students to respond to reading through a repertoire of writing formats. In this way, the students can demonstrate their ability to think through text, and they can show how they have acquired flexibility in their purposes and forms of writing. We advocate this process, as long as the purposes for the assessment are very clear. Are you assessing the students' understanding of the text? (That is text comprehension.) Are you assessing their responses to see how they integrate what they know with what they read? (That is personal response.) Or are you assessing their ability to write several drafts with grade-appropriate grammar, mechanics, and other conventions? (That is writing—both process and product.) Students have a right to know what you are assessing. Each task is different, so each task needs to be assessed in a way that explicitly takes into account its intended purpose.

From kindergarten to grade 6, we have seen students masterfully crafting efferent responses to literature through aesthetic means. At times, while it is hard to decipher the difference between efferent and aesthetic responses, we are reminded that Rosenblatt (1978) has stated that we should *not* require *only* efferent responses from students. Look at Figures 12.18 and 12.19, which depict kindergartners' responses to the book, *Officer Buckle and Gloria* (Rathmann, 1995). In this book, readers are introduced to Officer Buckle, a safety officer who is not quite taken seriously by the students until he decides to bring along his dog, Gloria. After this kindergarten class had read the text, the kindergarten teacher asked the students to draw and label what they felt to be important safety rules. The kindergartners could not help putting their own ideas into the writing task the teacher assigned. They tapped into their prior knowledge as they wrote and illustrated some of the safety rules they had previously learned.

In the next set of figures, Figures 12.20 and 12.21 (page 270), you can see that the voices of students can be loud and clear if we change the audience from ourselves to

FIGURE 12.18. Kindergartner's response to *Officer Buckle and Gloria* (Rathmann, 1995).

FIGURE 12.19. Kindergartner's response to *Officer Buckle and Gloria* (Rathmann, 1995).

others when we ask students to respond to text. In these samples, second-grade students who had read *The Quicksand Book* (dePaola, 1977) were asked to write letters to family members warning them about the dangers of quicksand. You can see in these pieces of writing that they combined both efferent and aesthetic responses. They demonstrated their knowledge of the main ideas, responding in ways consistent with second graders' understanding of an unlikely yet horrifying event.

In the next example, Figure 12.22 (page 271), a fifth grader was learning how to write a narrative account. She asked if she could write about the book she was reading, *War Comes to Willy Freeman* (Collier & Collier, 1983). When the teacher agreed, she wrote a well-developed narrative, trying to convince someone living in the 1750s to visit Sam Fraunces's Tavern in New York.

All of these examples show us creative and enjoyable ways students can demonstrate their understanding of text. These types of authentic writings are viable means for you to assess their comprehension abilities.

Assessing Comprehension and Response through Literature Circles

We have emphasized the importance of peer talk throughout this book. In Chapter 2, we have discussed literature circles ranging from highly structured contexts for teaching reading to informal ones in which students talk about their self-selected books for independent reading. We have observed students in kindergarten through grade 6 participating in peer-led discussions in such circles, when participation is well scaffolded and the responsibility of the teacher is gradually diminished until the students can take over the discussions themselves. Younger children may always need a prompt; older students can respond to what they have read when given some guidance by the teacher or a group leader.

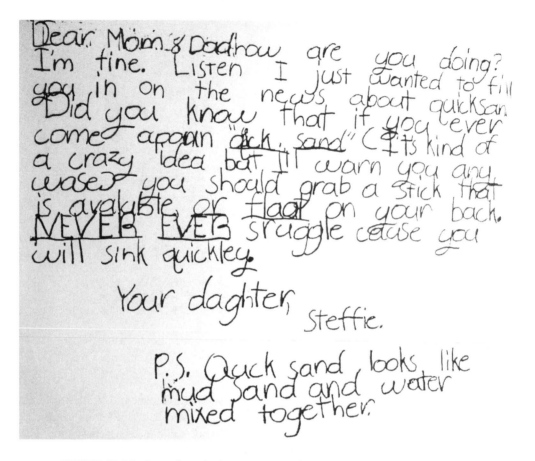

Dear Mom & Dad how are you doing?
I'm fine. Listen I just wanted to fill
you in on the news about quicksan
Did you know that if you ever
come apoain "dick sand" (& Its kind of
a crazy idea but I'll warn you any
wase) you should grab a stick that
is ayalubte or float on your back.
NEVER EVER sruggle cause you
will sink quickley.

Your daghter,
Steffie.

P.S. Quck sand looks like
mud sand and water
mixed together.

FIGURE 12.20. Second grader's response to *The Quicksand Book* (dePaola, 1977).

> Dear David, I know you're sort of young to understand what quicksand is. So…I will try to make it simple to understand. Quicksand is dangerous. That means I am going to warn you about it.
>
> If you ever go near the pond and see mushy sand that looks like dry sand read my lips, Do not go near it. It is quicksand! Do this if you fall in. Stay put. If you move you will sink faster. You should put a stick in it first.
>
> From Rick
> p.s. Watch out!

FIGURE 12.21. Response to *The Quicksand Book* (dePaola, 1977).

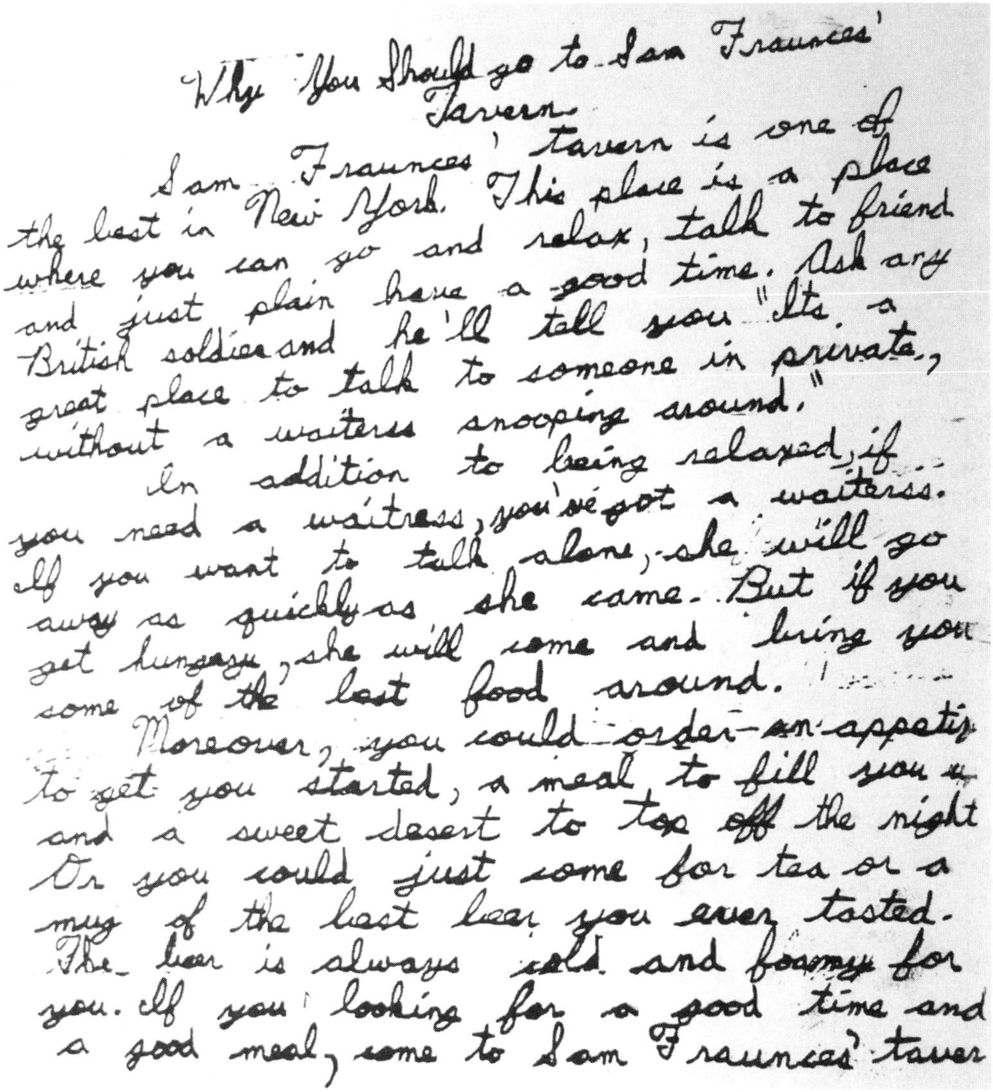
Why You Should go to Sam Fraunces' Tavern

Sam Fraunces' tavern is one of the best in New York. This place is a place where you can go and relax, talk to friend and just plain have a good time. Ask any British soldier and he'll tell you "Its a great place to talk to someone in private, without a waiterss snooping around."

In addition to being relaxed, if you need a waitress, you've got a waiterss. If you want to talk alone, she will go away as quickly as she came. But if you get hungary, she will come and bring you some of the best food around.

Moreover, you could order an appetiz to get you started, a meal to fill you up and a sweet desert to top off the night. Or you could just come for tea or a mug of the best bear you ever tasted. The bear is always cold and foamy for you. If you looking for a good time and a good meal, come to Sam Fraunces' taver

FIGURE 12.22. Fifth grader's persuasive composition: Response to *War Comes to Willy Freeman* (Collier & Collier, 1983).

Literature circles provide an authentic context for talking about literature, and you will learn a great deal about how your students use oral language to demonstrate their knowledge about the literary elements of stories and other texts. You can assess their ability to make personal connections; you will learn how they understand plot or text structure; you can observe the kinds of connections they make between texts; you will learn how they make sense of their world.

Figure 12.23 is a form you can use to record your observations while students are engaging in a peer-led discussion. During the discussion, your role is to observe. Set the boundaries and limits with your students beforehand, so they will understand your

Name of text: _____   Date: _____

Group member	Makes personal connections	Supports ideas through text	Demonstrates knowledge of plot or text	Makes intertextual connections	Builds on ideas of other group members	Uses words from text

FIGURE 12.23. Teacher observation form for literature circles.

role as an observer. In the process, you will also gain knowledge about your own teaching. You may hear your voice echoed in the voices of the children. After listening to a discussion, you might ask yourself: "Am I putting too much emphasis on the literal elements of the text? How can I help them to make more connections to themselves? In what ways can I help them provide text support when offering an idea or stating an opinion?"

Talking about books is a meaningful way for your students to learn—and practice— the give and take of conversations: participating in appropriate turn taking, challenging each other's ideas politely, listening to others, and taking risks with new words.

DESIGNING RUBRICS

You have seen throughout this chapter different tools for assessing your students in vocabulary, comprehension, and response. We have offered you examples of checklists, observation charts, and other informal assessments to give you an idea of the wide range of ways to assess your students' reading performance. You have no doubt noticed that we have included scoring *rubrics* as a way to collect information and analyze your students' performance. A rubric can be defined as "a scoring system that uses a prescribed set of criteria to evaluate student work" (Bell & McCallum, 2008, p. 305). The system can include samples of responses at varying degrees. Ideally, rubrics should be developed in collaboration with your students.

We summarize the guidelines suggested by Cooper and Kiger (2006, pp. 46–47) for using rubrics to assess student performance:

1. Identify the strategies, skills, and knowledge the task will demand.
2. Devise a task that requires the use of these strategies, skills, and knowledge.
3. Develop a rubric to evaluate the performance task.
4. Share the rubric with all students as the task begins.
5. Invite the students to use the rubric to evaluate themselves independently.

We have devised a strategy to help you design a rubric; it is described in Figure 12.24 (page 274). Some examples of teacher-made rubrics can be found in Figures 12.25 (page 275) and 12.26 (pages 276–277).

PUTTING TOGETHER
A PERFORMANCE ASSESSMENT DESIGN

By now, we have described almost every aspect of your students' reading knowledge, from the word levels they recognize to the processes they use to understand and respond to text. Several years ago, we designed many *performance assessments* that encompass all those aspects. A performance assessment we have used with second graders is included in Appendix B. The information we have received from this assessment and others like it has been very valuable; we are very satisfied with the amount and quality of information we learn about our students and the evidence that we collect.

To design each of our performance assessments, we did the following:

1. Identified a particular grade level.
2. Chose a text for the identified grade level. We found that every grade level included a short selection such as a fable, which served us well because the text is a complete story and is typically short (less than 300 words). In addition, we knew that each student would be able to read from a real text if we did not want to use a typed version.
3. Prepared a retelling sheet to record and analyze the retelling.
4. Devised a set of follow-up questions about the story. We followed the QAR protocol described in Chapter 7.
5. Designed an interview to assess metacognition.

---

1. Begin gathering evaluation criteria by taking a look at the nature of the task. In other words, what are the elements of the task? List them. For example, if the assessment is to write a summary, you have to determine first what a good summary looks like, and your list may begin to look like this:

   - Contains mostly main ideas.
   - Contains all salient details.
   - etc.

2. Look up the elements of that task in your standards manual to see if there are any additional criteria. If so, add them to your list.

3. Take your list of elements and turn them into evaluation criteria—for example, "The writing demonstrates clear, accurate identification of main ideas."

4. After you have determined all of your evaluation criteria, try to group them in some way for rubric categories. Your original evaluation criteria then become the criteria for the highest score on the rubric. For example:

	Organization	Content	Grammar
4 points		• Writing demonstrates clear, accurate identification of main ideas. • All main ideas are included.	

5. Reduce the rubric categories by using different qualifiers to determine lower scores. For example, if you give 4 points for identification of *all* main ideas, then you would give 3 points for identification of *most* main ideas.

FIGURE 12.24. Strategy for developing a rubric to match standards.

Score each bulleted item separately.

	4 Exceeds standard	3 Meets standard	2 Nearly meets standard	1–0 Below standard
Content	• Summary contains accurate information that matches the original text. • Summary contains concise inclusion of all story elements. • Summary contains concise inclusion of all important plot details. • Summary contains no redundant or trivial ideas.	• Summary contains some inaccurate information that does not match the original text. • Summary contains all story elements. • Summary contains all important plot details. • Summary contains one idea that is redundant or trivial.	• Summary contains significant inaccurate information that does not match the original text. • Summary contains most story elements. • Summary contains most important plot details. • Summary contains a few ideas that are redundant or trivial.	• Summary contains so much inaccurate information that a new graphic organizer must be completed and the summary must be rewritten. • Summary is missing too many story elements and must be rewritten. • Summary is missing too many important plot details and must be rewritten. • Summary needs a full revision to delete redundant or trivial details.
Organization	• Very well organized; text structure appropriate for topic. • Clear transitions are used to make the summary cohesive.	• Organized, text structure appropriate for topic. • Some transitions are used to make the summary cohesive.	• Weak organization or text structure does not match topic. • The summary needs revision to include transitions to help with cohesiveness.	• Poorly organized or no text structure. • The summary needs complete revision for cohesiveness.
Sentence structure and conventions	• Well-developed sentences with good variety of sentence beginnings. • Few or no errors in spelling, grammar, or punctuation.	• Most sentences are well developed with some variety in sentence beginnings. • Some grammatical errors, but they do not interfere with meaning.	• Some run-on or incomplete sentences with little variety in sentence beginnings. • Several grammar errors that make writing unclear.	• Many run-ons or incomplete sentences with no variety in sentence beginnings. • Grammatical errors interfere with readers' understanding.
Writing process	• All stages of the process are included. • Graphic organizers are complete and detailed. • Significant growth from draft to draft.	• Most stages of the process are included. • Graphic organizers are complete but not detailed. • Shows adequate growth from draft to draft.	• Some stages of the process are included. • Incomplete graphic organizers that led to lack of information in the summary. • Shows little or no growth from draft to draft.	• No stages of the process are included. • No graphic organizers included. • There is only one draft.

FIGURE 12.25. Narrative summary rubric.

Score each bulleted item separately.

	4 Proficient	3 Developing	2 Beginning to develop	1 Not yet
Writing process	• All graphic organizers are detailed and complete. • All stages of the writing process are included. • Significant growth from draft to draft.	• All graphic organizers are complete. • Most stages of the writing process are included. • Adequate growth from draft to draft.	• Incomplete graphic organizers. • Some stages of the writing process are included. • Some growth from draft to draft.	• No graphic organizers. • No stages of the writing process are included. • Little or no growth from draft to draft.
Book review elements	• The introduction paragraph has a captivating lead and states the title and author of the book. • The summary of the story line is brief and leaves the reader wanting to know more. • Character analysis is clear, with detailed examples. • Setting analysis is clear, with detailed examples. • Plot analysis is clear, with detailed examples. • Theme analysis is clear, with detailed examples. • Reflection expresses opinion and leaves the reader in suspense.	• The introduction paragraph is missing one of the following: captivating lead, title, or author. • The summary of the story line is brief and doesn't give away the ending. • Character analysis is clear, with some examples. • Setting analysis is clear, with some examples. • Plot analysis is clear, with some examples. • Theme analysis is clear, with some examples. • Reflection expresses opinion but is not suspenseful.	• The introduction paragraph is missing two of the following: captivating lead, title, or author. • There are too many details in the summary, but it doesn't give away the ending. • Character analysis is unclear, with few examples. • Setting analysis is unclear, with few examples. • Plot analysis is unclear, with few examples. • Theme analysis is unclear, with few examples. • Reflection does not express opinion and is not suspenseful.	• The introduction paragraph doesn't have a captivating lead, title, or author. • There is no summary, or the summary gives away the ending. • Character analysis is unclear, with no examples. • Setting analysis is unclear, with no examples. • Plot analysis is unclear, with no examples. • Theme analysis is unclear, with no examples. • There is no reflection.

276

Writing style	• Writing is fluent and uses clear transitions. • All ideas and opinions are clearly expressed.	• Writing is generally fluent and uses some transitions. • Most ideas and opinions are clearly expressed.	• Writing is not fluent and uses few transitions. • Some ideas and opinions are clearly expressed.	• Writing is not fluent and doesn't use transitions. • Ideas and opinions are not clearly expressed.
Content accuracy	• All details from the story are accurate.	• Most details from the story are accurate.	• Some details from the story are accurate.	• Details are not accurate.
Sentence structure and conventions	• All sentences are complete sentences. There are no fragments or run-ons. • Few or no errors in spelling, capitalization, or punctuation. • Few or no errors in grammar.	• There are some fragments and run-ons. • Some errors in spelling, capitalization, or punctuation. • Some errors in grammar.	• There are many fragments and run-ons. • Several errors in spelling, capitalization, or punctuation. • Several grammatical errors.	• Sentence structure inhibits readers' understanding. • Errors in spelling, capitalization, and/or punctuation make writing unclear. • Grammatical errors make writing unclear.

FIGURE 12.26. Book review assessment.

When we administered the performance assessments to the students at the beginning of the school year, it gave us information about (1) approximately how well the students could access the core reading text, and the level of support we might need to give each student; (2) how well the students could retell a story and answer questions; (3) the amount of explicit instruction in comprehension the students might need; and (4) the amount of knowledge they had about the processes they used as developing readers (i.e., the extent of their metacognition). We were able to take the components of the trustworthy assessments we typically used in classrooms to assess literacy (Paratore & McCormack, 2005) and combine them with the district-adopted reading text that the students would be reading that year.

COLLECTING EVIDENCE FOR STUDENT PORTFOLIOS

In Chapter 11, we have described how you can collect evidence of your students' performance and put it together with your students as part of a portfolio process. You have learned about various types of assessment in phonological/phonemic awareness, phonics, and fluency, and about the evidence for students' performance and growth in these aspects of reading that you can collect in the portfolios.

In this chapter, you have learned about methods for assessing students' metacognition, vocabulary knowledge, comprehension, strategy use, and response and about ways you and your students can collect evidence in these areas. You are now ready to add to your list of artifacts that you and your students can include in their portfolios.

Make a list of the artifacts you can collect about your students to learn what they know and can do.

FINAL WORDS ABOUT ASSESSING READING

In the last two chapters, we have described ways to assess your students in the classroom context. Whenever you assess your own students in the context of a real classroom, you have a great deal of data to analyze and to use in making decisions about your pedagogy. This is why learning about new assessments, trying them out, and sharing the results with others are important: Doing these things can only make you better at assessing.

If you are a teacher, you will be asked to assess your students in ways that are not always as authentic as the ones described in this book. This is all the more reason why you should be diligent about collecting as much evidence as you can about the things that your students know and can do well.

One last word of caution: Although instruction and assessment go hand in hand, please do not confuse assessment with instruction or with *assigning*. Assigning students to write in response to reading without teaching them how to do it is an ineffective practice. Assigning them to answer questions after reading a text is not teaching them how to think while they are reading and negotiating text so that it makes sense to them. We would like to see far more *teaching* of comprehension than we see on a day-to-day basis in the classrooms we observe. We hope that our explanations of explicit instruction and our suggestions for authentic assessment will inspire you to take a good look at your own pedagogy and motivate you to align your practices with what we know as excellent teaching of reading.

Before you read the next chapter, take a few moments to assess your comprehension of this chapter by referring to the Key Terms Chart in Figure 12.27 (page 280). Write definitions for these terms in your own words to assess your own understanding. In Chapter 13, we present ways to demonstrate your professionalism through self-study, inservices, and other professional development activities.

REFLECTION ON ARTIFACTS FOR YOUR SELF-STUDY

For your self-study, record on Figure 12.28 (page 281) the artifacts you created while you read this chapter.

KEY TERMS FOR CHAPTER 12

In this chapter, the following key terms are essential to your understanding of reading instruction. Think about what they mean, and try to define them in your own words.

anticipation guide

intervention assessment

story frame

word bank

rubric

performance assessment

FIGURE 12.27. Key Terms Chart for Chapter 12.

SELF-STUDY REVIEW CHART FOR CHAPTER 12

Name of Artifact	Teacher Instructional Actions and Language	Provisions for Individual Differences	Variety of Modes of Communication	Critical Thinking and Active Engagement	Opportunities for Assessment

FIGURE 12.28. Self-Study Review Chart for Chapter 12.

CHAPTER 13

Viewing Ourselves as Professional Teachers of Reading

Recently at a local gym, I (RLM) noticed a young woman, Thea, whom I instantly recognized as a student I had taught in second grade. I approached her and introduced myself. She said, "Of course I remember you, but I didn't think you would recognize me." During the conversation, Thea told me that she had just cleaned out a closet at her mother's house. In a box at the bottom of the closet, she found a dog-eared paperback copy of *Frog and Toad All Year* (Lobel, 1976). When she opened the book, there was a handwritten inscription from her mother: "Thea, I'm so proud of you! You are a great reader! Always remember your second-grade teacher, who taught you how to read." I wondered if Thea had struggled as an early reader, and I told her that I did not remember her struggling. She replied that she had had a very unsuccessful first-grade experience, but that she'd finally learned to read when she was a student in my second-grade class. "I have always been grateful to you," she said. She then told me, her voice swelling with pride, that she had just graduated from college and had been on the dean's list all 4 years.

Anyone who has been teaching children to read for a long time can tell many stories like this one. It is not unusual. We have chosen to include it here to illustrate the importance and impact of teaching children to read. Our students' early experiences with learning to read affect the rest of their lives. There is no job more difficult; there is no job more rewarding.

As good teachers of reading, we put great demands on our students. We must also put demands on ourselves as teachers of reading. Sometimes that means stepping out of our own comfort zones, trying new things, and being open to new ideas. We know that being a good teacher means more than receiving good training in a teacher education program. Learning to be an effective teacher of reading is ongoing and hard work. Members of other professions, such as medicine, law, and architecture, are required to engage in ongoing professional development throughout their careers as methods change, technologies advance, and research is conducted and disseminated. The same is true for the teaching profession. Fortunately, most school districts offer teachers many opportunities to update their skills and engage in professional development in the teaching of reading. But we have seen teachers go far beyond what their school districts require and expect.

MEETING PROFESSIONAL STANDARDS

In Rhode Island, the state in which we prepare our teachers, we have the following professional standard: "Teachers reflect on their practice and assume responsibility for their own professional development by actively seeking and participating in opportunities to learn and grow as professionals" (Rhode Island Department of Education, p. 17). We know that similar teaching standards exist in many other states we have investigated.

When you collect artifacts and engage in self-study, you are engaging in an important aspect of professional development. This is one way to investigate how to improve your practice of teaching reading. Read more about the research-based activities suggested in the text, try them out, and discuss them with others. Then, as suggested in the Preface, gather and organize your artifacts into a physical or electronic portfolio. We encourage you to make this process a consistent element of your practice. Our intention is to help you get started on a habit that can only lead to your becoming a better professional and a better teacher of reading.

There are many other ways to become involved in your own professional development activities. Ten important ones are listed in Figure 13.1 and are described in the rest of this chapter. Figure 13.2 contains links, websites, and online resources for your further investigation. We suggest that you participate in some or all of the professional activities and find the ones that suit you best. Choose the ones that provide you with the appropriate experiences to be the best professional you can be.

---

1. Become a member of professional organizations, and take advantage of their benefits.
2. Learn about and read award-winning literature for children.
3. Form or join a professional study group with other teachers of reading.
4. Start or join a professional book group.
5. Conduct action research, and share the results with your colleagues.
6. Keep a journal of your reflections about yourself as a teacher of reading.
7. Subscribe to online professional journals, to stay current with the latest research in the teaching of reading.
8. Visit other classrooms to learn new strategies for teaching reading.
9. Invite other teachers to your classroom to show them new strategies you have learned; ask them to model strategies for you.
10. Attend workshops, conferences, or courses in teaching reading, and share what you have learned with your colleagues.

FIGURE 13.1. Ten ways to show professionalism.

Professional Portfolios

www.eduscapes.com/tap/topic82.htm

content.scholastic.com/browse/article.jsp?id=4148

hagar.up.ac.za/catts/ole/oro1999/resources/portfolio/Professional.PDF

Professional Organizations

International Reading Association: *www.reading.org*

National Council of Teachers of English: *www.ncte.org*

National Reading Conference: *www.nrconline.org*

Children's Literature

American Library Association: *www.ala.org*

Multicultural Children's Literature: *www.lib.msu.edu/corby/education/multicultural.htm*

Professional Study Groups and Book Clubs

teacher.scholastic.com/products/instructor/jointheclub.htm

teachers.net/gazette/AUG00/fisher.html

www.choiceliteracy.com/public/department29.cfm

Action Research

gse.gmu.edu/research/tr

www.madison.k12.wi.us/sod/car/carhomepage.html

Online Journals

www.readingonline.org

aera-cr.asu.edu/ejournals

FIGURE 13.2. Websites and links for engaging in professional activities.

Become a Member of Professional Organizations

Becoming a member of one or more professional organizations opens the doors to a number of benefits and opportunities. Complete access to these organizations' websites is among the most advantageous. Members can access online journals, contribute to discussions forums, join committees, vote on officers and issues, and receive reduced rates for annual and regional conference fees. In addition, membership often provides discounts on professional books published by these organizations.

National organizations often have regional, state, or local affiliates. Become actively involved in these affiliates, and you can meet with other professionals who live and work near you.

Learn about and Read Award-Winning Literature for Children

If you love teaching children to read, you no doubt love to read yourself. Modeling a love for reading makes reading contagious for many children. Knowing good books is beneficial; being an avid reader is a must. Lapp, Fisher, and Flood (2008) suggest that teachers use authentic children's literature as a significant part of their reading programs, for three reasons. The first reason is that using real literature (both narrative and expository) models for children the language structures they will encounter as they become more competent readers. Second, reading real literature helps students connect what they are reading to their prior knowledge. Third, reading real literature is more motivating.

Each January, the American Library Association announces the winners of its awards for children's and young adults' books on its website (*www.ala.org*). Bookmark the site as a "favorite," because it is frequently updated. Figure 13.3 lists these awards and provides a short description of each.

The number of new books published each year can be overwhelming, especially for new teachers or for teachers who change grade levels. We suggest that you start by reading as many of the award winners and honor books as you can. Multicultural picture books and selections for older children are wonderful for reading aloud. Keeping up with the latest popular and recognized titles demonstrates to the students that you know about and care about the books they will read. Teacher endorsement is critical. Students and parents rely on teachers to recommend good literature, and contemporary titles are among the most popular ones with students.

- **John Newbery Medal**, for the most outstanding contribution to children's literature.
- **Randolph Caldecott Medal**, for the most distinguished American picture book for children.
- **Michael L. Printz Award**, for excellence in literature written for young adults.
- **Coretta Scott King Book Award**, recognizing an African American author and illustrator of outstanding books for children and young adults.
- **Schneider Family Book Award**, for books that embody the artistic expression of the disability experience for child and adolescent audiences.
- **Theodor Seuss Geisel Award**, for the most distinguished book for beginning readers.
- **Margaret A. Edwards Award**, for lifetime achievement in writing for young adults.
- **The Pura Belpré Award**, honoring Latino/Latina authors and illustrators whose work best portrays, affirms, and celebrates the Latino/Latina cultural experience in children's books.
- **Robert F. Sibert Medal**, for most distinguished informational book for children.
- **Andrew Carnegie Medal**, for excellence in children's video.
- **Mildred L. Batchelder Award**, for the most outstanding children's book translated from a foreign language and subsequently published in the United States.
- **Odyssey Award for Excellence in Audiobook Production.**
- **Alex Awards**, for the 10 best adult books that appeal to teen audiences.
- **May Hill Arbuthnot Honor Lecture**, recognizing an individual of distinction in the field of children's literature, who then presents a lecture at a winning host site.

FIGURE 13.3. The annual American Library Association youth media awards (*www.ala.org*).

There are many other professionals who can help you select books to read and use with students: your school librarian, the children's librarians at public libraries, and owners of independent booksellers. They know the books that are frequently requested, checked out, and purchased by students and their parents.

Form or Join a Professional Study Group

Participating in a study group is an interactive way to engage in professional development. Study groups can investigate topics in reading, pilot-test new programs, look at student work, and discuss teaching methods. They are flexible and allow for different ways of investigating topics in literacy, ranging from reading books to downloading online journal articles. The possibilities are endless. Participants can try out different techniques they read about. Later, they can bring student work and artifacts to the group for analysis and discussion by the group members. Bean (2004) states that when teachers are participants in study groups, "they become more engaged in the process and are generally more willing to apply what they are learning to their classroom practices" (p. 91).

In some districts, study groups meet during the school day, and the participants are released from their classrooms for an hour or so every month for the meetings. Teachers have told us that this structure works well for them, and it sends them a message that the study group meeting is an integral part of a teacher's working life.

Because study groups are gaining popularity, we have suggested some websites in Figure 13.2 (page 284) that contain information and guidelines for participating in such a group.

Form or Join a Professional Book Group

Professional book groups or clubs are increasing in many school districts. Teachers have informed us that they can meet as often as once a week, but they usually meet once a month after a professional book is read. This format is effective for several reasons. First, professional books *should* be discussed with other professionals. According to Walpole and McKenna (2008), professional book clubs "foster collaborative discussion of texts that have been selected for their match to the goals of the building" (p. 52). It is through reading and responding to the books that members can share their understanding and can seek clarification from each other. Second, the social aspect of a book group makes reading the texts more enjoyable. Moreover, in many districts and states, participating in a professional book club is considered valid professional development, and the hours can be collated or logged for recertification purposes.

Conduct Action Research

Action research is a systematic process for investigating a method, a program, or an authentic school or classroom situation. Its overarching purpose is to improve instructional actions (Johnson, 2002).

We would argue that good teachers are always conducting research; it is impossible to teach effectively without making ongoing assessments of your students' performance and then making the necessary adjustments. But, in our busy and hectic schedules, we often do the data analysis in our heads and keep going. What is different in

- The data collected in action research can be used to provide a more complete picture of your students and the students in your school or district.
- Your colleagues are often interested in hearing about the findings of your research project.
- Action research can be used to make a case for a particular methodology or program, or to evaluate new programs.
- Professional conferences, academic journals, and online journals are possible venues for sharing your action research projects.
- Local community organizations are often interested in hearing about the latest trends in education.

FIGURE 13.4. Why present your action research? Based on Johnson (2002).

action research is that the data collection and analysis are more systematic and often more purposeful. In addition, the results lend themselves to being shared with others.

Mraz, Vacca, and Vintinner (2008) have found three trends when investigating teachers as researchers. First, they have found that teachers who do action research feel more involved in their own practice of teaching. Moreover, teacher action researcher teams exhibit increased collegiality as a result of working closely with each other on their shared goals, investigations, and practice. Furthermore, the studies they conduct can produce data that are focused and measurable.

Johnson's (2002) work has guided us through well-structured action research projects with teachers from many districts. Figure 13.4 summarizes Johnson's rationale for engaging in action research and sharing the results. Your colleagues, your school administration, and the community are truly interested in hearing about the findings of your research project.

Keep a Journal

If you have been gathering evidence for your self-study, you already know the importance of reflection for pedagogy. Keeping a teaching journal has similar results. It is perhaps the easiest way to engage in professional development.

Yinger and Clark (1981) have suggested that keeping a journal of feelings, thoughts, and reflections provides teachers with the means to learn more about themselves in four important ways. First, it enhances what they know. When teachers write about their prior knowledge in a journal, things that may have become routine are once again made explicit in their minds. This act enables teachers to construct new meaning as they make connections with newly acquired knowledge. Yinger and Clark add that this process also allows teachers to identify gaps or inconsistencies in their thinking.

Second, the act of journal writing provides teachers with connections to their emotions and feelings. Yinger and Clark have suggested that by making symbolic representations of affective knowledge, teachers can examine their emotional conflicts and resolve personal issues related to their classrooms.

Third, Yinger and Clark believe that journal writing is an opportunity for teachers to explore what they do and how they do it. Journal writers who produce written records of their actions have opportunities to reflect outside the classroom and to evaluate their actions and procedures in quiet moments separate from the demands of teaching.

Finally, Yinger and Clark have suggested that through journal writing, teachers have occasions to reflect on "why" or the reasons for their actions. They state that this process provides teachers with knowledge that results from evaluating and judging personal motives and making changes to their rationales accordingly. These four provisions of classroom journal writing give teachers opportunities for systematic reflection on their teaching.

Journal entries can be structured around a series of questions, such as "What did I learn about myself today?", "What were the strengths of my lesson?", or "How could I have differentiated my instruction to meet the needs of all the students?" Responding to such questions in writing, learning from them, and making the changes or revisions to instruction can make a journal valuable.

Many teachers require their students to keep journals; your own journal is a perfect complement to their activity. It can model for students the importance of maintaining a written log as a self-evaluation tool. One of our professors once said, "Never ask your students to write anything you haven't written yourself." We agree.

Subscribe to Online Professional Journals

Reading professional journals is the best way to stay current. Many online versions of professional journals and publications are now offered as alternatives to paper copies. Figure 13.2 (page 284) provides links to two journals that are available online; there are many others. Many of these journals are peer-reviewed research journals. Reading the research often validates the good practice that excellent teachers use. More importantly, it helps teachers stay on the cutting edge of the latest research in reading. We feel that professional development should include a fair amount of reading the research. As previously mentioned, if you belong to professional organizations, you will have increased access to online journals and other publications. These websites are frequently updated, and they include summaries of research and the organizations' position papers.

Visit Classrooms of Other Excellent Teachers

Teaching can be a solitary experience, even with a classroom full of energetic children. Classroom teachers are seldom able to work outside their own classrooms. When we were reading specialists, we spent time in many classrooms while providing services to students, modeling lessons, and consulting with teachers. We were surprised at how different teachers were, and how reading methods varied from teacher to teacher. Not everything we saw was best practice, but many things were. We remember thinking as we saw terrific lessons, "Everyone should see this!" If you are able to take a professional day from your job or class to visit the classroom of an excellent teacher or to shadow one, it will be well worth your while. The classroom you want to visit may be in your own school, or it may be outside your district. An exemplary lesson modeled by a teacher is far easier to replicate than one that is only described to you. In addition, you will find that excellent teachers have well-designed classroom spaces and routines that support literacy learning.

If you decide to visit, arrive prepared. Equip yourself with a notebook to take field notes and write questions. Bring a camera to take photos of classroom spaces. Immediately afterward, be sure to record all your thoughts and observations, so you do not forget anything: "What can I try tomorrow? What is going to involve more study? What will require follow-up with the teacher or teachers I observed?" Visiting other class-rooms or shadowing an excellent teacher is a powerful way to engage in professional development.

Attend Workshops, Conferences, or Courses in Teaching Reading

Be thoughtful in your choices for workshops, conferences, or courses. Do not choose them just because they are convenient or inexpensive (or free), or because they are a quick and easy way to gather professional development points. Rather, make decisions based upon your needs and upon the credentials and reputations of the instructors or presenters. Be sure the information and methods are current and research-based. Talk to others who have attended similar events or who have experience working with the presenters.

After attending a workshop or conference, it is a good idea to talk with others about what you have learned. Once again, this requires a process of deep reflection as you decide which aspects of the conference or workshop are beneficial to share with others and what format in which to present them. We once had a principal who was very generous in granting professional days to attend workshops and conferences, provided that the attendees would share what was learned with the rest of the faculty at a faculty meeting or at an after-school workshop. We got lots of practice in making presentations to our peers, because we never passed up an opportunity to attend an outstanding workshop or a national conference. By offering up front to present to your faculty what you have learned at a workshop, you may increase your chances of getting permission to take professional days to attend conferences and workshops.

A FINAL THOUGHT

Recently we came across this letter from a second grader to his parents:

> Dear Mom and Dad
> Evrething has ben fin
> we just finisht tomie Depaola
> I thingk my techer has a crush on him
> Becas we have ben stodeing
> him for a month.

We cannot emphasize enough the effects that our knowledge, actions, and enthusiasm about reading have on our students. We are convinced that teaching children to read is the most important job in the world. We applaud all teachers who choose to take on—and excel at—this profession.

The Most Common Phonetic Elements and the Most Common Onsets and Rimes

The Most Common Phonetic Elements

Consonants

Name	What you hear	Examples
Single consonants	The sound of the individual letter is heard.	c<u>a</u>t b, c, d, f, g, h, j, k, l, m, n, p, q, r, s, t, v, w, x, y, z
Consonants—two-letter blends	The sound of each of the two letters is heard.	<u>st</u>op r family: br, cr, dr, fr, gr, pr, tr, wr l family: bl, cl, fl, gl, pl, sl s family: sc, sk, sm, sn, sp, st, sw t family: tr, tw
Consonants—three-letter blends	The sound of each of the three letters is heard.	<u>str</u>ip scr, squ, str, spr, spl
Consonant digraphs	Two letters combine to make a whole new sound.	<u>ch</u>oose <u>sh</u>eet <u>th</u>e <u>wh</u>o

Vowels

Name	What you hear	Examples
Single vowels—short	The short sound.	c<u>a</u>t a, e, i, o, u, and sometimes y
Single vowels—long	The long sound (the vowel says its name).	g<u>o</u> a, e, i, o, u, and sometimes y
Silent vowels	No sound.	fac<u>e</u>
R-controlled vowels	The vowel combines with the r to make a new sound.	c<u>ar</u> sh<u>or</u>t f<u>ir</u> f<u>ur</u> aft<u>er</u>

Vowel digraphs	Only one vowel sound is heard. The first vowel is long and the second is not sounded.	Long a: b<u>ai</u>t
		        h<u>ay</u>
		Long e: sh<u>ee</u>p
		        <u>ea</u>t
		Long o: b<u>oa</u>t
		        t<u>oe</u>

Vowel diphthongs	Two vowels come together to make a whole new sound.	oo: l<u>oo</u>k, m<u>oo</u>n oi: <u>oi</u>l oy: b<u>oy</u> ou: <u>ou</u>t au: t<u>au</u>ght ow: <u>ow</u>n, sn<u>ow</u>

The Most Common Onsets and Rimes

Onsets—single letter	Examples
b	*b/ig = big*
c	*c/at = cat*
d	*d/og = dog*
f	*f/an = fan*
g	*g/et = get*
h	*h/at = hat*
j	*j/am = jam*
k	*k/eep = keep*
l	*l/og = log*
m	*m/an = man*
n	*n/ap = nap*
p	*p/en = pen*
r	*r/ag = rag*
s	*s/ad = sad*
t	*t/ap = tap*
w	*w/et = wet*

Onsets—double letter	Examples
bl	*bl/og = blog*
br	*br/at = brat*
ch	*ch/at = chat*
cl	*cl/ap = clap*
cr	*cr/ab = crab*
dr	*dr/op = drop*
fl	*fl/ag = flag*
fr	*fr/og = frog*
gl	*gl/ad = glad*
pl	*pl/um = plum*
sh	*sh/op = shop*
sk	*sk/unk = skunk*

(cont.)

The Most Common Onsets and Rimes

Onsets—double letter (cont.)	Examples
sl	*sl/ip = slip*
sm	*sm/all = small*
sp	*sp/ot = spot*
st	*st/op = stop*
sw	*sw/eat = sweat*
th	*th/ing = thing*
tr	*tr/am = tram*
tw	*tw/in = twin*

Onsets—triple letter	Examples
scr	*scr/ap = scrap*
shr	*shr/ink = shrink*
spr	*spr/ing = spring*
squ	*squ/id = squid*
str	*str/ap = strap*

Rimes—double-letter endings	Examples
ad	*bad, sad, mad*
ag	*sag, brag, tag*
am	*clam, spam, cram*
an	*pan, plan, tan*
ap	*tap, scrap, map*
at	*cat, fat, hat, sat*
ed	*bed, fed, led*
eg	*beg, leg, peg*
en	*den, hen, then*
et	*pet, met, jet*
ig	*big, fig, pig*
in	*bin, fin, tin*
ip	*dip, hip, lip*
it	*bit, fit, hit*

The Most Common Onsets and Rimes *(page 3 of 3)*

Rimes— double-letter endings *(cont.)*	Examples
ob	*job, mob, slob*
og	*frog, hog, flog*
ot	*jot, slot, plot*
ud	*mud, bud, spud*
un	*fun, nun, sun*

Rimes— triple-letter endings	Examples
ace	*face, trace, grace*
ake	*bake, make, lake*
amp	*damp, cramp, lamp*
and	*band, hand, land*
ang	*bang, gang, sang*
eat	*meat, treat, pleat*
eep	*keep, sheep, jeep*
eet	*greet, feet, meet*
end	*bend, fend, lend*
ent	*bent, cent, dent*
est	*best, nest, pest*
ilk	*milk, silk*
ing	*king, spring, thing*
ink	*pink, mink, sink*
int	*lint, tint, print*
ist	*fist, gist, twist*
ond	*bond, pond, frond*
uck	*pluck, truck* (be careful with this rime)
ump	*dump, lump, pump*
unk	*bunk, punk, sunk*
usk	*dusk, tusk, musk*

APPENDIX B

Second-Grade Sample
Reading Performance Assessment

Affective Survey

Ask students these questions and record their responses.

1. How would you describe yourself as a reader?

2. What would you like to be able to read?

3. Do you like to read aloud? Read silently?

4. What kinds of things do you like to read or read about?

5. How can you improve as a reader?

6. What is the title of the last book you read on your own?

7. What do you think teachers can do to motivate their students to read?

Second-Grade Text:

"The Fox and the Stork"

On a summer day, Fox went for a walk in the forest and met Stork. Stork was happy to meet Fox and said,

"Hello, Fox!"

"Hello," replied Fox. As Fox bowed deeply, he added, "I was just thinking of you, Stork. Would you like to have dinner with me tonight at my house?"

Stork was delighted and said, "I would love to have dinner with you tonight! What time would you like me to come?"

"At sundown," Fox replied.

Now I hope you do not think that Fox was being a good friend. Fox really thought a lot of himself and liked others to know how smart he was, too. He was planning to play a trick on Stork so he could brag about it to his other animal friends. So when Stork arrived for dinner that night, Fox outwitted her and put the soup into two shallow bowls.

Well, you can imagine what happened! Because Stork's beak was so long, she was not able to eat any of the soup. Fox, of course, knew Stork could not eat out of the shallow bowl, but asked Stork anyway, "Why aren't you eating your soup?"

Stork replied that she wasn't very hungry even though the soup was quite delicious. Stork wanted to be polite so she asked Fox to come to her nest for dinner the next night. Fox said he would like to come and the two made plans to meet again.

The next night, when Fox approached Stork's nest, he smelled a delicious dinner being prepared. He was very hungry and could not wait to eat the porridge that Stork had prepared. Well, Stork was also very clever and served the porridge in two very tall vases that had very narrow necks. Of course Fox's snout could not fit in the vase so he could not eat a thing! Fox realized right then and there that Stork was smarter than he was because she tricked him back!

Moral: If you trick others, they may trick you back!

Based on LaFontaine's version of Aesop's fable (1989).

Running Record Sheet

Child's name: _____

Date: _____   Grade: _____

	Uses meaning? structure? visual?
Put running record here:	

Based on Clay (1979).

Fluency Assessment and Analysis (Three Parts)

CALCULATE ACCURACY

100 words – number of incorrectly read words = accuracy percentage

CALCULATE AUTOMATICITY

- Choose a 100- to 200-word passage from a text in the literacy curriculum. Ask the student to read aloud for 1 minute from the beginning of the text.
- As the student is reading, count the number of correct words. Stop after 1 minute.
- Calculate the score as correct words per minute (cwpm; WCPM, or words correct per minute, in the chart below).
- Find child's rate in the chart below.

ORAL READING FLUENCY TARGET RATE NORMS

Grade	Fall (WCPM)	Winter (WCPM)	Spring (WCPM)
1		10–30	30–60
2	30–60	50–80	70–100
3	50–90	70–100	80–110
4	70–110	80–120	100–140
5	80–120	100–140	110–150
6	100–140	110–150	120–160
7	110–150	120–160	130–170
8	120–160	130–170	140–180

(cont.)

DETERMINE PROSODY

While you are listening to the student's oral reading, use the following Likert scale we designed to score the elements of prosody.

Elements of prosody	All of the time Score = 3	Some of the time Score = 2	None of the time Score = 1
Student uses consistent and appropriate volume.			
Student uses punctuation for effective phrasing.			
Student reads easily and efficiently, making more self-corrections than errors.			
Student reads at a steady conversational pace.			
Student uses expression while reading aloud. For example, student changes tone for dialogue or to differentiate among characters.			
Student reads with the appropriate tone for the mood of the story or to exemplify the emotions of the character.			
Score tally.			

Procedure for calculating automaticity is based on Kuhn (2007). Oral reading fluency norms chart was retrieved February 20, 2008, from *www.prel.org/products/re_/assessingfluency.htm*; reprinted by courtesy of Pacific Resources for Education and Learning. Prosody information is based on Rasinski (2003).

Final score: _____

INTERPRETATION OF PROSODY SCORE:

18–15: Prosody is exemplary for level of text read.

15–6: Prosody needs intervention according to area(s) of need.

Story-Retelling Assessment and Analysis

	Narrative	NI	P	Q	V	R
Setting						
Names main character(s)	• _Fox and Stork_					
Names other characters	• _None_					
Time and place	• _Forest during a summer day_					
Problem/Goal						
Refers to problem and/or primary goal	• _Fox asks Stork to dinner_ • _Stork accepts_ • _Fox plans on tricking Stork so he can brag to other animals_ • _Fox serves soup in shallow bowls_ • _Stork can't eat soup because her beak is too long_					
Major Events						
Relates event(s) leading to solution	• _Before leaving, Stork invites Fox to dinner_ • _Fox says yes_					
Resolution						
States how problem is solved or goal is attained	• _Stork serves porridge in tall jars with narrow necks_ • _Fox can't eat and goes home hungry_					
Consequence						
Ends retelling with a concluding statement	• _Fox realizes he can't brag to other animals_ • _Stork has tricked him as well_ • _Moral: If you trick others, they may trick you back!_					
Sequence						
Retells the story in structural order						

(Header above NI/P/Q/V/R columns: **Interventions**)

Key

NI =	No intervention	V =	Visual cues
P =	Prompt	R =	Reread
Q =	Questioning		

Adapted from Paratore and McCormack (2005). Copyright 2005 by The Guilford Press. Adapted by permission.

Probe Questions Assessment and Analysis

1. In which season did the Fox meet the Stork in the forest?
   (Right There question)

2. Why did Fox want to trick Stork?
   (Right There question)

3. What was Fox's plan?
   (Think and Search question)

4. When Stork was eating at Fox's house, why do you think Fox asked Stork, "Why aren't you eating your soup?"
   (Author and Me question)

5. How did Fox feel at the end of the story?
   (Author and Me question)

6. If you were Stork, how would you feel at the end of the story?
   (Author and Me question)

7. Tell about a time that you tricked someone or someone tricked you.
   (On My Own question)

Percentage correct: _____

Types of question–answer relationships student answers well:

_____

_____

_____

_____

Interventions needed for question–answer relationships:

_____

_____

_____

_____

Question–answer relationships based on Raphael (1982, 1984, 1986).

Metacognitive Process Interview and Qualitative Analysis

Interview

1. What is reading?

2. If someone asked you how to read, what would you say?

3. What's hard about reading?

4. What's easy about reading?

5. What do you do before you start reading? (You want students to explain the process.)

6. What do you do when you come to a word you don't know? (You want students to explain the process.)

7. What do you do to help you remember what you have read? (You want students to explain the process.)

8. What do you do when you finish reading? (You want students to explain the process.)

9. What is a story? (You want students to tell you specific information, such as "It has characters and a plot.")

Analysis

Based on a student's answers to the questions, design appropriate interventions.

Reading Performance Assessment and Intervention Report Form

AFFECTIVE SURVEY

Summarize what you have learned about the student's interests and motivations. Write an intervention plan to help him or her improve in this area or maintain positive attitudes.

Summary:

Intervention plan:

RUNNING RECORD

Accuracy percentage: _____

Self-correction rate: _____

Check one: *Independent* ____   *Instructional* ____   *Frustrational* ____

What did the student use to help him or her decode the difficult words? Meaning? Structure? Visual? A combination? Explain.

Error analysis: List any phonemes or strategies with which the student had difficulty.

Intervention plan: Make a *list of strategies* and/or *list of phonemes* the student needs to learn/ review to improve decoding ability.

(cont.)

FLUENCY ASSESSMENT

Accuracy percentage: _____

Automaticity percentage: _____

Prosody score: _____

Fluency intervention plan: Make a list of strategies the student needs to learn/review to improve his/her fluency.

STORY-RETELLING ASSESSMENT AND ANALYSIS

Rate the following as NI, P, Q, V, or R.

Names main character(s): _____

Names other characters: _____

Time and place: _____

Refers to problem and/or primary goal: _____

Relates event(s) leading to solution: _____

States how problem is solved or goal is attained: _____

Ends retelling with a concluding statement: _____

Retells the story in structural order: _____

Retelling intervention plan: Make a *list of strategies* the student needs to learn/review to improve his/her understanding of retelling a story.

(cont.)

PROBE QUESTIONS ASSESSMENT AND ANALYSIS

Percentage correct: _____

Analysis: What kinds of questions did the student get right? Get wrong?

Probe questions intervention plan: Make a list of strategies the student needs to learn/review to improve comprehension ability.

METACOGNITIVE PROCESS INTERVIEW AND QUALITATIVE ANALYSIS

Results: Summarize what strategies the student knows and doesn't know.

Intervention plan: Make a list of strategies the student needs to learn/review to improve comprehension ability.

References

Adams, M. J. (1990). *Beginning to read.* Cambridge, MA: MIT Press.

Afflerbach, P. (1990). The influence of prior knowledge on expert readers' main idea construction of strategies. *Reading Research Quarterly, 25,* 31–43.

Alexander, P. A., & Jetton, T. L. (2000). Learning from text: A multidimensional and developmental perspective. In M. L. Kamil, P. B. Mosenthal, P. D. Pearson, & R. Barr (Eds.), *Handbook of reading research* (Vol. 3, pp. 285–310). Mahwah, NJ: Erlbaum.

Allington, R. (2006). *What really matters for struggling readers: Designing research-based programs* (2nd ed.). New York: Allyn & Bacon.

Allington, R. L. (1983). Fluency: The neglected reading goal. *The Reading Teacher, 36,* 556–561.

Allington, R. L. (2001). *What really matters for struggling readers: Designing research-based programs.* New York: Addison Wesley Longman.

Allington, R., & Cunningham, P. (2007). *Schools that work.* Boston: Pearson.

Alvermann, D., Swafford, J., & Montero, M. K. (2004). *Content area literacy instruction for the elementary grades.* New York: Pearson.

Anderson, R. C. (1985). Role of the reader's schema in comprehension, learning and memory. In F. Singer & R. Ruddell (Eds.), *Theoretical models and processes of reading* (pp. 372–384). Newark, DE: International Reading Association.

Anderson, R. C., Hiebert, E. H., Scott, J., & Wilkinson, I. (1985). *Becoming a nation of readers.* Washington, DC: U.S. Department of Education.

Anderson, R. C., & Pearson, P. D. (1984). A schema-theoretical view of basic processes in reading. In P. D. Pearson (Ed.), *Handbook of reading research* (pp. 255–292). New York: Longman.

Anderson, R. C., Spiro, R. J., & Anderson, T. H. (1978). Schemata as scaffolding for the representation of information in connected discourse. *American Educational Research Journal, 15,* 433–440.

Anderson, R. C., Wilson, P. T., & Fielding, L. G. (1988). Growth in reading and how children spend their time outside of school. *Reading Research Quarterly, 23,* 285–303.

Armbruster, B. B., Lehr, F., & Osborn, J. (2001). *Put reading first: The research building blocks for teaching children to read: Kindergarten through grade three.* Washington, DC: U.S. Department of Education.

Armento, B .J, Nash, G. B., Salter C., & Wixson, K. (1991). *Some people I know.* Boston: Houghton-Mifflin.

Atsma, A. J. (2000–2008). Typhoeus I. In *Theoi Greek Mythology.* Retrieved March 4, 2009, from *www.theoi.com/Gigante/Typhoeus.html*

Banks, J. A. (2007). Multicultural education: Characteristics and goals. In J. A. Banks & C. A.

Banks (Eds.), *Multicultural education issues and perspectives* (6th ed., pp. 3–30). Hoboken, NJ: Wiley.

Barton, J. (2001). *Teaching with children's literature.* Norwood, MA: Christopher Gordon.

Beach, R. (2000). Reading and responding at the level of activity. *Journal of Literacy Research, 32,* 237–251.

Bean, R. M. (2004). *The reading specialist.* New York: Guilford Press.

Bear, D., Invernizzi, M., Templeton, S., & Johnston, F. (2008). *Words their way: Word study for phonics, vocabulary, and spelling* (4th ed.). Boston: Pearson.

Beck, I. L. (2006). *Making sense of phonics: The hows and whys.* New York: Guilford Press.

Beck, I. L., McKeown, M. G., Hamilton, R. L., & Kucan, L. (1997). *Questioning the author: An approach for enhancing student engagement with text.* Newark, DE: International Reading Association.

Bell, S., & McCallum, R. (2008). *Handbook of reading assessment.* Boston: Pearson.

Bergman, J. (1992). SAIL—A way to success and independence for low-achieving readers. *The Reading Teacher, 45,* 598–602.

Best of Sicily. (2007). Mount Etna. Retrieved November 25, 2007, from *www.bestofsicily.com/etna. htm*

Blachowicz, C., Buhle, R., Frost, S., & Bates, A. (2007). Formative uses of assessment cases from the primary grades. In J. R. Paratore & R. L. McCormack (Eds.), *Classroom literacy assessment: Making sense of what students know and do* (pp. 246–262). New York: Guilford Press.

Blachowicz, C., & Fisher, P. (2002). *Teaching vocabulary in all classrooms.* Upper Saddle River, NJ: Merrill.

Bouffard, S., & Weiss, H. (2008). Thinking big: A new framework for family involvement policy, practice, and research. *The Evaluation Exchange, 14,* 1–40.

Bowen, N. K., & Bowen, G. L. (1998). The effects of home microsystem risk factors and school microsystem protective factors on student academic performance and affective investment in schooling. *Social Work in Education, 20,* 219–231.

Brabham, E., & Villaume, S. (2001). Building walls of words. *Reading Teacher, 54*(7), 700–703.

Bromley, K. (2007). Assessing student writing. In J. R. Paratore & R. L. McCormack (Eds.), *Classroom literacy assessment: Making sense of what children know and do* (pp. 210–226). New York: Guilford Press.

Brown, A. L., Armbruster, B. B., & Baker, L. (1986). The role of metacognition in reading and studying. In J. Orasanu (Ed.), *Reading comprehension: From research to practice* (pp. 49–76). Mahwah, NJ: Erlbaum.

Brown, A. L., Campione, J. C., & Day, J. D. (1981). Learning to learn: On training students to learn from text. *Educational Researcher, 10*(2), 14–21.

Brown, A. L., & Day, J. D. (1983). Macrorules for summarizing texts: The development of expertise. *Journal of Verbal Learning and Verbal Behavior, 22,* 1–14.

Brown, R., & Coy-Ogan, L. (1993). The evolution of transactional strategies instruction in one teacher's classroom. *Elementary School Journal, 94,* 221–234.

Bruner, J. S. (1975). The ontogenesis of speech acts. *Journal of Child Language, 2,* 1–40.

Caldwell, J. S. (2002). *Reading assessment: A primer for teachers and tutors.* New York: Guilford Press.

Caldwell, J. S. (2008). *Reading assessment: A primer for teachers and coaches* (2nd ed.). New York: Guilford Press.

Calkins, L. (1994). *The art of teaching writing.* Portsmouth, NH: Heinemann.

Cazden, C. (2001). *Classroom discourse: The language of teaching and learning* (2nd ed.). Portsmouth, NH: Heinemann.

Centers for Disease Control and Prevention (n.d.). What is MRSA (methicillin-resistant Staphylococcus aureus)? Retrieved June 24, 2009, from *www.cdc.gov/ncidod/dhqp/ar_mrsa_ca_public. html#2*

Chinn, C. A., Anderson, R. C., & Waggoner, M. A. (2001). Patterns of discourse in two kinds of literature discussion. *Reading Research Quarterly, 36,* 378–411.

Clay, M. (1979). *An observation survey of early reading achievement.* Portsmouth, NH: Heinemann.

Cooper, D., & Kiger, N. (2006). *Literacy: Helping children construct meaning.* Boston: Houghton Mifflin.

Cross, D. R., & Paris, S. G. (1988). Developmental and instructional analyses of children's metacognition and reading comprehension. *Journal of Educational Psychology, 80*(2), 131–142.

Cunningham, P. (2005). *Phonics they use: Words for reading and writing* (4th ed.). Boston: Pearson.

Cunningham, P., & Allington, R. (2007). *Classrooms that work: They can all read and write.* Boston: Pearson.

Dearing, E., McCartney, K., Weiss, H. B., Kreider, H., & Simpkins, S. (2004). The promotive effects of family educational involvement for low-income children's literacy: How and for whom does involvement matter? *Journal of School Psychology, 42,* 445–460.

Diller, D. (2003). *Literacy work stations.* Portland, ME: Stenhouse.

Dolch, E. W. (1950). *Teaching primary reading.* Champaign, IL: Garrard Press.

Donovan, C. A., & Smolkin, L. B. (2001). Genre and other factors influencing teachers' book selections for science instruction. *Reading Research Quarterly, 36,* 412–440.

Dorn, L., & Soffos, C. (2001). *Scaffolding young writers: A writer's workshop approach.* Portland, ME: Stenhouse.

Dudley-Marling, K., & Searle, D. (1991). *When students have time to talk.* Portsmouth, NH: Heinemann.

Duffelmeyer, F. (1994). Effective anticipation guide statements for learning from expository prose. *Journal of Reading, 37,* 452–455.

Duke, N. (2000). 3.6 minutes per day: The scarcity of informational texts in first grade. *Reading Research Quarterly, 35,* 202–224.

Duke, N., & Pearson, P. D. (2002). Effective practices for developing reading comprehension. In A. Farstrup & S. J. Samuels (Eds.), *What research has to say about reading instruction* (pp. 205–242). Newark, DE: International Reading Association.

Durkin, D. (1978–1979). What classroom observations reveal about reading comprehension instruction. *Reading Research Quarterly, 4,* 481–533.

Enciso, P. E. (1997). Negotiating the meaning of difference: Talking back to multicultural literature. In T. Rogers & A. O. Soter (Eds.), *Reading across cultures: Teaching literature in a diverse society* (pp. 13–41). New York: Teachers College Press.

Ensle, A. (1996). A study of current trends in parental involvement programs for parents of limited English proficient children. In A. Ensle (Ed.), *Critical issues in parental involvement.* Clear Lake City, TX: UHCL Research Center for Language and Culture, and U.S. Department of Education, Educational Resources Information Center.

Epstein, J. L. (1986). Parents' reactions to teacher practices of parent involvement. *Elementary School Journal, 86,* 277–294.

Evans, K. S. (2002). Fifth-grade students' perceptions of how they experience literature discussion groups. *Reading Research Quarterly, 37,* 46–69.

Flavell, J. H. (1985). *Cognitive development.* Englewood Cliffs, NJ: Prentice-Hall.

Flower, L., Stein, V., Ackerman, J., Kantz, M. J., McCormick, K., & Peck, W. C. (1990). *Reading to write: Exploring a cognitive and social process.* New York: Oxford University Press.

Freeman, E. B., & Person, D. G. (1992). *Using nonfiction trade books in the elementary classroom: From ants to zeppelins.* Urbana, IL: National Council of Teachers of English.

Fry, E., & Kress, J. E. (2006). *The reading teacher's book of lists* (5th ed.). San Francisco: Jossey-Bass.

Fry, E., Polk, J. K., & Fountoukidis, D. L. (1985). *The reading teacher's book of lists.* Englewood Cliffs, NJ: Prentice-Hall.

Galda, L. (1982). Assuming the spectator stance: An examination of the responses of three young readers. *Research in the Teaching of English, 16,* 1–20.

Galda, L., Ash, G. E., & Cullinan, B. E. (2000). Children's literature. In M. L. Kamil, P. B. Mosenthal, P. D. Pearson, & R. Barr (Eds.), *Handbook of reading research* (Vol. 3, pp. 361–379). Mahwah, NJ: Erlbaum.

Gambrell, L. B. (1996). Creating classrooms that foster reading motivation. *The Reading Teacher, 50,* 14–25.

Gambrell, L. B. (2004). Literacy motivation: Implications for urban classrooms. In D. Lapp, C. C. Block, E. J. Cooper, J. Flood, N. Roser, & J. V. Tinajero (Eds.), *Teaching all the children: Strategies for developing literacy in an urban setting* (pp. 193–201). New York: Guilford Press.

Garner, R. (1987). *Metacognition and reading comprehension.* Norwood, NJ: Ablex.

Gaskins, I. W., & Elliot, T. T. (1991). *Implementing cognitive strategy instruction across the school: The Benchmark manual for teachers.* Cambridge, MA: Brookline Books.

Gaskins, I. W., Gensemer, E., & Six, L. (2005). Tailoring a middle school language arts curriculum to meet the needs of struggling readers. In R. L. McCormack & J. R. Paratore (Eds.), *After early intervention, then what?: Teaching struggling readers in grades three and beyond* (pp. 137–157). Upper Saddle River, NJ: Pearson.

Gay, G. (2000). *Culturally responsive teaching: Theory, research, and practice.* New York: Teachers College Press.

Gee, J. P. (2000). Discourse and sociocultural studies in reading. In M. L. Kamil, P. B. Mosenthal, P. D. Pearson, & R. Barr (Eds.), *Handbook of reading research* (Vol. 3, pp. 195–207). Mahwah, NJ: Erlbaum.

Glazer, S. M. (2007). A classroom portfolio system: Assessment is instruction. In J. R. Paratore & R. L. McCormack (Eds.), *Classroom literacy assessment: Making sense of what students know and do* (pp. 227–245). New York: Guilford Press.

Graves, D. (1994). *A fresh look at writing.* Portsmouth, NH: Heinemann.

Graves, M. F., Juel, C., & Graves, B. B. (2001). *Teaching reading in the 21st century* (2nd ed.). Needham Heights, MA: Allyn & Bacon.

Guthrie, J. T., & Wigfield, A. (2000). Engagement and motivation in reading. In M. Kamil, P. Mosenthal, P. D. Pearson, & R. Barr (Eds.), *Handbook of reading research* (Vol. 3, pp. 403–422). Mahwah, NJ: Erlbaum.

Harris, V. (Ed.). (1992). *Teaching multicultural literature in grades K–8.* New York: Christopher-Gordon.

Harvey, S. (1998). *Nonfiction matters: Reading, writing, and research in grades 3–8.* York, ME: Stenhouse.

Haynes, N., Comer, J., & Hamilton-Lee, M. (1989). School climate enhancement through parental involvement. *Journal of School Psychology, 27*(1), 90–97.

Henderson, A. T. (Ed.). (1987). *The evidence continues to grow: Parent involvement improves student achievement.* Columbia, MD: National Committee for Citizens in Education.

Henderson, A. T., & Berla, N. (1994). *A new generation of evidence: The family is crucial to student achievement.* Columbia, MD: National Committee for Citizens in Education.

Idol, L. (1987). Group story mapping: A comprehension strategy for both skilled and unskilled readers. *Journal of Learning Disabilities, 20,* 196–205.

Idol, L., & Croll, V. J. (1987). Story-mapping training as a means of improving reading comprehension. *Learning Disability Quarterly, 10,* 214–229.

International Reading Association. (2000). *Making a difference means making it different: Honoring children's rights to excellent reading instruction.* Newark, DE: Author.

Irving, J. (1998). *A widow for one year.* New York: Random House.

Johnson, A. P. (2002). *A short guide to action research.* Boston: Allyn & Bacon.

Johnson, D. (2000). Just the right word: Vocabulary and writing. In R. Indrisano & J. Squire (Eds.), *Perspectives on writing: Research, theory, and practice* (pp. 162–186). Newark, DE: International Reading Association.

Johnson, D., & Pearson, P. D. (1984). *Teaching reading vocabulary.* New York: Holt, Rinehart & Winston.

Johnston, P. (1997). *Knowing literacy.* York, ME: Stenhouse.

Johnston, P. (2000). *Running records: A self-tutoring guide.* Portland, ME: Stenhouse.

Johnston, P. (2002). *The language of assessment.* Paper presented at the annual meeting of the Rhode Island Department of Education, Warwick, RI.

Kamil, M. L. (1994, April). *Matches between reading instruction and reading task demands.* Paper presented at the annual meeting of the American Educational Research Association, New Orleans, LA.

Kamil, M. L., & Lane, D. (1997). *A classroom study of the efficacy of using information text for first grade reading instruction.* Paper presented at the annual meeting of the American Educational Research Association, Chicago.

Kintsch, W., & van Dijk, T. A. (1978). Toward a model of text comprehension production. *Psychological Review, 85,* 363–394.

Kletzien, S. B., & Dreher, M. J. (2004). *Informational text in K–3 classrooms: Helping children read and write.* Newark, DE: International Reading Association.

Kong, A., & Fitch, E. (2002–2003). Using book club to engage culturally and linguistically diverse learners in reading, writing, and talking about books. *The Reading Teacher, 56,* 352–362.

Kuhn, M. (2007). Effective oral reading assessment. In J. R. Paratore & R. L. McCormack (Eds.), *Classroom literacy assessment: Making sense of what students know and do* (pp. 101–112). New York: Guilford Press.

Kuhn, M., & Morrow, L. M. (2005). Taking computers out of the corner. In R. L. McCormack & J. R. Paratore (Eds.), *After early intervention, then what?: Teaching struggling readers in grades three and beyond* (pp. 172–189). Upper Saddle River, NJ: Pearson.

LaBerge, D., & Samuels, S. (1974). Toward a theory of automatic information processing in reading. *Cognitive Psychology, 6,* 293–323.

Ladson-Billings, G. (1994). *The dreamkeepers.* San Francisco: Jossey-Bass.

Lahanas, M. (n.d.). Mount Etna. In *Hellenica.* Retrieved March 4, 2009, from *www.mlahanas.de/Greeks/LX/MountEtna.html*

Lapp, D., Fisher, D., & Flood, J. (2008). Selecting instructional materials for the literacy program. In S. Wepner & D. S. Strickland (Eds.), *The administration and supervision of reading programs* (pp. 105–117). New York: Teachers College Press.

Lapp, D., Flood, J., Ranck-Buhr, W., Van Dyke, J., & Spacek, S. (1997). Do you really just want us to talk about this book?: A closer look at book clubs as an instructional tool. In J. R. Paratore & R. L. McCormack (Eds.), *Peer talk in the classroom: Learning from research* (pp. 6–25). Newark, DE: International Reading Association.

Lubliner, S., & Smetana, L. (2005). The effects of comprehensive vocabulary instruction on Title I students' metacognitive word-learning skills and reading comprehension. *Journal of Literacy Research, 37*(1), 11–39.

Maloch, B. (2002). Scaffolding student talk: One teacher's role in literature discussion groups. *Reading Research Quarterly, 37,* 94–112.

Mandler, J. M. (1984). *Stories, scripts, and scenes: Aspects of schema theory.* Hillsdale, NJ: Erlbaum.

Many, J. E., & Wiseman, D. L. (1992). The effects of teaching approach on third-grade students' response to literature. *Journal of Reading Behavior, 24,* 265–287.

Martinez, M. G., Roser, N. L., Hoffman, J. V., & Battle, J. (1992). Fostering better book discussions through response logs and a response framework: A case description. In C. K. Kinzer & D. J. Leu (Eds.), *National Reading Conference yearbook* (Vol. 41, pp. 303–311). Chicago: National Reading Conference.

McCormack, R. L., & Carney, M. (2005). Making reading look like a cool thing to do. *The California Reader, 39,* 3–15.

McGee, L. M. (1992). An exploration of meaning construction in first graders' grand conversations. In C. K. Kinzer & D. J. Leu (Eds.), *National Reading Conference yearbook* (Vol. 41, pp. 177–186). Chicago: National Reading Conference.

McKenna, M. C., & Stahl, S. A. (2003). *Assessment for reading instruction.* New York: Guilford Press.

Mehan, H. (1979). *Learning lessons.* Cambridge, MA: Harvard University Press.

Melzi, G., Paratore, J. R., & Krol-Sinclair, B. (2000). Latino mothers' revelations of reading and writing in their daily lives. In F. Rodriguez-Brown & T. Shanahan (Eds.), *National Reading Conference Yearbook* (Vol. 49, pp. 178–193). Chicago: National Reading Conference.

Meyer, B. J. F. (1987). Following the author's top-level structure: An important skill for reading comprehension. In R. Tierney, J. Mitchell, & P. Anders (Eds.), *Understanding readers' understanding* (pp. 59–76). Hillsdale, NJ: Erlbaum.

Meyer, B. J. F., & Rice, E. (1984). The structure of text. In P. D. Pearson (Ed.), *Handbook of reading research* (pp. 319–351). New York: Longman.

Morrow, L. M. (1984). Effects of story retelling on young children's comprehension and sense of story structure. In J. A. Niles & L. A. Harris (Eds.), *Changing perspectives on research in reading/language processing and instruction* (pp. 95–100). Rochester, NY: National Reading Conference.

Morrow, L. M. (1985). Retelling stories: A strategy for improving young children's comprehension, concept of story structure, and oral language complexity. *Elementary School Journal, 85*(5), 647–661.

Morrow, L. M. (1986). Effects of structural guidance in story retelling on children's dictation of original stories. *Journal of Reading Behavior, 18*(2), 135–152.

Morrow, L. M. (2005). *Literacy development in the early years: Helping children read and write* (5th ed.). Boston: Pearson.

Moskal, M. K., & Blachowicz, C. (2006). *Partnering for fluency.* New York: Guilford Press.

Mraz, M., Vacca, J. L., & Vintinner, J. P. (2008). Professional development. In S. Wepner & D. S. Strickland (Eds.), *The administration and supervision of reading programs* (pp. 133–143). New York: Teachers College Press.

Nagy, W. (1988). *Teaching vocabulary to improve comprehension.* Newark, DE: International Reading Association.

Nagy, W., & Scott, J. (2000). Vocabulary processes. In M. Kamil, P. Mosenthal, P. D. Pearson, & R. Barr (Eds.), *Handbook of reading research* (Vol. 3, pp. 269–284). Mahwah, NJ: Erlbaum.

National Geographic Society. (1996). Retrieved December 1, 2007, from *animals.nationalgeographic.com/animals/mammals/african-elephant.html?nav=A-Z*

National Zoo. (n.d.-a). African elephants. Retrieved December 1, 2007, from *nationalzoo.si.edu/Animals/AfricanSavanna/fact-afelephant.cfm*

National Zoo. (n.d.-b). Asian elephants. Retrieved December 1, 2007, from *nationalzoo.si.edu/Animals/AsianElephants/factasianelephant.cfm*

National Zoo. (n.d.-c). Giant pandas: Meet Mei Xiang, Tian Tian, and Tai Shan. Retrieved June 24, 2009, from *nationalzoo.si.edu/Animals/GiantPandas/MeetPandas/default.cfm*

Nieto, S. (1996). *Affirming diversity: The sociopolitical context of multicultural education* (2nd ed.). White Plains, NY: Longman.

Ogle, D. M. (1986). A teaching model that develops active reading of expository text. *The Reading Teacher, 39,* 564–570.

Palincsar, A. S., & Brown, A. L. (1989). Instruction for self-regulated reading. In L. Resnick & L. Klopner (Eds.), *Toward the thinking curriculum: 1989 yearbook of the Association for Supervision and Curriculum Development* (pp. 19–39). Alexandria, VA: Association for Supervision and Curriculum Development.

Pappas, C. C., & Pettegrew, B. S. (1998). The role of genre in the psycholinguistic guessing game of reading. *Language Arts, 75,* 36–44.

Paratore, J. R. (2000). Grouping for instruction in literacy: What we've learned about what's working and what's not. *The California Reader, 33,* 2–7.

Paratore, J. R., & McCormack, R. L. (Eds.). (1997). *Peer talk in the classroom: Learning from research.* Newark, DE: International Reading Association.

Paratore, J. R., & McCormack, R. L. (2005). *Teaching literacy in second grade.* New York: Guilford Press.

Paratore, J. R., Melzi, G., & Krol-Sinclair, B. (2003). Learning about the literate lives of Latino families. In D. M. Barone & L. M. Morrow (Eds.), *Literacy and young children: Research-based practices* (pp. 101–118). New York: Guilford Press.

Paris, S. G., & Lindauer, B. K. (1976). The role of inference in children's comprehension and memory for sentences. *Cognitive Psychology, 8,* 217–227.

Paris, S. G., Lipson, M. Y., & Wixson, K. K. (1983). Becoming a strategic reader. *Contemporary Educational Psychology, 8,* 293–316.

Paris, S. G., & Winograd, P. (1990). How metacognition can promote academic learning and instruction. In B. Jones & L. Idol (Eds.), *Dimensions of thinking and cognitive instruction* (pp. 15–51). Mahwah, NJ: Erlbaum.

Pasquarelli, S. L. (1997). What is strategic reading instruction?: Addressing the Rhode Island English language arts frameworks. *Rhode Island Reading Review, 14,* 8–13.

Pasquarelli, S. L. (2006a). The practice of teaching genre by genre. In S. L. Pasquarelli (Ed.), *Teaching writing genres across the curriculum: Strategies for middle school teachers* (pp. 1–14). Greenwich, CT: Information Age.

Pasquarelli, S. L. (Ed.). (2006b). *Teaching writing genres across the curriculum: Strategies for middle school teachers.* Greenwich, CT: Information Age.

Pearson, P. D. (1984). Direct explicit teaching of reading comprehension. In G. G. Duffy, L. R. Roehler, & J. Mason (Eds.), *Comprehension instruction* (pp. 222–233). New York: Longman.

Pearson, P. D. (2007). An endangered species act for literacy education. *Journal of Literacy Research, 39,* 145–162.

Pearson, P. D., & Dole, J. A. (1987). Explicit comprehension instruction: A review of research and a new conceptualization of instruction. *Elementary School Journal, 88,* 151–165.

Pearson, P. D., & Gallagher, G. (1983). The gradual release of responsibility model of instruction. *Contemporary Educational Psychology, 8,* 112–123.

Pressley, M. (2000). What should comprehension instruction be the instruction of? In M. L. Kamil, P. B. Mosenthal, P. D. Pearson, & R. Barr (Eds.), *Handbook of reading research* (Vol. 3, pp. 545–562). Mahwah, NJ: Erlbaum.

Pressley, M. (2002a). Comprehension strategies instruction: A turn-of-the-century status report. In C. C. Block & M. Pressley (Eds.), *Comprehension instruction: Research-based best practices* (pp. 11–27). New York: Guilford Press.

Pressley, M. (2002b). Metacognition and self-regulated comprehension. In A. Farstrup & J. Samuels (Eds.), *What research has to say about reading instruction* (pp. 291–309). Newark, DE: International Reading Association.

Pressley, M., & El-Dinary, P. B. (1993). Introduction. *Elementary School Journal, 94,* 105–108.

Pressley, M., El-Dinary, P. B., Gaskins, I., Schuder, T., Bergman, J. L., Almasi, J., et al. (1992). Beyond direct explanation: Transactional instruction of reading comprehension strategies. *Elementary School Journal, 92,* 511–554.

Pressley, M., Goodchild, F., Fleet, J., Zajchowski, R., & Evans, E. D. (1989). The challenges of classroom strategy instruction. *Elementary School Journal, 89,* 301–342.

Pressley, M., Wharton-McDonald, R., Mistretta-Hampston, J., & Echevarria, M. (1998). Literacy instruction in 10 fourth- and fifth-grade classrooms in upstate New York. *Scientific Studies of Reading, 2*(2), 159–194.

Probst, R. (1981). Response based teaching of literature. *English Journal, 70,* 43–47.

Purves, A., & Beach, R. (1972). *Literature and the reader: Research in response to literature, reading interests, and the teaching of literature.* Urbana, IL: National Council of Teachers of English.

Raphael, T. (1982). Question-answering strategies for children. *The Reading Teacher, 36,* 186–191.

Raphael, T. (1984). Teaching learners about sources of information for answering comprehension questions. *Journal of Reading, 27,* 303–311.

Raphael, T. (1986). Teaching question–answer relationships, revisited. *The Reading Teacher, 39,* 516–522.

Raphael, T., & Au, K. (2005). QAR: Enhancing comprehension and test taking across grades and content areas. *The Reading Teacher, 5,* 20–32.

Raphael, T., Florio-Ruane, S., & George, M. (2001). Book club plus: A conceptual framework to organize literacy instruction. *Language Arts, 79,* 159–168.

Raphael, T., & McMahon, S. (1997). *The book club connection: Literacy, language, and classroom talk.* New York: Teachers College Press.

Rasinski, T. (2003). *The fluent reader.* New York: Scholastic.

Rasinski, T. V., Padak, N. D., Linek, W., & Sturtevant, E. (1994). Effects of fluency development on urban second-grade readers. *Journal of Educational Research, 87,* 158–165.

Reutzel, R., & Morrow, L. M. (2007). Promoting and assessing effective literacy learning class-room environments. In J. R. Paratore & R. L. McCormack (Eds.), *Classroom literacy assessment: Making sense of what students know and do* (pp. 33–49). New York: Guilford Press.

Rhode Island Department of Education. (2007). *Rhode Island professional teaching standards.* Providence: Author.

Rhodes, L. K., & Shanklin, N. L. (1993). *Windows into literacy: Assessing learners K–8.* Portsmouth, NH: Heinemann.

Roehler, L., & Duffy, G. (1991). Teacher's instructional actions. In P. D. Pearson, R. Barr, M. Kamil, & P. Mosenthal (Eds.), *Handbook of reading research* (Vol. 2, pp. 861–884). New York: Longman.

Rosenblatt, L. M. (1938). *Literature as exploration.* New York: Appleton-Century.

Rosenblatt, L. M. (1978). *The reader, the text, the poem: The transactional theory of the literary work.* Carbondale: Southern Illinois University Press.

Rosenblatt, L. M. (1983). *Literature as exploration* (4th ed.). New York: Modern Language Association of America.

Rosenblatt, L. M. (1991). Literary theory. In J. Flood, J. Jensen, D. Lapp, & J. Squire (Eds.), *Handbook of research on teaching the English language arts* (pp. 57–62). New York: Macmillan.

Rosenblatt, L. M. (1995). *Literature as exploration* (5th ed.). New York: Modern Language Association of America.

Rosenblatt, L. M. (2004). The transactional theory of reading and writing. In R. B. Ruddell & N. J. Unrau (Eds.), *Theoretical models and processes of reading* (5th ed., pp. 1363–1398). Mahwah, NJ: Erlbaum.

Rosenblatt, L. M. (2005). *Making meaning with texts.* Portsmouth, NH: Heinemann.

Roser, N. L., Strecker, S., & Martinez, M. (2000). Literature circles, book clubs, and literature discussion groups. In K. Wood & T. Dickinson (Eds.), *Promoting literacy in grades 4–9* (pp. 295–305). Needham Heights, MA: Allyn & Bacon.

Rumelhart, D. (1980). Schemata: The building blocks of cognition. In R. J. Spiro, B. Bruce, & W. Brewer (Eds.), *Theoretical issues in reading comprehension* (pp. 33–58). Hillsdale, NJ: Erlbaum.

Samuels, S. J. (1979). The method of repeated reading. *The Reading Teacher, 32,* 403–408.

Samuels, S. J. (1983). A cognitive approach to factors influencing reading comprehension. *Journal of Educational Research, 76,* 261–266.

Saul, E. W., & Dieckman, D. (1995). Theory and research into practice: Choosing and using information trade books. *Reading Research Quarterly, 40,* 502–513.

Short, E. J., & Ryan, E. B. (1984). Metacognitive differences between skilled and less skilled readers: Remediating deficits through story grammar and attribution training. *Journal of Educational Psychology, 76,* 225–235.

Sipe, L. R. (2000). The construction of literary understanding by first and second graders in oral response to picture storybook read-alouds. *Reading Research Quarterly, 35,* 252–275.

Snow, C., Burns, S. M., & Griffin, P. (Eds.). (1998). *Preventing reading difficulties in young children.* Washington, DC: National Academy Press.

Stanovich, K. E. (1986). Matthew effects in reading: Some consequences of individual differences in the acquisition of reading. *Reading Research Quarterly, 21,* 360–407.

Stein, N. L., & Glenn, C. G. (1979). An analysis of story comprehension in elementary school children. In R. D. Freedle (Ed.), *Advances in discourse processes: Vol. 2. New directions in discourse processing* (pp. 53–119). Norwood, NJ: Albex.

Sweet, A. P., & Snow, C. E. (Eds.). (2003). *Rethinking reading comprehension.* New York: Guilford Press.

Tracey, D. H., & Morrow, L. M. (2002). Preparing young learners for successful reading comprehension. In C. C. Block & M. Pressley (Eds.), *Comprehension instruction: Research-based best practices* (pp. 319–333). New York: Guilford Press.

Vacca, R., & Vacca, J. (2005). *Content area reading literacy and learning across the curriculum.* Boston: Pearson.

Vygotsky, L. S. (1978). *Mind in society: The development of higher psychological processes.* Cambridge, MA: Harvard University Press.

Wagstaff, J. (2001). Word walls that work. *Instructor, 45,* 2–3.

Walpole, S., & McKenna, M. (2008). Literacy coaches: Their emerging literacy roles. In S. Wepner & D. S. Strickland (Eds.), *The administration and supervision of reading programs* (pp. 45–56). New York: Teachers College Press.

Winograd, P., Flores-Duenas, L., & Arrington, H. (2003). Best practices in literacy assessment. In L. Morrow, L. Gambrell, & M. Pressley (Eds.), *Best practices in literacy instruction* (2nd ed., pp. 210–244). New York: Guilford Press.

Wood, K. D., Taylor, D. B., Drye, B., & Brigman, M. J. (2007). Assessing students' understanding of informational text in intermediate- and middle-level classrooms. In J. R. Paratore & R. L. McCormack (Eds.), *Classroom literacy assessment: Making sense of what students know and do* (pp. 195–209). New York: Guilford Press.

Worthy, J., & Roser, N. (2004). Flood ensurance: When children have books they can and want to read. In D. Lapp, C. C. Block, E. Cooper, J. Flood, N. Roser, & J. V. Tinajero (Eds.), *Teaching all the children: Strategies for developing literacy in an urban setting* (pp. 179–192). New York: Guilford Press.

Yinger, R., & Clark, C. (1981). *Reflective journal writing: Theory and practice.* Lansing, MI: Institute on Research and Teaching.

Yopp, H. K. (1993). Developing phonemic awareness in young children. *The Reading Teacher, 45,* 696–703.

Yopp, H. K. (1995). Yopp–Singer Test of Phoneme Segmentation. *The Reading Teacher, 49,* 40–49.

CHILDREN'S BOOKS

Aardema, V. (1975). *Why mosquitoes buzz in people's ears.* New York: Dial.

Adler, D. (1996). *Picture book of Thomas Alva Edison.* New York: Holiday House.

Asch, F. (1980). *The last puppy.* Englewood Cliffs, NJ: Prentice-Hall.

Brown, M. (1947). *Stone soup.* New York: Scribner.

Chardiet, B., & Schwartz, C. (1995). *Hide and seek science #02: Where's that reptile?* New York: Cartwheel.

Collier, J., & Collier, C. (1983). *War comes to Willy Freeman.* New York: Delacorte.

Cowley, J. (1980). *Mrs. Wishy-Washy.* New York: Wright Group.

dePaola, T. (1977). *The quicksand book.* New York: Holiday House.

Dewdney, A. (2005). *Llama, llama, red pajama.* New York: Viking.

Earle, S. (2006). *Sea critters.* Washington, DC: National Geographic Society.

Edwards, P. D. (2005). *The bus ride that changed history: The story of Rosa Parks.* Boston: Houghton Mifflin.

Fleischman, S. (1986). *The whipping boy.* New York: Greenwillow Books.

Fritz, J. (1976). *What's the big idea, Ben Franklin?* New York: Coward, McCann & Geoghegan.

Fritz, J. (1977). *Can't you make them behave, King George?* New York: Coward, McCann & Geoghegan.

Galdone, P. (1984). *The teeny-tiny woman.* New York: Clarion.

Gardiner, J. R. (1980). *Stone fox.* New York: Crowell.

Gauch, P. (1972). *Grandpa and me.* New York: Coward, McCann & Geoghegan.

Giovanni, N. (2005). *Rosa.* New York: Henry Holt.

Green, M. (2002). *A strong right arm: The story of Mamie "Peanut" Johnson.* New York: Dial Books for Young Readers.

Hamilton, V. (1968). *The House of Dies Drear.* New York: Macmillan.

Heller, R. (1982). *Animals born alive and well.* New York: Grosset & Dunlap.

Hesse, K. (1997). *Out of the dust.* New York: Scholastic.

Hiaasen, C. (2002). *Hoot.* New York: Random House.

Hoffman, M. (1991). *Amazing Grace.* New York: Dial Books for Young Readers.

Hutchins, P. (1986). *The doorbell rang.* New York: Greenwillow Books.

LaFontaine, J. (1989). The fox and the stork. In *Fables* (pp. 10–11). Boston: Houghton Mifflin.

Lobel, A. (1972). *Frog and Toad together.* New York: Harper & Row.

Lobel, A. (1976). *Frog and Toad all year.* New York: Harper & Row.

Lunde, D. (2007). *Hello bumblebee bat.* New York: Charlesbridge.

Maestro, B. (1996). *Coming to America: The story of immigration.* New York: Scholastic.

Martin, B. (1967). *Brown bear, brown bear, what do you see?* New York: Holt, Rinehart & Winston.

Meddaugh, S. (1992). *Martha speaks.* Boston: Houghton Mifflin.

Nesbitt, K. (2007). *Revenge of the lunch ladies.* Minnetonka, MN: Meadowbrook Press.

Park, F., & Park, G. (2000). *The royal bee.* Honesdale, PA: Boyds Mill Press.

Park, L. S. (2001). *A single shard.* New York: Clarion Books.

Patron, S. (2006). *The higher power of Lucky.* New York: Atheneum/Richard Jackson Books.

Paulsen, G. (1987). *Hatchet.* New York: Bradbury Press.

Rathmann, P. (1991). *Ruby the copycat.* New York: Scholastic.

Rathmann, P. (1995). *Officer Buckle and Gloria.* New York: Putnam.

Rosen, M. (1989). *We're going on a bear hunt.* New York: Margaret K. McElderry.

Say, A. (1993). *Grandfather's journey.* Boston: Houghton Mifflin.

Shaw, N. (1986). *Sheep in a jeep.* Boston: Houghton Mifflin.

Taback, S. (1977). *Joseph had a little overcoat.* New York: Random House.

Wheeler, L. (2007). *Jazz baby.* Orlando, FL: Harcourt.

White, E. B. (1952). *Charlotte's web.* New York: Harper & Row.

Willems, M. (2007). *There is a bird on your head!* New York: Hyperion.

Woods, A. (1984). *The napping house.* San Diego, CA: Harcourt Brace Jovanovich.

Index